THE NEW SULTAN

ERDOGAN AND THE CRISIS OF MODERN TURKEY

SONER CAGAPTAY

I.B.TAURIS

LONDON · NEW YORK · OXFORD · NEW DELHI · SYDNEY

I.B. TAURIS
Bloomsbury Publishing Plc
50 Bedford Square, London, WC1B 3DP, UK
1385 Broadway, New York, NY 10018, USA

BLOOMSBURY, I.B. TAURIS and the I.B. Tauris logo
are trademarks of Bloomsbury Publishing Plc

First published in Great Britain 2017
This edition published 2020

Cover design by www.paulsmithdesign.com
Cover image © Evrim Aydin/Anadolu Agency/Getty Images

A catalogue record for this book is available from the British Library.

A catalog record for this book is available from the Library of Congress.

ISBN: PB: 978-1-8386-0058-7
ePDF: 978-1-8386-0060-0
eBook: 978-1-8386-0059-4

Typeset by Newgen KnowledgeWorks Pvt. Ltd., Chennai, India
Printed and bound in Great Britain

To find out more about our authors and books visit
www.bloomsbury.com and sign up for our newsletters.

To the loving memory of my mother

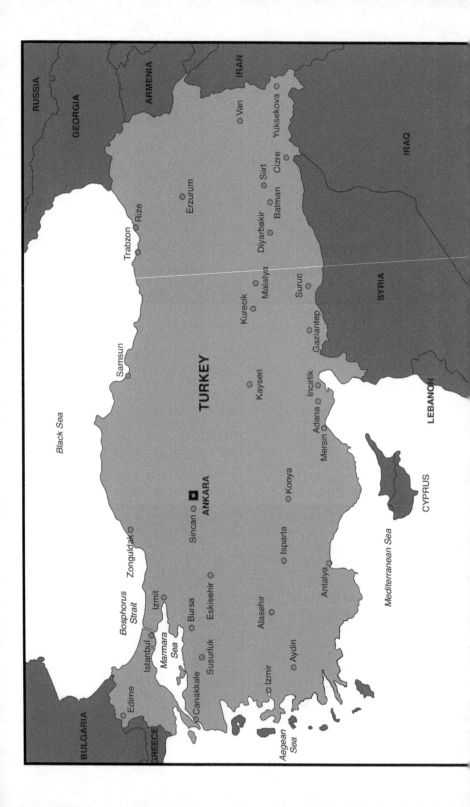

Contents

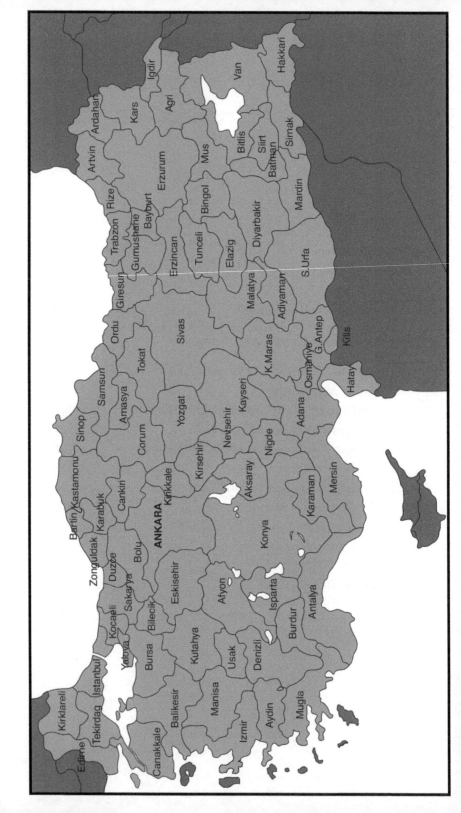

List of Illustrations

Maps

Figures

Plates

Acknowledgments

I could not have finished this book had it not been for the dedication of my research assistant Oya Rose Aktas and research intern Nicholas Masada. Oya and Nick worked with me tirelessly from the very early stages of this project, helping bring it to completion. I am especially grateful to Oya for her commitment and passion for scholarly work, including this book. Oya and Nick together have done a masterful job, drafting, editing, formatting, and fact-checking the manuscript. We went through each page together as a team, and I am indebted to both for their contributions.

I am also thankful to my former research assistant Tyler Evans for his assistance. Tyler helped draft some of the chapters in the original manuscript, and also reviewed it. My research assistant Cem Yolbulan helped prepare the first outline, and interns Cagatay Ozdemir and Yaman Ege Ercan carried out research to build the manuscript in its earlier stages, and for this I am in their debt. I am also thankful to Washington Institute research assistants and interns Omar Alhashani, Joe Baka, Kendall Bianchi, Jillian Bowen, Benjamin Brown, Emily Burlinghaus, Jackson Doering, Yousif Kalian, Josh Kaye, Jacob Magid, and Aryeh Mellman, who edited various parts of the manuscript. Over the years, I have been blessed with a great group of research assistants and interns. In this regard, I am grateful to Ayca Ariyoruk, Mark Bhaskar, Esin Efe, Bilge Menekse, and Ege Cansu Sacikara for helping in the research stage of this book.

I am grateful to my colleagues at the Washington Institute for Near East Policy, one of the best places to work, for their support. The institute is my intellectual home, and I owe special thanks to its director Rob Satloff, who has believed in my work and supported it over the years. I am also grateful to the institute's research director Patrick Clawson and my colleague and friend Ambassador Jim Jeffrey, who provided me with useful feedback on the initial draft of this book.

I am also indebted to John Espinoza, Hasan Bulent Kahraman, Yuri Kim, Alan Makovsky, Sabri Sayari, Rich Outzen, Soli Ozel, William Tuttle, Sinan Ulgen and Akin Unver, and other colleagues and friends who have reviewed my manuscript. Their contributions helped improve the book. I am also grateful to Tomasz Hoskins, my editor at I.B.Tauris, for his help in shepherding me through the publication process, to his colleague Tom Stottor, who also provided comments on an earlier draft, and to Alex Middleton for copy-editing the manuscript and helping to sharpen it.

I would like to thank Vanessa and Tony Beyer for their dedication to my work and the Turkish Research Program at the Washington Institute. I am indebted to Madeline and Michael Silverman for their support for me and for the mission of the program. I am also deeply thankful to the memory of Yvonne Silverman for her commitment to my scholarship. Finally, I owe gratitude to my friend Jen Moore, who inspired me to write this book. Of course, any errors or omissions are mine.

Abbreviations

AKP	Justice and Development Party
ANAP	Motherland Party
ANC	African National Congress
AP	Justice Party
CHP	Republican People's Party
CUP	Committee of Union and Progress
DP	Democrat Party (the name of two Turkish political parties)
DSP	Democratic Left Party
DYP	True Path Party
ECHR	European Court of Human Rights
EEC	European Economic Community
FDI	Foreign direct investment
FP	Virtue Party
HDP	Peoples' Democratic Party
HSYK	High Council of Judges and Prosecutors
IETT	Istanbul Electricity, Tramway, and Tunnel Company
IMF	International Monetary Fund
ISIS	Islamic State in Iraq and Syria
ISKI	Istanbul Water and Sewerage Administration
KRG	Kurdistan Regional Government
LDP	Liberal Democratic Party (Japan)
MB	Muslim Brotherhood
MGK	National Security Council (Turkey)
MHP	Nationalist Action Party
MIT	National Intelligence Organization (Turkey)
MNP	National Order Party

MSP	National Salvation Party
MTTB	National Turkish Student Union
OSCE	Organization for Security and Co-operation in Europe
PKK	Kurdistan Workers' Party
PRI	Institutional Revolutionary Party (Mexico)
PYD	Democratic Union Party (a PKK affiliate)
RP	Welfare Party
SAP	Swedish Social Democratic Party
SHP	Social Democratic People's Party
TAF	Turkish Armed Forces
TAK	Kurdistan Freedom Falcons (a PKK affiliate)
TOBB	Union of Chambers and Commodity Exchanges of Turkey
TUSIAD	Turkish Industry and Business Association
YPG	People's Protection Units (a PYD affiliate)

Introduction to the New Edition

The nefarious coup attempt of July 2016 exacerbated Turkey's entrenched political crisis under its president Recep Tayyip Erdogan. Although the attempt failed, thanks in part to the efforts of broad segments of the Turkish society, which resisted military takeover, Erdogan has used the post-coup state-of-emergency powers to carry out a broader crackdown on large parts of Turkish society. He has gone after not only alleged coup plotters but also many of his secular, leftist, and liberal opponents, as well as Kurdish nationalists organized under the Peoples' Democratic Party (HDP).

In truth there was no good outcome of the coup attempt: If the putschists had won, then Turkey would have become an oppressive country run by generals. And if Erdogan won, as he did, Turkey still became more oppressive compared to the pre-coup years. According to Freedom House rankings, Turkey went from being considered "Partly Free" in 2015 to "Not Free" in 2016 and has remained that way ever since.[1]

Since this book was first published, Turkey's economic growth has slowed down. In foreign policy, Ankara is increasingly squeezed between Moscow and Washington. Turkey's decision to purchase the Russian-made S-400 missile defense system has led to the United States threatening to impose military and financial sanctions on Ankara should Erdogan go ahead with his decision. Those potential US sanctions could seriously undermine Turkey's already fragile economy, and meanwhile the raging war in Syria in

2019 threatens not only Turkey's security but also the bedrock of US–Turkish ties.

To make matters worse, Erdogan's increasingly authoritarian grip since the coup attempt has only aggravated Turkey's crisis. Each election held since early 2017 has demonstrated a persistent political divide in the country, which Erdogan's strategy has exacerbated. Turkey is still split starkly down the middle, between those who adore the country's president and those who loathe him.

In June 2018, allying with the Nationalist Action Party (MHP), a hard Turkish nationalist faction, Erdogan's Justice and Development Party (AKP) won nearly 52 percent of the vote, giving the president another five-year mandate to run the country. Less than a year later, although Erdogan's party (again in alliance with the MHP) maintained its support at 52 percent in the nationwide local elections held on March 31, 2019, it lost mayoral races in all but one of the country's six largest cities—despite the fact that the president spent weeks personally rallying for his party. Just two days prior to the elections, he made over half a dozen speeches across Istanbul for his candidate.[2]

Most strikingly, Erdogan lost Istanbul, the city of his birth and political ascent. His candidate Binali Yildirim was defeated in Istanbul's mayoral race by opposition Republican People's Party (CHP) candidate Ekrem Imamoglu, suggesting that the CHP, long considered a lethargic opposition faction, may present a fresh challenge to Turkey's president if it sticks to Imamoglu's inclusive political tactics.

Imamoglu's victory is not a small feat. He and other opposition candidates faced a completely unfair playing field during the election campaign. I followed the Turkish election results live on CNN Türk—a heavily pro-Erdogan station these days. Yildirim, Erdogan's candidate, prematurely declared victory in the contested race, well before all the votes were counted. Poignantly, when it became apparent that Imamoglu had won, CNN Türk refused to put him on air. CNN Türk's election panel for the night then discussed Imamoglu's victory speech by making only oblique references to it. Never in my life have I witnessed a more Kafkaesque political scene.

Only a few years ago, many believed that Erdogan's extraordinary popularity could have got a dead man elected, if that was what was required. Yildirim was no stranger to the electorate; he had previously served as Turkey's prime minister under Erdogan. Now, it appeared, Erdogan could not even get his right-hand man elected.

In many ways Erdogan no longer represents change in Turkey, but rather the status quo. In short, Erdogan has lost his magic touch.

Prime minister of Turkey since 2003 and president since 2015, he has already ruled Turkey for over a decade and a half, becoming the country's most powerful politician in recent history.

However, here is the catch: Nearly 33 million Turks, just under 40 percent of the country's population, have come of voting age under him. These citizens hold Erdogan responsible for the country's problems, including renewed conflict with the Kurdistan Workers' Party (PKK) and a collapsing economy, not to forget an increasingly oppressive political and social environment.

Nor does Erdogan inspire voters the way he used to. I was reminded of this once again while watching a campaign video of him being driven across a Black Sea city under extreme security, with dozens of police cars guarding his vehicle, in a well-formed cortege.[3] Numerous police officers, standing on both sides of the street every ten feet, closely monitor the thin crowd, which is only one or two lines deep. And Erdogan, remote and distant, throws goody bags to this unenthusiastic crowd from behind the bullet-proof shield of his fortified motorcade.

This is not to say that Erdogan is unpopular in Turkey. Until recently, he had delivered phenomenal economic growth, lifting desperate people, especially his conservative supporters, out of poverty. His movement, the AKP, still emerged as the most popular from the June 2019 elections with nearly 45 percent of the vote. While Erdogan's opponents, including many leftists, seculars, and liberals, abhor his authoritarian style of government, many of his core conservatives still give him total support.

Nevertheless, Erdogan's dilemma is that he has reached an inflection point in his career where many of the country's voters, a majority in urban centers, are turning away from him. Turkey entered recession in June 2019, right before the vote, and the painful economic downturn has peeled off more supporters.

If he wants to make a comeback, Erdogan needs to—again— become the face of positive change in Turkey.

To this end, he has an opportunity. Turkey has had nationwide polls (total of seven) or cataclysmic events (such as the 2016 coup attempt) every year since 2014. Erdogan faces no new polls—and hopefully no further cataclysmic events—until 2023. I believe that the Turkish president is pragmatic, and should use this opportunity to reach out, normalize the country's political system, and end the repression of the opposition.

This would be the Erdogan whom history will remember well. The alternative is an Erdogan whose legacy rapidly depreciates, and who will be "remembered" as a leader who oppressed his people to retain power. This Erdogan will wither away in history.

---

1 https://freedomhouse.org/report/freedom-net/2015/turkey. Accessed on April 10, 2019.

2 https://www.sabah.com.tr/gundem/2019/03/29/baskan-erdogandan-tuzla-da-onemli-aciklamalar. Accessed on April 10, 2019.

3 https://twitter.com/fahrettinaltun/status/1102541879709782022. Accessed on April 10, 2019.

INTRODUCTION

Meet Recep Tayyip Erdogan

O n Friday, July 15, 2016, as I was driving home for the weekend, a terrifying text message popped up on my phone from my assistant. "Coup in Turkey!" she said. "How?" I asked myself. Although the country had seen its share of coups in the twentieth century, as a student of Turkish politics for more than 20 years I believed that the time for revolutions in Turkey had passed. I was wrong. Less than an hour later, I was at the CNN studio in Washington DC, where I joined Wolf Blitzer on his show *The Situation Room* to discuss the unfolding situation.

On air, Wolf showed me a live video of the spiraling chaos, including pictures of Turkish Air Force planes bombing the country's capital, Ankara, and asked me to comment. I felt speechless, almost frozen for a second. For over two decades I have enjoyed analyzing and writing about Turkey, a democratic Muslim-majority country and a NATO member, which I thought presented itself as the exception to the relative disorder and instability in the Middle East. But that evening, as I looked at pictures of Turkey's capital being bombed by its own military—the last time Ankara came under military attack was in 1402, when Tamerlane's army swept through it—changed my mind. And that night, for the first time, I did not enjoy studying Turkey. I felt somewhat melancholic as I sat down at 2 a.m. to pen an op-ed for the *Washington Post*.[1]

Although the coup plot against president Recep Tayyip Erdogan and the Justice and Development Party (AKP) government was soon, and thankfully, thwarted, my views of Turkish politics have not changed: Turkey is in trouble, very deep trouble. The country is polarized between supporters and opponents of Erdogan, who has

1

won successive elections in Turkey since 2002 on a platform of right-wing populism. He is the archetype of the anti-elitist, nationalist, and conservative politicians on the rise around the world. He has demonized and cracked down on electoral constituencies that are not likely to vote for him, a strategy that has dramatically worsened the polarization in Turkey, which is now sharply split between pro- and anti-Erdogan camps: the former, a conservative and Turkish-nationalist right-wing coalition, believes that the country is paradise; the latter, a loose group of leftists, secularists, liberals, and Kurds, thinks that it lives in hell.

More alarmingly, terror groups such as the hard-leftist Kurdistan Workers' Party (PKK) and the jihadist Islamic State in Iraq and Syria (ISIS) are taking advantage of this chasm in Turkey, adding to the bloodshed and widening the divide even further. Between summer 2015 and the end of 2016 alone, Turkey suffered 33 major ISIS and PKK terror attacks, which killed almost 550 people. Each time the PKK attacks, the pro-Erdogan bloc targets the opposition, as happened on December 17, 2016, when, following a PKK terror attack that killed 14 off-duty Turkish soldiers, pro-government mobs firebombed branches of the pro-Kurdish Peoples' Democratic Party (HDP). And when ISIS attacks, the anti-Erdogan bloc blames him and the government for not protecting them. This is what happened on December 31, when ISIS targeted a New Year's celebration at an Istanbul nightclub, killing 39 people—in the aftermath of the attack, secular Turks immediately started to blame the government and the pro-government media for inciting hatred by, for instance, labeling New Year's Eve celebrations as belonging to "other cultures and other worlds."[2] To make things even worse, international actors, from the Assad regime in Damascus, which Ankara tried to oust during the Syrian civil war, to Russia and Iran, which support Assad, are eager to see Erdogan fall and Turkey descend into chaos.

In short, Turkey is in crisis. Could it implode under such pressure? It certainly could, and, if it did, it would be nothing short of a disaster. Turkey occupies a crucial position—geographically and ideologically—between Europe, the Middle East, and Central Asia.

It is the oldest democracy and largest economy between Italy and India; its implosion would plunge the world into chaos far greater in scale than that currently raging in Syria and Iraq.

But can Turkey walk away from such an unfortunate future? Any answer to this is impossible without a full understanding of Erdogan's ascendancy and political aspirations. The Turkish president is one of the most influential statesmen of our time. He and the party he leads—at first *de jure*, currently de facto—have won five parliamentary elections, three sets of nationwide local elections, one presidential election by popular vote, and two referenda between 2002 and early 2017. Understanding Erdogan requires dissecting his upbringing in secularist Turkey as a pious man, the mistreatment he faced at the hands of the country's Westernized elites, and his subsequent rise to power amid—and indeed almost as the personification of—an ascendant movement: political Islam. Since he first entered national politics in the 1990s, Erdogan has presented himself as a poor man from the other side of the tracks. Like Turkey's populist leaders in the past, such as Suleyman Demirel and Bulent Ecevit, Erdogan's political identity has always been based on the claim that he represents the voice of the common people, advocating their interests against the elites.

Erdogan cut his teeth in Turkish politics in the Islamist National Salvation Party (MSP) and its National Outlook school, a deeply nationalist, conservative, anti-Western, and avowedly anti-secular movement in the 1970s. He subsequently rose through the hierarchy of the Welfare Party (RP), the MSP's successor, in the 1990s. He then used his own political party, the AKP (a refurbished incarnation of the RP established in 2001 with help from RP leader and later Turkish president Abdullah Gul) to become the most powerful person in the country. Born in 1954 to a working-class family in a gritty neighborhood of Istanbul, Erdogan is a product of Turkey's greatest city and commercial capital. He is business-minded, pragmatic, and in pursuit of global recognition, but, as an Islamist politician, he is also deeply hostile toward the secular elites who dominated his city throughout the twentieth century. Erdogan conquered the historical Ottoman capital, serving a successful stint as its mayor between 1994 and 1998, before setting his sights on the takeover of Turkey at large. His AKP entered the country's parliament as the largest party in November 2002.

Erdogan's rise to power was by no means smooth, though, and members of the secularist elite tried to block him every step of the way. In 1998, for example, he was forced to step down as Istanbul's mayor and sent to jail for reciting an allegedly incendiary poem that judges concluded incited religious hatred. Speaking to a crowd in the southeastern Turkish province of Siirt the previous year, Erdogan had delivered the following lines: "The mosques are our barracks, the domes our helmets, the minarets our bayonets, and the faithful our soldiers."[3] Although his original ten-month prison sentence was eventually reduced to four months and ten days, his imprisonment from March to July 1999 resulted in a ban from politics. This development, despite temporarily wounding Erdogan, actually empowered him by casting him as a martyr. That, in return, boosted his appeal among the country's conservative constituencies. Ironically, the attempts of Turkey's secularist system to undermine him, in the end, helped him.

The narrative of the political underdog assisted Erdogan's AKP victory in the parliamentary election of November 2002. But even then his struggles with the country's secularist establishment did not end. The Turkish constitution stipulates that the prime minister be a member of parliament, and Erdogan, who had not been able to run for parliament in the 2002 election due to his 1998 political ban, could not take office as prime minister even though his party had won in the polls. It was only in March 2003, when he was allowed to run in a by-election, that he was able to enter the legislature, finally taking office as Turkey's prime minister on March 14 of that year.

After 2003, Erdogan ran Turkey for three terms as prime minister, winning two more general elections, in 2007 and 2011. In 2014, he won yet another election, becoming president and rising to head of state, thereby occupying a position once held by Mustafa Kemal Ataturk, the country's first president, who established modern

Turkey in 1923 after the collapse of the Ottoman Empire. Since 2014, in addition to his powers as head of state, Erdogan has tightly controlled the government and the AKP through his proxies. In other words, he has been successful in his attempt to become unassailably the most powerful person in the country.

But what will Erdogan's enduring legacy be? Buried under all the criticism, his record has many positive elements, namely, his successful delivery of economic growth and improved living standards. This is Erdogan's bright side. He has lifted many Turks out of poverty and has given more people a piece of the economic pie. For this, many will be eternally grateful to him. Turkey's per capita gross domestic product more than doubled during Erdogan's first six years in government (measured according to current prices).[4] Under Erdogan, the country even escaped the global recession of 2008 relatively unscathed.

When Erdogan's AKP came to power in 2002, Turkey was a country of mostly poor people; it is now a country of mostly middle-income citizens. Life has improved, and citizens enjoy better infrastructure and services overall. In 2002, Turkey's maternal-mortality rate was roughly comparable to prewar Syria's; now it is close to Spain's. In other words, Turks used to live like Syrians, but now they live like Spaniards. This is why Erdogan remains wildly popular and wins elections, even though Turkey's per capita income has inched up only incrementally since that "miracle" surge between 2002 and 2008.[5] Going forward, the economy will be Erdogan's Achilles heel. If Turkey continues to grow, his base will continue to support him. However, his political success could easily be undermined by global shocks—Turkey's economy is big, but not big enough to emerge unscathed from a global downturn or domestic slowdown and instability. During the third quarter of 2016 the country's economy shrank by 1.8 percent, the biggest downturn since the 2008 global economic crisis.[6]

In any case, and barring economic meltdown, Erdogan will go down in history as one of Turkey's most memorable, effective, and influential leaders, likely ranking alongside Ataturk, who believed that the secular, Westernized political system he built in the twentieth century would never be torn down. As Andrew Mango has written of Turkey's first president:

> Mustafa Kemal Atatürk is one of the most important statesmen of the twentieth century. He established and shaped the Turkish republic, today the strongest state between the Adriatic and China in the broad Eurasian land belt south of Russia and north of the Indian subcontinent. He influenced the history of his country's neighbours [...] Atatürk is usually known today as a radical modernizer and westernizer [...] the cultural revolution he wrought was genuine and wide-ranging. Secularism was central to it. True, the secularization of the Turkish ruling class and of the state which it ran had started in the nineteenth century. It was pushed forward vigorously by the CUP [Committee of Union and Progress, the Young Turk party that led the Ottoman Empire during its final years] after 1908. But it was Atatürk who decided that religion should have no say at all in government.[7]

Secularism has been a hallmark of Ataturk's reforms and legacy in Turkey. Since Ataturk established the religion-regulating Presidency of Religious Affairs ("Diyanet" in Turkish, later renamed the Directorate for Religious Affairs) in 1924, responsible for operating mosques and training Islamic prayer leaders (imams), the secularist state has tried to control religion. From the beginning, this model faced challenges, especially from the religious, including the Kurds, and those in positions of local authority during the Ottoman era. Most tellingly, in 1925 a Kurdish religious leader (sheikh) led the most serious anti-Kemalist uprising. A total of 18 rebellions broke out during the 1920s and 1930s against Ataturk.[8] He would crush the mostly Kurdish uprisings, but the Kurdish issue, discussed in Chapter 10, would later come to haunt the country.

Ataturk, an officer in the Ottoman military, was a product of the late Ottoman Empire: he was decidedly secularist and pro-Western.

His attempt at the radical Westernization and Europeanization of Turkey was his response to the collapse of the empire, dubbed the "sick man of Europe." He believed that the Ottomans had failed because they had not secularized and Europeanized enough. If Turkey could become as powerful as the European countries of the day, which included many of the world's great powers, then it might avoid the dark fate of the Ottoman Empire, which was dismembered by the European states at the end of World War I. Ataturk wanted to make Turkey completely European so it would become invincible again.

The theme of making Turkey great again would be picked up by later generations of Turkish leaders, most recently by Erdogan, whose plan to this end would be to make the country a powerful Middle Eastern nation able to compete with the Europeans and other great powers. The collapse of the Ottoman Empire continues to shape Turkey's view of its place in the world, creating myths and goals that resonate in the Turkish psyche. Nations that were great empires never forget that fact, and they often have a malleable, exaggerated sense of their glory days and a story about why they are no longer an empire—a combustible blend of pride in an idealized past, grievance over greatness lost or stolen, and readiness to be inspired (less flatteringly, vulnerability to manipulation) by effective politicians.

Ataturk's answer to Turkey's loss of greatness was to make it completely European in the interwar-era fashion. Accordingly, the country's founder and first president, who ruled for 15 years, between 1923 and 1938, used his complete control of the state to shape Turkey from the top down and in his own European and secularist image. Of course, Ataturk did not eliminate religion. Rather, he created a secularist system that essentially controlled it and even marginalized citizens who defined their identity first and foremost through their faith. Ataturk and his followers, named Kemalists after the second name of the Turkish leader, were supremely confident about the system they had built.

Having governed Turkey for 15 years, from 2002, Erdogan has amassed powers sufficient to undermine Ataturk's legacy and, were they alive, make those original Kemalists question their absolute confidence in their system. He has dismantled Ataturk's secularism in just over a decade and has done so with little mercy for his opponents. He has flooded the country's political and education systems with rigidly conservative Islam and pivoted Turkey away from Europe and the West. This is—paradoxically—Erdogan's "Ataturk" side. Of course, Erdogan does not share Ataturk's values, just his methods. Just as Ataturk shaped Turkey in his own image following the collapse of the Ottoman Empire, Erdogan is shaping a new country, but one that sees itself as profoundly Islamist in politics and foreign policy—to make it a great power once again.

Erdogan is an "anti-Ataturk Ataturk." Having grown up in secular Turkey and faced social exclusion at a young age due to his piety and conservative views, Erdogan is motivated by deep-rooted animosity toward his predecessor's ways. And yet he has dismantled Ataturk's system by using the very tools that the country's founding elites provided him with: state institutions and top-down social engineering—both hallmarks of Ataturk's reforms. Erdogan has used Ataturk's means and methods to replace even Ataturk himself. The end result is that now Turkey discriminates against citizens who do not first and foremost identify through Islam, more specifically conservative Sunni Islam, the branch to which Erdogan belongs.

However, Erdogan has a problem: whereas Ataturk came to power as a military general, Erdogan has a democratic mandate to govern. Furthermore, Turkey is split almost down the middle between pro- and anti-Erdogan camps. Despite these facts, Erdogan desperately wants to change Turkey in his own image in the way that Ataturk did, and herein lies the crisis of modern Turkey: half of the country embraces Erdogan's brand of politics, but the other half vehemently opposes it. So long as Turkey is genuinely democratic, Erdogan cannot complete his revolution.

This has given birth to Erdogan's dark, illiberal side: in order to push forward with his platform of revolutionary change in the face of a split society, he has subverted the country's democracy. Exploiting his popularity, he has eroded democratic checks and balances, including the media and the courts. Instead of delivering more liberties for all, he has cracked down on his opponents and locked up dissidents, providing freedoms only for his conservative and Islamist base. Although he has won elections democratically, Erdogan has gradually become more autocratic, ensuring, once he has won an election, that the political playing field is uneven in order to prevent power from escaping his hands. He has accomplished this by playing the "authoritarian underdog." Building on his narrative of political martyrdom under the secularist system in the 1990s, Erdogan now portrays himself as a victim who is grudgingly forced to suppress those conspiring to undermine his authority. He has intimidated the media and the business community through politically motivated tax audits and by jailing dissidents, scholars, and journalists. His police regularly crack down on peaceful opposition rallies. Accordingly, although Turkey's elections continue to be free, they are increasingly unfair. Erdogan's electoral strategy has created deeply entrenched polarization in Turkey: his conservative base, constituting about half of the country, has zealously rallied around him in his defense; the other half of the country, brutalized by Erdogan, holds a profound resentment for him. Increasingly, there is little common ground between these constituencies.

The failed coup of July 2016 ironically increased Erdogan's power because the nefarious attempt to create a junta traumatized the entire Turkish nation. The plotters bombed the Turkish capital of Ankara, which had not come under military attack for 600 years. Erdogan escaped an attempt on his life by minutes, leaving the resort where he was vacationing just before an assassination squad descended on his hotel. In the immediate aftermath, much of the country rallied behind Erdogan. This is not because the opposition had suddenly decided that they liked their authoritarian leader, but rather because the citizenry and Erdogan chose to unite in their common trauma.

Where does Turkey go from here? I see three possible paths for the country, in each of which Erdogan is the central character. He could continue with his polarizing politics, in which case Turkey will be entrenched in a permanent state of crisis, accompanied by a deepening societal schism. Alternatively, he could become completely authoritarian, forcing the country to bend to his powerful persona. The third and final scenario is an extension of the second: since nearly half the population will never entirely acquiesce to being held in his iron grip, and given the covert anti-Erdogan policies of Russia, the fallout from the Syrian war, the jihadist threat and Kurdish violence, developments could catapult Turkey into a terrible civil war.

Going forward, Erdogan can only continue his divisive politics until he consolidates or loses power, leaving Turkey deeply polarized. ISIS and PKK terror attacks and tensions with the Kurds in the country and in Syria, where Ankara has been battling the PKK-allied Democratic Union Party (PYD), will exacerbate the situation, leaving Turkey to muddle through its most crippling crisis of modern times. Erdogan's foreign-policy vision will present Turkey with further challenges. Whereas Ataturk and the late Ottoman sultans envisioned Turkey as European, Erdogan has pivoted the country toward the Middle East and often practiced Islamist solidarity in foreign policy to make Turkey a great regional power. To Erdogan's disappointment, this policy has not brought Turkey greatness. He has played his hand poorly against Russia and Iran in the Syrian civil war, and also against Iran in Iraq. In both countries, Turkey and Ankara-backed forces are being overwhelmed by Russia and Iran as this book goes to print. Across the Middle East, Erdogan has thrown his support exclusively behind the Muslim Brotherhood (MB), a now-outcast Islamist movement. Because of these moves, Erdogan's Turkey has become dangerously isolated in the region. Not only is Ankara left with few friends in the Middle East, but two chaotic countries, Iraq and Syria, and the jihadists nested therein, now flank the country.

Erdogan's controversial path, which must wind through regional aggression and the threat of terrorism, promises little glory. The president may continue to consolidate power by acting as a divisive figure, thereby exposing Turkey to deep tensions and further violence, in which case he will be crowned an "autocratic sultan." Obviously, if that trajectory comes to fruition, his legacy will not be a positive one: about half the electorate will vehemently oppose his platform and work to undermine it. Add to this the influence of nefarious outside actors, including the jihadists, and Turkey could even descend into an unfortunate civil conflict.

Can Erdogan hold Russia, Iran, Iraq, Syria, and the jihadists at bay, while moving forward with his polarizing revolution at home? The choice is his. He will go down in history as the person who transformed Turkey economically and lifted so many of its citizens out of poverty. He might also be remembered as the man who transformed Turkey politically and launched it on a path to global greatness once again. I believe that Erdogan is truly interested in making modern Turkey a major power so that it does not meet the fate of the Ottoman Empire or Poland, once-powerful countries which were painfully dismembered by greater powers. Erdogan's vision is that Turkey needs to become a strong nation so it can survive in a rapacious global system. But the path to a strong Turkey is through a healthier democracy, and not illiberal politics. As I wrote in *The Rise of Turkey*, after transforming Turkey economically, Erdogan must transform the country into a liberal democracy in order for the Turks to rise as a global power.[9] Thanks to Erdogan, Turkey has become a middle-income society and a middle power in the last decade. It can become an advanced economy and a global power only if it remains an open and democratic society, keeping and attracting talent and capital, two ingredients without which this transformation cannot take place.

To this end, Erdogan must bring together the country's disparate halves, resolving Turkey's crisis around a new liberal order. This would require a new constitution, which would have to promise freedom *of* religion for Turkey's religious half, and freedom *from* religion for the other half. It is not only sensible, but also necessary for Erdogan to remodel the country into a liberal democracy in order for this rise to global prominence to take place. This is Erdogan's "good sultan" trajectory. A new liberal constitution would also help him solve the country's Kurdish issue. This would pave the way for Turkish peace with Kurds in the Middle East, turning the Syrian and Iraqi Kurdish regions (the latter already a friend of Turkey) into an effective cordon sanitaire against the jihadist threat, sectarian warfare, and instability that will emanate from Iraq and Syria for decades. This trajectory would crown Erdogan as Turkey's Erdogan the Great in the mold of Suleyman the Magnificent—the best known of the great Ottoman rulers.

As this book goes to press, Erdogan seems to have pivoted away from this direction. After emerging as a unifying figure in the aftermath of the failed July 2016 coup, he has cast himself as a polarizing, autocratic leader once again. In November 2016, in a report by the US-based NGO Freedom House, Erdogan's Turkey joined Putin's Russia in being designated "not free" in terms of internet freedom for the first time, as a result of, among other things, "network shutdowns, social media blocking, lengthy prison sentences, and nationwide cyber-attacks [against opposition forces]," as well as receiving a "downward" designation overall as a "partly free" country, suggesting further deterioration of its democracy.[10]

There is, of course, a fourth possible path for Turkey, one that excludes Erdogan but is nevertheless driven by his economic success. Thanks to him, Turkey has become a middle-class society whose citizens are increasingly making very middle-class demands and asking Erdogan to respect basic rights, such as freedom for the media and freedoms of association, assembly, and expression. This trajectory (the case for a liberal Turkey), however, looks a little weak at the moment. While the country's conservative half has Erdogan, their "Ataturk," secular and liberal Turks lack a similarly charismatic leader. Furthermore, the anti-Erdogan camp is woefully divided among various factions. However, if secular and liberal Turks can find a captivating, Western-leaning man or woman to unite them and lead the country, the long-term future could be theirs after Erdogan exits.

To shed light on the crisis of modern Turkey and what it means for the world, this book will explore Erdogan's dramatic rise against the backdrop of the ascendancy of political Islam. It will also provide "report cards", evaluating Erdogan's record on democracy and foreign policy with periodic snapshots. The first two chapters describe Erdogan's childhood and youth in secular Turkey, at which time political Islam was a peripheral movement. Chapters 3 to 5 depict the rise of political Islam in Turkey and Erdogan's ascent to the national stage as mayor of Istanbul, the country's biggest city. Chapter 6 details the perfect storm that caused the secular system to implode, thereby catapulting Erdogan and his new AKP to power in 2002. The next three chapters chronicle Erdogan's three terms as prime minister, beginning with his first term in 2002–7, as described in Chapter 7, during which he delivered phenomenal economic growth and helped elevate the majority of the Turkish population to the middle class. These events also boosted Erdogan's popularity, bringing his party within reach of 50 percent support. Chapter 8 outlines Erdogan's subsequent illiberal turn between 2007 and 2011, when he took down the secularist state and democratic checks and balances in Turkey with the help of allies, including the Islamic Gulen movement, which later reportedly turned against him to instigate the failed July 2016 coup. Chapter 9 describes Erdogan's crackdown on his erstwhile allies, including the Gulen movement and leftists, after 2011. The following two chapters present Turkey's Kurdish problem and Erdogan's failed gambit to make Turkey a key Middle East actor, setting the stage for Turkey's current predicament. The final chapter outlines the political crisis that Erdogan's actions have unleashed, but also presents ways that Turkey might end its plight.

1

Growing up Poor and Pious in Secular Turkey

The boy from the other side of the tracks

In his 2015 novel *A Strangeness in My Mind*, Turkish Nobel laureate Orhan Pamuk introduces Mevlut, a poor, conservative immigrant from Anatolia (the Asian part of Turkey) who grew up in Istanbul in the 1960s and 1970s, only to come to hate the city's secular, Westernized elites.[1] Recep Tayyip Erdogan could well be an earlier and real-life version of Mevlut. Erdogan, whose family migrated to Istanbul from a conservative town, grew up in the working-class neighborhood of Kasimpasa in the 1950s and 1960s when Turkey was a poor, "third-world" country. Located in the heart of the city, Kasimpasa sits at the bottom of a hill that ascends to Istanbul's bohemian Beyoglu district, and then to Nisantasi, the city's exclusive upper-crust and old-money enclave. During Erdogan's childhood, Nisantasi was a refuge for the privileged few, who would sip cocktails in high-end hotels and shop for expensive clothing on nearby leafy boulevards. The sights and sounds of Kasimpasa along the Golden Horn—a thin waterway that cleaves into the downtown European side of Istanbul—could not have been more different from those of Nisantasi. The Golden Horn was the hub of Turkey's industrial revolution. As early as the eighteenth century, the Ottoman Empire established factories along this inlet to take advantage of the waterway's central location and easy maritime access.

By the time Erdogan was a child growing up along the Golden Horn, this busy inlet had become the most polluted area in Turkey. Open sewers and industrial waste flew into it. During the summer, the breeze from the estuary would carry an overwhelming stench into the narrow alleyways of Kasimpasa, and with every rainstorm the rough cobbled streets would fill with mud. It was a decaying industrial neighborhood, populated mostly by recent arrivals to Istanbul from the Anatolian hinterland. Indeed, Erdogan himself is descended from a generation of Anatolian Turks fleeing the grinding poverty of rural Turkey in an attempt to make a better life in Istanbul.

Ever since the Ottoman period, when it was a popular area for sailors, Kasimpasa has been known for its culture of bravado. To this day, the expression *Kasimpasali* ("of Kasimpasa") is used in Turkey to describe local street toughs who abide by a distinctive code of honor that values unadorned bluntness. A *Kasimpasali* Turk will not shy away from humiliating his counterpart to undermine him—a characteristic Erdogan has displayed readily in his political career.

There is, though, a gentler side to growing up in Kasimpasa. Erdogan remembers fondly the richly woven social fabric of the local streets: "In my time, we were close with everyone in the neighborhood," he once mused in a televised interview, recounting how families would look after one another's children and share meals with each other. "We had solidarity. The bonds of the neighborhood were very strong."[2] Erdogan has been known to boast of Turkey's technological and economic advancements in recent years, but he has also mourned the passing of this traditional social unit, a consequence of Turkey's rapid socio-economic transformation since the 1980s.

So much of the old Kasimpasa helps explain Erdogan. The experience of growing up in this rough-hewn, conservative area, "the bad zip code" part of Istanbul, would forever shape his view of the "other," that is, Turkey's elite, rich, Westernized communities and their secularist, Kemalist ideology. Even when Erdogan entered business in the 1990s and became wealthy, he maintained his contempt for this elite. In some ways, Erdogan eternally remains the guy from the other side of the tracks. Rising to power within Islamist parties, considered peripheral movements in Turkey until the 1990s, he has dominated Turkish politics after taking office as prime minister in

March 2003. Gradually, he has amassed so much political power that he has become Turkey's most powerful leader since Ataturk. But still Erdogan carries a chip on his shoulder: a deep grudge against secular Turks, as if to remind them of how unkindly they treated him as a poor, conservative, and pious youth from Kasimpasa. Erdogan has rarely let his guard down against his secular opponents, whose power is waning next to his. This is a result of his persistent fear that one day those opponents could push him back to Kasimpasa. Erdogan's biggest strength as a politician and biggest weakness as a citizen is that despite being in tight control of the country, he feels as if he is still an outsider.

Summers on the Black Sea

In the summer, Erdogan would travel with his family to Rize, a province on the eastern Black Sea coast in northeast Anatolia populated by Georgians, Greek- and Armenian-speaking Muslims, Turks, and Lazes (an ethnic group related to Georgians). There they would stay with relatives for a few weeks, sometimes a month, joining them in the fields to harvest tea in the remote village of Dumankaya. His father would also arrange for him to take lessons with local religious teachers to supplement his education.[3] The eastern Black Sea coast is one of Turkey's most conservative regions and was the last to convert from Christianity to Islam. It was governed by the Byzantine Empire of Trebizond until its capture in 1461 by the Ottomans, following which it was Islamicized. This late conversion has created a brand of Islam in the region that is especially fiery and pious. Located in its heart, Rize Province is notoriously one of the most conservative in all of Turkey.

Traveling to Rize each summer exposed the young Erdogan to this particularly ardent and observant brand of Islam. The province left an indelible mark on the future president, partly because Turkey has a traditional belief, going back to the Ottomans, that one's identity is shaped not necessarily by where one is born, but by where one's parents are from. For Erdogan, this is Rize. The province will always be his home. Similarly, the people there see Erdogan as one of their own. This goes some way to explaining his immense popularity in the region: in 2014, when he ran to become the country's first popularly elected president—following his passing of a constitutional amendment in 2007, before which Turkish presidents were elected by parliament—Erdogan received a stunning 80.6 percent of the vote in Rize. Whatever his legacy in Turkey at large, Erdogan will be lionized there for decades to come. Successive generations of this eastern Black Sea province will remember him as the local boy who changed Turkey.

Papa Erdogan

During the first decades of the Turkish republic, the government strictly controlled migration to Istanbul.[4] When rural travelers arrived from Anatolia at the city's Haydarpasa railway station, a German-built, Prussian-looking edifice, wooden suitcases in hand, they were detained by military police and sent back whence they came. The 1950 transition to a multi-party system paved the way for rural groups to migrate to cities more easily. Anti-migration measures were relaxed and, particularly after 1960, large numbers of workers began pouring into Istanbul's slums in search of jobs. The population of the city nearly tripled between 1940 and 1980, as people like Erdogan's father left their conservative hometowns and moved their families there.

Immigrants from Rize and the Black Sea coast were among the first group to arrive in Istanbul when the city started to experience industrialization soon after World War II. At that time, Turkey had few roads or railways in its interior, and for the inhabitants along the coast the Black Sea offered a convenient maritime connection to Istanbul, which lies at its mouth. Only with the improvement of Turkey's road network after the 1950s would the Anatolian hinterland be gradually opened up to mass migration into Istanbul.

Though his family was not directly involved in Kasimpasa's naval tradition, Erdogan's father, Ahmet Erdogan, chose to relocate to the neighborhood, a short walk from the city's passenger port in Karakoy, where ships from Rize and other Black Sea cities docked. Ahmet had originally moved to Istanbul from Rize as a teenager and worked at the city's Ottoman-era ferry company, Sehir Hatlari. He later became a ferryboat captain on the Bosphorus for the same company. According to Erdogan, people in the Kasimpasa neighborhood knew his father as "Uncle Skipper" and respected him as an accomplished seaman. Nevertheless, Ahmet Erdogan could not save the family from the everyday poverty that consumed most Turks until the 1980s. Erdogan said that during these years he sold snacks on the street with his mother to supplement the family income and to save money for books. Even during hard times, he says, he never went hungry, thanks to his mother's resourcefulness in the kitchen. As for his father, befitting his profession as a ship's captain, Ahmet had a reputation for being strict and authoritative: "When you cursed, you paid a heavy price," Erdogan once explained. "My father made sure to hold us accountable."[5]

Going to a religious school in a secular republic

Erdogan and his father grew up in Kemalist Turkey. According to Ataturk's secularist, Europeanizing, and nationalist principles, religion, local tradition, and ethno-national ideology were a volatile concoction that put the very survival of the new Turkish state at risk. National security demanded that the state extinguish these vestiges of the past. The Kemalist republic abolished the Caliphate, the ultimate representation of worldwide Sunni Islamic unity, in 1924, and Ataturk demoted Islam from its place as the state's official religion in 1928.

Against this cultural and political onslaught, religion retreated into the private sphere, within the walls of the home and the hushed conversations of the mosque. Ataturk also banned religious Sufi orders (Islamic brotherhoods, also known as *tariqats*) and shuttered their shrines (*tekkes*). Nevertheless, the religious managed to survive, and Islamic orders simply burrowed underground, later surfacing after Turkey became a multi-party democracy—but not completely, as they always feared persecution. Learning to maintain a semi-subterranean existence endowed their members with a strong sense of solidarity, and injected them with a desire to thrive. A code of secrecy has shrouded all but the most liberal of these orders, and to this day many Turks who affiliate with them shy away from making such connections public. For instance, Erdogan himself is rumored to be a member of the Naksibendi order, but he has neither confirmed nor denied such allegations.

For those with strong attachments to their faith, like Erdogan's family, most things were an uphill battle in secular Turkey until the twenty-first century. For the young Erdogan, the educational system served as a dramatic reminder of religion's estrangement from mainstream life. Erdogan grew up in a staunchly secular society in which the state relegated religion to the private sphere and kept it under strict control.

The roots of this phenomenon lie in the Ottoman Empire and Ataturk's reforms. Although the Ottoman state's legitimacy rested on Islamic authority, in practice the sultans sought to make Muslim clerics their servants. For political leaders, Sunni Islam was supposed to provide a transcendental framework that would bind the empire's many diverse communities together and encourage loyalty to the state. But this agenda collapsed when the empire finally crumbled in the crucible of World War I. Much to the chagrin of Ottoman stalwarts, the victors in the ensuing war for control of Turkey, led by Ataturk, did not seek to restore the Ottoman order (although they could not escape all of its accretions).

Ardent proponents of European thought and lifestyles, Ataturk and his followers set about realizing their vision of a modern republic built on a European template. For their new state, they adopted the Civil Code of Switzerland. They also adopted criminal laws from Italy and commercial laws from interwar Germany (thankfully for

Turks, it was not the other way around). Finally, Ataturk turned to France for a centralized and nationalist model of territorial administration to replace the looser bonds that had tied the sultan to his far-flung provinces. France was also the model for a system of European-style secularism predicated on the political philosophy of *laïcité*—the assurance of no religion in state affairs. Accordingly, Ataturk established a strict firewall between religion and government, which would last until the AKP's rise after 2002. Turkey became one of the most ideologically secular Muslim-majority states in the twentieth century.

In organizing the relationship between religion and politics on the basis of *laïcité*, Kemalism confined religion to the private sphere and then mandated freedom from religion in government, education, and public policy. An exception to this secularization of education were the Imam Hatip schools—for imams and *hatips* (preachers)—founded to train Muslim men for state employment. This initial effort at establishing state-administered religious instruction, launched in 1924 under Ataturk, lasted only six years before being closed down due to an "apparent lack of students willing to enroll."[6] After this closure, Turkey was left without a formal system of religious education, raising the prospect that uncertified local religious figures might take on these roles.

Nevertheless, recognizing the dominance of Islam in Turkish society, successive governments used educational institutions to mold a state-sanctioned version of the religion that would provide a religious outlet without threatening the secular tenets of the state. Erdogan grew up in these state-created Imam Hatip schools (discussed in Chapter 3). Erdogan's father made his son's education a priority, never tiring of the mantra "study and become a man."[7] But the education system that young Erdogan entered as a child presented pious families with a frustrating dilemma: place their children in institutions that depicted religion as a backward mentality that stood in the way of progress and civilization, or enter them in religious institutions, a choice that risked subjecting them to long-lasting stigma in Kemalist society.

21

In 1965, going with his gut and heart, Ahmet Erdogan registered his son as a student at Istanbul Imam Hatip High School's middle-school section as an 11-year-old pupil. Because the young Erdogan's school lay across the Golden Horn in Istanbul's old city, his father enrolled him as a boarding student.[8] Ahmet Erdogan likely sent his son to a boarding school away from home due to poverty (Imam Hatip schools were free of charge and boarding was largely subsidized), but also to remove distractions. Erdogan loved soccer, and as a teenager he wished one day to become a star player. His father didn't share his son's passion for sports, and sending the young Erdogan away ensured that he would not be sneaking out to play for his team. As Ahmet would learn years later, boarding school did not curb his passion for soccer: the young Erdogan continued playing secretly around the neighborhood until he was drafted onto Camialti Spor, one of Kasimpasa's amateur teams, at which point he confessed to his father his continued love of the sport.[9]

Ultimately, though, Papa Erdogan decided to send his son to the Imam Hatip school because he believed his son needed to receive a proper and more formal religious upbringing. Erdogan would later explain that he began his religious education after a teacher at his primary school noticed his enthusiasm for religious instruction and proposed an Islamic education to his father. A pious man himself, Ahmet was pleased and encouraged his son to take the Imam Hatip entrance exams, which he passed.[10] Living in a secular republic, young Erdogan would not have necessarily been introduced at a young age to a religious curriculum. It is thanks to his father, a willing teacher, and the Imam Hatip school system that he had access to such an education.

2

Turkey after Ataturk

E rdogan was born in 1954, four years after Turkey held its first
free and fair elections, and his life story follows the history
of democracy and rise of political Islam there. After Turkey
switched to a multi-party democratic system in the second half of
the twentieth century, a diverse array of Sunni religious and political
groups gradually formed a close alliance—one that would eventually
crumble, resulting in the July 2016 coup attempt against Erdogan—
to counter the Kemalist state, which was trying to pigeonhole all
Muslims in the country into a strictly controlled brand of Islam.

By the late 1940s, the Kemalists' ambitious agenda of social transformation had begun to sputter. The local cadres of the Republican
People's Party (CHP)—Ataturk's political vanguard, which acts as
the main secularist opposition party to the AKP today—found themselves battling the enduring patterns of authority in Anatolian rural
life.[1] Awakening to these realities—and responding to the impending
expansion of the political system to electoral competition—the CHP,
which dominated the Turkish parliament between 1923 and 1950,
passed a spate of reforms that dulled the Jacobin edge of the Kemalist
project, even as it continued to seek to maintain a firm hold over
the dreaded forces of religion and regionalism. In 1946, the CHP
ended the exile of more than 2,000 Kurdish tribal and sheikh-level
leaders who had been forcibly relocated to western Turkey after the
anti-Kemalist rebellions of previous decades.

In 1947, the Turkish Ministry of Education reintroduced religious
education with the inception of private seminars that would last five
years for middle-school graduates and two years for high-school

graduates.[2] Two years later, the CHP also rescinded the 1925 law that had closed Sufi shrines, bringing them under state care.[3] Indeed, there could hardly have been a clearer admission of the state's inability to stamp out grassroots Islam.[4]

Turkey's first democrat

The limits of the Kemalist project became all the more apparent when the public was allowed to express its preferences at the ballot box. Ismet Inonu, who became president after Ataturk's death in 1938, inherited a single-party state. Like Ataturk, Inonu was a former officer in the Ottoman army. Born in Izmir to a Kurdish father from Malatya Province in east-central Turkey and a Turkish mother from Bulgaria, Inonu epitomized High Kemalism: he was a European-style elitist, a staunch secularist, and a decidedly nationalist Turk. Under Inonu, all high-level government officials were members of the ruling CHP and the boundaries between state and party were blurry.[5] After the conclusion of World War II, however, Ankara sought to move closer to the community of Western nations to protect itself against Soviet Russia—its historical nemesis. The shift towards Washington meant paying greater heed to the loyal opposition in Ankara, who had long been clamoring for more democratization, arguing that Ataturk's vision of modern Turkey demanded it. Inonu's decision to make Turkey a democracy probably owed more to his personal, Kemalist-inspired conviction that Turkey should follow the West than to outside factors, such as the protection offered by the Western alliance against the Soviet Union. Had he wanted, Inonu could have stayed in power until his death, like Salazar did in Portugal (Portugal was admitted to NATO in 1949, Salazar's authoritarian leadership notwithstanding). In the multi-party general election of July 1946, the CHP managed to hold on to a large majority of seats in the legislature, due in part to vote-rigging by local CHP loyalists.[6] But in the 1950 election the party suffered a brutal rout, only holding on to 69 of the legislature's 487 seats.[7]

The winner of this election was the Democrat Party (DP). In reality, most of the DP's leadership came from the same top echelons of state and military elites, many of whom belonged to the secularist–nationalist Committee of Union and Progress (CUP), a Young Turk faction that had run the Ottoman Empire during its waning years, and had later served alongside Ataturk to build the Turkish republic.[8] Celal Bayar—an economist and banker by profession, who took the presidency from Inonu after the DP victory—had, like Inonu, been a close associate of Ataturk since his days in the CUP. Bayar, whose family came from Bulgaria, was typical of the Western-oriented and secular-minded CUP members, many of whom had family roots in the Balkans (Ataturk himself was born in what is today Thessaloniki, Greece). Bayar served with Ataturk in Turkey's War of Independence of the early 1920s, and assumed the office of prime minister after Inonu fell out with Ataturk in 1937.[9]

But the lifeblood of the DP was of a different sort. The party rose to power atop an outpouring of grievances, from landowners and small manufacturers who felt stifled by the state's interventionist economic policies, as well as from villagers who had grown resentful toward the heavy-handedness of state bureaucrats. Their champion was the new prime minister, Adnan Menderes, a landowner from Aydin Province on Turkey's Aegean coast: a region that had been integrated into the global economy in the nineteenth century, when railway construction had opened its rich produce, such as figs, raisins, and tobacco, to export. As the scion of a prominent landowning family, Menderes possessed social cachet among Turkey's agricultural class, which still constituted the vast majority of Turkey's population. Indeed, the DP deputies, who for the first time filled the seats of the legislature, came overwhelmingly from professions outside the bureaucracy and the military, two constituencies synonymous with High Kemalism at the time.[10] The broad array of Anatolian interests that carried Menderes into office would become the backbone of the center-right, an enduring political force in Turkey whose appeal was based largely on ambivalence toward High Kemalism's elitist and secularist agenda.

Fighting the elites: the DP and its legacy

The DP era marks a milestone in the conservatives' rendition of their history in modern Turkey. To be sure, Erdogan began his political ambitions within Islamism, a social movement with its own distinct history (which will be explored further in Chapter 3). But his AKP, an Islamist movement, also owes a political debt to the DP. Although the DP was a center-right movement, one that embraced secularism, AKP members often pay homage to Menderes as the first politician in Turkey's republic to stand up to the Kemalists, and AKP politicians draw liberally from the rhetorical devices pioneered by the DP. With the wildly popular slogan "Enough! It is the nation's turn to speak!" the DP appointed itself the spokesperson for the people against the indifferent elitism of the CHP.

This juxtaposition has been a powerful trope ever since, and it is a common theme in Erdogan's political rhetoric, which stresses continuity between the DP's legacy and his own role as the voice of the people. Remarking on this legacy in 2010, Erdogan proclaimed: "The torch of democracy that Menderes and his friends lit has been passed from hand to hand, and carried to [our party] today."[11] Importantly, democracy is not just an abstract ideal in this discourse; it is about the interests and identity of the common people of Muslim Anatolia. Even the DP's name suggested this symbolism. For many in rural and illiterate Anatolia in the 1950s, "Democrat" alluded to "Demir Kirat" (Grey Iron Horse), the fabled steed of Koroglu, a hero of Anatolian and Turkish folklore who defended the peasantry against the injustices of the powerful.[12] Tellingly, the emblem of the DP was a horse, an image that its successor, the Justice Party (AP), would adopt as well. Pitting "the people" against the minority elite is a political tradition that the Islamists would carry on with gusto in later decades. Sevki Yilmaz, a candidate in the Islamist Welfare Party (RP), a movement from which Erdogan rose to national prominence in the 1990s, declared in 1991 that voting gives the people a powerful weapon against the exclusive minority elite, and, with this weapon, "either we will shoot ourselves or we will shoot the ones who have been shooting us for 60 years."[13]

Democracy first became a weapon against the Kemalists with the DP victory in 1950. To capitalize on their recently won mandate to govern, the party framed its platform of economic liberalization as a measure that would break down the privileges of the entrenched elite and create opportunities for the farmers and tradesmen of Anatolia. Indeed, the free trade that landowners such as Menderes promoted benefitted them and Turkey tremendously in the 1950s, when the country became a supplier of foodstuffs to Europe's recovering states and the surging US economy, and demand pushed export prices higher. Turkey's economic growth, following the devastating destruction of World War I and the crippling effect of World War II, truly began with the export of high-quality cotton, golden sultana raisins, dried Smyrna figs, and rosy Malatya apricots to American and European consumers in the 1950s. By unleashing this energy, the DP created opportunities for the common man, and, as DP leader and Turkish president Celal Bayar famously remarked, transformed Turkey into a prosperous "little America" in a matter of decades.[14]

Of course, Erdogan is not Bayar or Menderes. Those men represented the center-right, pro-secular brand of Turkish politics, and they were also pro-Western (specifically pro-United States) in their philosophy. In today's political environment, Erdogan, who hails from the country's traditionally anti-Western Islamist movement, assiduously avoids favorable comparisons between his country and the United States. But he, too, is fond of equating economic liberalization with the empowerment of the excluded, and he blames the Kemalists for stifling these productive energies. Improvising on the theme so successfully employed by the DP during the early years of his tenure, Erdogan would often chafe at what he called the "bureaucratic oligarchy" comprising Kemalist state elites who had become deeply entrenched in the capillaries of power in the judiciary and civil service.[15] Erdogan painted these interests as obstinately opposing his agenda of privatization, liberalization, and pro-growth economics. If only these naysayers would stand aside,

27

Erdogan would often opine, the AKP could bring progress and development to ordinary Turks.

The DP also established the precedent of using mass religious sentiment as a means of mobilizing voters. It should be emphasized that this pre-dated the worldwide ascendancy of contemporary political Islam. Unlike the movement that would emerge a few decades later, the DP's nod to religion did not constitute a political program advocating Islam as a solution to the pressing economic and social problems facing the country. Still, secularist critics were upset by the DP's favorable attitude to religion, evidenced by the fact that one of its first actions after its election victory was to permit the Islamic call to prayer (*ezan*) to be made in Arabic.[16] Under Ataturk and Inonu, the government had required that it be performed in Turkish, as part of an attempt to sever Turkey's Muslims from Arabic, the liturgical tongue of Islam. The DP's counter-move in 1950 of reinstating Arabic *ezan* dashed any lingering hopes that state reformers might be able to reshape Turkish Islam fundamentally to better conform to the Kemalist rubric.[17]

The DP's deification of Ataturk

However, it was also the DP that institutionalized the deification of Ataturk. In spite of the above, in many ways the DP was a Kemalist movement, demonstrating the success of this ideology in shaping the minds of Turks of so many political stripes, including its detractors and opponents. Accordingly, none of the DP's leaders, Menderes included, ever attempted to eclipse the "father" of modern Turkey—Mustafa Kemal's surname, Ataturk, given to him by legislation in the Turkish parliament in 1934, means "Father of the Turks." The DP responded harshly when members of underground religious orders began to deface the Ataturk busts that were becoming an inescapable feature of Turkey's landscape.[18] It was also the DP that completed construction of Anitkabir, a Doric-style and imposing mausoleum situated on a hill overlooking Ankara, where Ataturk's body is interred. At night, when Ankara descends into the blackness of the Anatolian steppe, Anitkabir is bathed in pure white light, shining over the city as the Turkish version of the Athenian Acropolis.

How Erdogan sees it

Erdogan has broken with this tradition not only by attempting to place himself on a par with Ataturk in the public imagination, but also, in 2012, by trying to gain an even more significant foothold there by ordering the construction of a massive mosque on Istanbul's Camlica Hill, at 268 meters (879 feet) the city's highest spot. When finished later in 2017, this "Erdogan Mosque" will dominate Istanbul's skyline, soaring above even Ottoman-era mosques built by the country's great sultans on the seven hills of the old city. The construction on Camlica Hill, which is not one of the seven, is symbolic on multiple levels. It would not be surprising if Erdogan asked to be buried next to this mosque one day, following the tradition of Ottoman sultans, who constructed monumental mosques in the Ottoman capital next to which they would be interred after death. Furthermore, this mosque (an attempt to outshine Ataturk's non-religious mausoleum) will overlook Istanbul, the Ottoman capital Ataturk abandoned as part of his secularist project. As the boy from the other side of the tracks in Istanbul, Erdogan does not care much for Ankara, Ataturk's city and a symbol of High Kemalism.

Turkey in the late 1950s

Erdogan's life story tracks the gradual demise of High Kemalism in Turkey. Erdogan was only a child during the DP era. Nevertheless, policy changes aimed at diluting High Kemalism altered the course of his life and it was the DP's cautious warming toward religion that made it possible for the young Erdogan to attend an Imam Hatip school. In 1951, the DP opened numerous such institutions across seven cities, including Istanbul and Ankara. Before Erdogan was old enough to matriculate into the Imam Hatip system, however, Turkey's political winds changed once again and the status of the schools was once more in jeopardy. A decade that had begun with an upbeat attitude to Turkey's democratic prospects ended with a drift toward authoritarianism and the first military coup in the history of the republic. As the 1950s wore on, the Menderes government grew increasingly intolerant of opposition to its rule. To weaken the electoral opposition, the DP targeted the vast material assets that the CHP had accrued during its time in power. To weaken the CHP's allies in the state, the DP granted itself the authority to dismiss civil servants, including judges and university professors who had served for more than 25 years. This effectively gave the DP the power to clear out the ranks of the Kemalist old guard with the stroke of a pen, as well as to swap Kemalist judges with jurists sympathetic to the DP. When the opposition press denounced these measures, the DP responded with laws restricting press freedom; when students took their opposition to the streets, the DP passed a law banning political demonstrations outside election seasons.[19] Having won three straight elections—in 1950, 1954, and 1957—the DP drifted into majoritarianism in the late 1950s, much like the AKP would after winning three elections with solid mandates in 2002, 2007, and 2011. Majoritarianism, a philosophy that indiscriminately respects the will of a plurality, would ultimately sound the death knell for the DP.

Modern Turkey's first coup (1960)

Amid these heavy-handed measures, the DP continued to keep the bulk of the electorate on its side, and it probably could have dismissed these pockets of opposition had it not failed to placate a far more important institution: the military. The 1950s had not been kind to the prestige of the mid-level officer corps of the Turkish Armed Forces (TAF). Once a privileged group in socio-economic terms, the corps saw its relative wealth decline as inflation eroded fixed salaries, and as a new class of Anatolian businessmen took flight under the protective wing of the DP.[20] And with its majoritarian turn, populist rhetoric, and opening up to religion, the DP stoked fears within the military of a dangerous departure from the political tenets of Ataturk's republic. On top of all this, after his visit to the United States in 1960—when President Dwight Eisenhower refused to bail out Turkey's slumping economy, suffering as a result of falling global food prices in the late 1950s—Menderes announced that he would visit the Soviet Union in July of that year. This raised concerns over Turkey's foreign-policy trajectory in the Cold War.

Military officers saw an opportunity as Turkey's university students and urban elites began to step up their demonstrations against the Menderes government. The government cracked down on peaceful student rallies, resulting in casualties. In May 1960, the TAF made its move. The military rounded up the DP leadership and set about cobbling together a new set of institutions to restore their vision of Kemalism. The coup, its manifesto forcefully broadcast to the country over the radio, was mostly bloodless, and since the majority of the top brass had little appetite for governing, the military quickly began preparations to restore civilian rule. But first the military organized a new state structure in which the bureaucratic elite and the military itself would continue to exercise power, with Inonu and the CHP at the helm. But the junta also executed Menderes, as well as minister of foreign affairs Fatin Rustu Zorlu and minister of finance Hasan Polatkan. The three would become martyrs and be adopted by the AKP when Erdogan embraced the center-right after 2000.[21]

From Menderes to Erdogan

The bloody denouement of the DP era is something of a lasting trauma for Turkey's conservative leaders, especially Erdogan. In his speeches, Menderes' death serves as a constant reminder of the

31

Kemalist elites' willingness to resort to unspeakable acts to defend its privileges. "This attitude has sunk into the genes of [the CHP]," Erdogan declared in a 2016 speech to commemorate Menderes' death. "And though the years may pass this attitude continues."[22] In Erdogan's retelling of history, Menderes' demise was but the first act in what became a continuous cycle of democratic empowerment thwarted by military intervention. Turkey would witness a "coup by memorandum" (not a complete military takeover, but a period of military-compliant governments initiated by a warning from the TAF) in 1971, followed by a complete military takeover in 1980. Another coup by memorandum in 1997 and two abortive coups in 2007 and 2016 followed. At each juncture, according to Erdogan, the privileged elite was bent on abusing the common man (until the failed 2016 coup, when the Gulenists became the abusive actors in this narrative).

Erdogan has long framed this cycle as an existential threat against which his followers must struggle. After 2010, young AKP radicals began wearing funerary shrouds to party rallies, suggesting their willingness to die for Erdogan and his cause.[23] During the abortive 2016 coup, members of the AKP's grassroots did indeed sacrifice their lives, standing up to the tanks and airplanes of the coup perpetrators. Fatma Sahin, the AKP mayor of the southern Turkish city of Gaziantep and an Erdogan loyalist, declared at a rally soon thereafter that these martyrs had foiled the attempts of the people's enemies to subject Erdogan to the same fate that had befallen Menderes.[24]

Erdogan can trace this struggle of everyday people against the military to the earliest years of his childhood. Even as a child, his life was affected by the military intervention that resulted in Menderes' death. The CHP government that followed the DP had a far less positive view of Imam Hatip schools. In 1963, two years before Erdogan's father decided to enroll him in the Imam Hatip system, the CHP minister of education declared: "As long as I hold this post, there will be no new Imam Hatip schools opened."[25] In the decades that followed, Imam Hatip graduates would complain of official and unofficial discrimination against them. Erdogan attended Istanbul Imam Hatip High School at the height of stigmatization and controversy, in the late 1960s and early 1970s, and graduated in 1973. In a televised interview in 2013, Erdogan explained how he felt "othered" along with his Imam Hatip peers, describing how he was repeatedly told that his education would disqualify him from any profession other than washing the bodies of the dead, a task traditionally reserved for the religiously trained in Islam.[26]

Even if Imam Hatip students were estranged from mainstream society, they were embraced within their own community. During the 1970s, Imam Hatip schools were centers of cultural and social activity among conservative Turks. In the evenings, students from such families would gather to perform talent shows and plays.[27] At these gatherings, students would take turns reciting verses from the Qur'an or from the works of contemporary Islamist poets who took issue with secularism, Kemalism, and Turkey's Western vocation, such as Necip Fazil Kisakurek. (One of Erdogan's favorite literary figures, Kisakurek was also a virulent anti-Semite and the publisher of *Buyuk Dogu*, whose title means "Great East," one of modern Turkey's first nationwide Islamist journals.) The Imam Hatip schools provided a refuge in secular Turkey, one in which Erdogan thrived. It was in these local gatherings that Erdogan developed his skills as an orator. Though an unimpressive student, he won several prizes for poetry recitation and composition.[28] His immersion in the social milieu of the Imam Hatip schools also led to his initiation into the conservative-cum-Islamist strain of Turkish politics in the late 1960s and 1970s, a period of instability and political violence.

3

The Foundations of Political Islam in Turkey

The conflict that roiled Turkey during Erdogan's teenage and early adult years was not between secularism and Islam. Rather, it was the Cold War contest between the left and the right that provided the symbols and labels for political unrest. The left began to rise in Turkey in the aftermath of the 1960 coup, with the liberal 1961 constitution allowing room for socialism. Before the decade was over, Turkey's students and workers had organized en masse, armed with the repertoire of ideas and protests of the worldwide socialist movement. In the febrile atmosphere, even this was enough to alarm the Turkish establishment. In January 1963, the parliament (under CHP rule) began establishing official associations for combating the imagined spread of communism in the countryside.[1]

Demirel: Turkey's first prime minister from the other side of the tracks

Efforts to mobilize against the left gained further impetus when the center-right AP took power in 1965. Suleyman Demirel, a US-trained engineer born to a poor, rural Anatolian family, had taken the AP's helm in 1964. His life story—he took office as prime minister seven times before becoming president in 1993—epitomizes Ataturk's success in providing upward mobility to poor Anatolians, catapulting them to power while integrating them into the Kemalist state—the opposite of Erdogan's story. Born in the

Isparta Province of western Anatolia in 1924, Demirel studied civil engineering at the prestigious Istanbul Technical University. He spoke with a thick Aegean-hinterland accent, analogous to a rural drawl in the United States, implying wholesomeness and country roots. This endeared him to Aegean farmers, a key voting bloc for his AP. According to Turkish political scientist Hasan Bulent Kahraman, Demirel, a devout Muslim, "entered politics to bring [the] peasantry and [the] state [to] good terms."[2] Demirel spent time in the United States, where he completed postgraduate work and was also awarded a prestigious Eisenhower Fellowship in 1954. His experience in the United States during the height of the Cold War made him strongly pro-American and pro-free market, but also virulently anti-communist.

Anti-communism in Turkey

Accordingly, Demirel made the communist threat a central theme of the party, invoking the "red menace" to rally supporters against the caricatured bogeymen of godless communism and foreign invasion. Demirel accused the CHP, moving to the left at that time, of flirting with the communists and Soviet Russia. Before long, leftist rallies began to face attacks from angry mobs who chanted "death to the communists" and sometimes beat up party delegates.[3] In a taste of what was to come in the late 1970s, ultra-nationalist (anti-Russian) and anti-communist groups formed in the 1960s began physically to intimidate leftist demonstrators. Their leader was Alparslan Turkes, a politician with a military background who promoted an ideology based on the ethnic superiority of Turks. Born in 1917 on the island of Cyprus, he was first initiated into ethnicist Turkish nationalism on the frontlines of the Greek–Turkish conflict over the Mediterranean island. He fell out with mainstream Kemalist Turkish nationalists after World War II when he was accused of having been too "cozy" with Nazi Germany as a young military officer. He was later part of the junta that carried out the 1960 coup, but was again sidelined by more moderate nationalist officers who sent him into exile in New Delhi. Several years later, Turkes returned to politics to take the helm of the Republican Peasants' Nation Party (CKMP), later renamed the Nationalist Action Party (MHP), an ultra-nationalist faction that sits in the Turkish legislature to this day, currently led by Devlet Bahceli. In the 1960s, the ultra-nationalists were a minor force at the ballot box, but, taking advantage of anti-communist sentiments, they soon became influential as shock troops in street battles that would virtually define Turkish politics during the 1970s.

The 1971 coup by memorandum

The Turkish left, too, was growing more radical and violent. A rising generation of university students got wind of the wars of liberation against the West across the world, and drew analogies with their own society. While the more bookish among them read the works of Marx and Lenin, the less intellectually inclined memorized revolutionary slogans, and proved themselves useful with their fists when vocal arguments with opposing groups became tiresome. By the end of the 1960s, a small number of these leftist students were robbing banks and engaging in scattered attacks against security forces. They imagined themselves as the spearhead of a revolution that would emancipate poor villages and shanty towns across Turkey. Soon, the campus became a battleground. By the 1970s, fights with sticks and knives had become gun battles and bombings. To stem the rising tide of anarchy, the TAF intervened in March 1971 by issuing a memorandum asking the government to resign, a request to which Demirel as prime minister acceded. For the next two years, technocratic governments approved by the TAF ran the country. These governments jailed thousands of leftist activists, as well as some rightists and Islamists. But this would provide only a brief intermission before the violence grew even worse.

Erdogan switches schools to eliminate penalty

Turkish politics in the 1970s was simply too tempting for Erdogan to ignore. The stigmatization Erdogan faced as a religious-school student in a secular society politicized him at a young age. His initiation into the tumult of student politics was a natural extension of the Imam Hatip community's growing activism in conservative and Islamist politics at the time, a backlash that would eventually tear down Turkey's secular political system. Erdogan participated in his early teenage years in the National Turkish Student Union (MTTB), a right-wing association dedicated to resisting communist ideology. Though devoted to his faith and trained to become a Muslim prayer leader at his Imam Hatip school, this was not the future he saw for himself. From an early age, he aspired to a life in politics, and he saw studying political science as the best preparation for this vocation. But having an Imam Hatip diploma would bar him from this academic path. At that point, Imam Hatip graduates were allowed only to become clerics or to study theology at university. In order to bypass this hurdle, he had to leave his school and friends and enroll in a public school with a secular curriculum in his final year. This tactic undoubtedly left a stigma in Erdogan's mind. Still, the detour helped him gain acceptance into Istanbul's Aksaray Business and Management School (today part of the Marmara University). Erdogan describes almost hiding his Imam Hatip pedigree because he could not use it in the outside world. As he once stated quite frankly, after going to an Imam Hatip in the 1970s, "you could not easily attend university."[4] This marginalization drove Imam Hatip-educated youths to seek out their own space in the politically febrile environment of 1970s Turkey.

Political Islam comes to Turkey

Erdogan and his conservative friends watched as the Marxist left and the nationalist right thrashed one another over their conflicting ideological visions. He found little to excite him in this contest. The Marxist jargon of the leftist students was foreign and obscure. The ultra-nationalists, at least, claimed to stand for patriotic values and traditional morality. But while some Imam Hatip youths were drawn into the ranks of these paramilitary gangs, the ultra-right's relationship with the Islamists was a fraught one, and many pious youths felt they held little common ground with Turkes' paramilitaries, who idolized the concept of a "Turkish race" along with "Islamic community." Among Erdogan's social circle and across Muslim-majority countries, however, a different political message was gaining traction, a new ideology that was aligned more closely with Erdogan's sensibilities. Theorists like Sayyid Qutb in Egypt and Ali Shariati in Iran argued that the "Muslim world" had taken a disastrous turn when it had begun to look to secular ideologies, whether nationalism or Marxism, for answers to society's problems. If the postwar decades had shown anything, it was that these ideologies had nothing to offer the Muslim nations except more of the same: poverty, repression, and cultural and political humiliation by the West. Returning to Islam, or rather, the version of Islam that this new movement's leaders were propounding, was the only way to lift the masses out of their misery.

Needless to say, these ideological currents were blatantly incompatible with the strict secularism enshrined in Turkey's official discourse. And yet the incipient Islamist movement mostly avoided the gaze of the Turkish authorities during the 1970s. Keenly aware of their vulnerability, the Islamists eschewed violence during these years. This period became a time for preparation and internal purification, one that was analogous to the *hijra*—the Prophet Muhammad's strategic retreat from Mecca to Medina. Like the Prophet during that era, the Islamists used this time to solidify their social base and construct alternative social spaces, which became insulated communities governed by the moral dictates of Islam and removed from the invasive influences of secularism and Kemalism. With bombs exploding in the streets, the Turkish authorities were too preoccupied to harass these pious enclaves. Moreover, some in Turkey's military and security establishment began to see Islam as a possible bulwark against communism.

Erbakan's dream

As an intellectual trend, Islamism was an answer to the extreme politicization of Turkish society during the Cold War era. The first man successfully to avail himself of these new symbols on the campaign trail was Necmettin Erbakan, the leader of the first Islamist party to enter the Turkish parliament. He would later, in 1996, briefly become the first Islamist prime minister of Turkey. Erbakan's background was prototypical of the rising Islamist political elite in the country in that, rather than boasting religious credentials, he was an exemplar of worldly accomplishment: born to a secularist family, he earned a doctorate in mechanical engineering from the university of Aachen in Germany. Following a successful stint in the German automotive industry, Erbakan could have had a lucrative career abroad had he joined the brain drain of engineers settling in America and Europe during those years. Instead, he returned to Turkey to become an advocate for small businesses at the Union of Chambers and Commodity Exchanges of Turkey (TOBB) in 1967. In this capacity, Erbakan cast himself as a spokesman for the conservative heartland of Turkey that was represented by TOBB, where antipathies were aimed toward the country's industrialists.[5] He soon came under fire from these Istanbul- and Izmir-based industrial elites and their allies in the corridors of power, and was quickly forced out of the position.[6]

Ejected by the elites, Erbakan tossed his hat into the electoral ring in 1969. When he could not find a home in any of the existing political parties (Demirel refused to let Erbakan, his classmate from Istanbul Technical University, run with the AP), he instead got elected as an independent candidate in the conservative central-Anatolian city of Konya.[7] Riding his growing popularity in the Turkish heartland, Erbakan established his movement, the National Order Party (MNP), in 1970. In so doing, he created Turkey's first Islamist party, which would eventually spawn Erdogan's AKP. Erbakan's bold Islamist rhetoric caught the attention of both the elites and Turkey's Constitutional Court, which, committed to protecting the country's secularist constitution, ordered the MNP to disband. Meanwhile, in the aftermath of the 1971 coup by memorandum, the TAF, in charge of the country behind the scenes, was cracking down on political dissenters across the country. Fearing his turn would be next, Erbakan fled to Europe.

Erbakan's worries and the Turkish leftists' hopes about the actions of the TAF were largely the same. In the 1960s, many on the left hoped for an alliance with the military under the rubric of a leftist interpretation of Kemalism. Influenced by Nasserism in Egypt, they envisioned the military taking charge and using force to uproot the conservative patterns of authority in Anatolian society. This would pave the way for a new socialist utopia. However, these dreams were dashed with the military crackdown of 1971. While Islamists and the nationalist right were lightly scathed by the military intervention, thousands of leftists were thrown in jail. Lifted by these political winds, Erbakan returned to Turkey in 1973. At that time, the young Erdogan was completing his Imam Hatip education and gaining a reputation within the Islamist youth movement as a vigorous leader. That year, Erbakan reincarnated the MNP as the National Salvation Party (MSP), which would soon become Erdogan's entry point into Turkish politics. The MSP's establishment marked the start of what would become a recurrent pattern for Turkish Islamist parties: each time the country's Constitutional Court shut down an Islamist faction, its leaders would found another. It would take two decades and three attempts—namely, the MSP, the Welfare Party (RP), and the Virtue Party (FP)—for the MNP's great-great-grandchild, Erdogan's AKP, to hold its ground against the Constitutional Court and its secularist allies.

Islamists are blocked by the center-right

But the Turkish Islamists had another adversary in the 1970s: the center-right parties that dominated the country's politics. Turkey is a fundamentally right-leaning country: between 1950, when it became a multi-party democracy, and 2002, when the AKP rose to power, center-right parties ran the country for 44 years, with center-right forces typically receiving 40–60 percent of the vote. The second pillar of Turkish politics in this era was the center-left, which generally received 20–40 percent of the vote, playing the role of main opposition. These blocs were followed by smaller groups, namely, the ultra-nationalists, led by the MHP, and the Islamists. Traditionally minor forces of Turkish politics, the ultra-nationalists and Islamists generally received 10–20 percent of the vote each.

The center-right's strength was in its platform, which appealed to the sensibilities of most Turks: in the economic sphere they embraced pro-market policies, and in foreign policy they were pro-Western, opting for strong ties with NATO, the United States, and, after the Cold War, the EU and Israel. Center-right leaders, such as Turgut Ozal and Suleyman Demirel, though they were conservative Muslims, considered themselves Western and believed Turkey's place was in the West. Tellingly, it was the center-right DP that brought Turkey into NATO in 1952. The DP also initiated Turkey's EU ambitions by applying to join the EU's predecessor, the European Economic Community (EEC), in 1959. The center-right Motherland Party (ANAP) took a key step in Turkey's EU journey by reapplying—Europe has been notorious in dropping the ball on Ankara's membership, hoping that the Turks will forget!—in 1987 (though a CHP-led government took the first major step in this regard by entering into an Association Agreement with the EEC in 1963). Another center-right group, the True Path Party (DYP) upgraded ties with Israel in the 1990s. The DYP also took Turkey into a customs union with the EU in 1995—a move that forced the country's hitherto protected industries to become competitive, with positive repercussions for economic growth later during the

Erdogan years. In domestic politics, the center-right prioritized protection of state unity over Kurdish rights. And with regards to the establishment of religion in the state, it promoted "soft secularism," supporting some but not total separation of religion from government and education.

By comparison, the center-left, mostly led by the CHP, traditionally stood for "hard secularism," that is, Kemalist *laïcité*, which demanded that an impenetrable firewall divide religion from education and politics. In the economic sphere, true to the statist origins of Kemalism, the center-left traditionally promoted state intervention. Following the Cold War, center-left parties made an effort to embrace free markets, though this has, at best, been half-hearted given the left's statist background. Along the same lines, the center-left's nationalist antecedents have meant that it has, for the most part, been hostile toward granting political or cultural rights to the country's Kurdish community and often adopted a nationalist line in foreign policy. Although the bloc formally switched to a pro-Western policy with the end of the Cold War, its nationalist instincts have remained a subcutaneous force. Between 1950 and 2002, leftist governments led Turkey for fewer than two years—all under Bulent Ecevit.

Of the smaller groupings, the ultra-nationalists traditionally stood for a "soft secularism" similar to that of the center-right, but often vacillated on free-market policies. In international affairs, they promoted a pro-Western doctrine to defend the country against Turkey's longtime enemy, Moscow, during the Cold War. Following the collapse of the Soviet Union, they adopted an anti-Western, and often virulently anti-US, foreign policy. Domestically, this faction, currently led by the MHP, strongly opposes not just the PKK, but often also Kurdish national identity.

The Islamists, however, promoted an anti-Western foreign policy, suggesting that instead of capitulating to the West, Turkey should become a stand-alone Muslim power, drawing strength from its Ottoman history. On the political side, the Islamist faction rejected secularism, strongly advocating that Sunni Islam play a larger role in politics and education. In the economic sphere, the Islamists have historically supported a "Third Way" policy, which they described as "outside capitalist and socialist systems."[8] On the Kurdish issue, they have promoted shared religious bonds between Turks and Kurds as an alternative to Kurdish national identity. Finally, again traditionally speaking, they have rejected democracy in principle—despite participating in elections. The somewhat politically erratic platform of the Islamist parties rendered them one of the smaller forces of Turkish politics until the rise of the AKP under Erdogan.

Enter Ecevit: Turkey's first (and last) leftist and Sanskrit-speaking prime minister

Nevertheless, the vicissitudes of democratic politics brought Erbakan and the Islamists center-stage in Turkish politics sooner than anyone expected. Ironically, it was a leftist leader, Bulent Ecevit, who would carry the Islamists to power as his coalition partners in the negotiations that followed the 1973 general election.

Ecevit had taken over the CHP from Inonu in 1972, successfully casting it as a leftist, working-class movement. A Sanskrit-reading journalist and poet educated in Istanbul's prestigious, American-founded Robert College, Ecevit was nevertheless able to connect with the man on the street, thanks to his charismatic, "man of the people" personality—he wore a signature worker's beret, spoke of workers' rights, and had been the minister of labor in the coalition government led by Inonu after the 1961 general election who provided workers with the right to strike. His eloquent command of the Turkish language, matched to this day only by Erdogan among Turkish politicians, captivated the poor and the dispossessed, boosting the CHP's popularity in the polls. His television appearances enthralled millions with pledges to reinvent the CHP as a party of the left and the poor. A moderate sort of socialism, Ecevit suggested, would provide answers to the economic and social challenges facing the common man.[9]

The Islamists flirt with the left...

The formula was a resounding success: Ecevit's CHP took 33 percent of the vote and 185 seats in the 450-member parliament in the 1973 election, up from 27 percent in the previous election in 1969. The CHP emerged as the largest party in the legislature, but failed to win the majority needed to form a government. The MSP had come in far behind Ecevit's CHP and Demirel's AP, taking slightly less than 12 percent of the vote. Still, Erbakan saw an opportunity to prove that Islamists could play a serious role in politics.[10] The MSP had worked hard to dispel the image of Islamists as backward and unqualified for government. In this 1973 election, less than 3 percent of the MSP's candidates were clerics, while more than half represented private industry and about 20 percent came from the government.[11] After the election, the MSP agreed to join the CHP in a coalition government, but also insisted on a role of substance in the Ecevit cabinet. Their demands were met. The MSP took the ministries of the interior and justice, among others.[12] The capture of the Interior Ministry by Islamists would begin the politicization of Turkey's police (a body administered by the Interior Ministry) and bureaucracy with right-wing cadres. In a few decades, few leftists or liberals, if any, would be left among the police chiefs and governors (also appointed by the Interior Ministry) responsible for Turkey's 81 provinces.

...then divorce the left, and swing to the right

This first attempt at bringing the Islamists into Ankara proved to be a short-lived and somewhat strange experiment. From the very first days of the Ecevit–Erbakan government, the personal and political incompatibility of the two men was obvious. Even after Erbakan's win, many in Turkey's Islamist movement felt that democratic politics had nothing to offer them. Erbakan was determined to prove them wrong and, to this end, he fought furiously for Islamist interests and refused to play second fiddle to Ecevit. For instance, in a defiant gesture, he came out strongly against Ecevit's 1974 proposal for granting an amnesty to political prisoners, most of whom were leftists.[13] With the two men badly out of sync with one another, the leftist–Islamist coalition collapsed in less than a year. Erbakan abandoned Ecevit and joined the parties of the right in a new coalition government, dubbed the Nationalist Front, an alliance of the center-right AP, the ultra-nationalist MHP—both driven by their fear of Russia—and Islamist MSP, motivated by its hatred for the "godless Soviet Union." The AP, still boasting the fabled Anatolian Grey Iron Horse as its symbol, headed by Demirel, led this coalition. Turkes and Erbakan joined him as deputy prime ministers, together with Turhan Feyzioglu, chair of the smaller Republican Reliance Party (CGP), a nationalist faction that had earlier split off from the CHP in protest at Ecevit's swing to the left.

The role of Erbakan in the Nationalist Front coalition would be minor, but still influential. Following the 1971 coup, the pro-military secularist government had closed the middle-school sections of Imam Hatip institutions over their concerns that religious education at a young age would influence children during their most impressionable years. Once civilian rule was restored, the CHP–MSP coalition had reopened the closed Imam Hatip middle schools, a concession from Ecevit to Erbakan. The right-wing Nationalist Front alliance that took over from Ecevit granted female students the right to study in Imam Hatip schools, a right they did not have during Erdogan's school years. Since women are not allowed to be clerics in traditional Sunni Islam, their admission to Imam Hatip schools, whose official purpose remains the training of clerics, exposed their true mission: to provide a vehicle for religious education in a secularist republic. Imam Hatip schools proliferated over the course of the 1970s, thanks to a burgeoning network of Islamic civil-society organizations that raised money from local communities, as well as backing from the Nationalist Front that went toward the construction of new schools.[14] By 1980 there were more than 200,000 students studying at 374 Imam Hatip middle schools and 333 Imam

Hatip high schools.[15] As a result of Erbakan's albeit brief period of influence over state institutions, his Islamist party would remain a voice in Turkish politics that secularists could disdain but hardly ignore; although Erbakan would be personally banned from politics in 1980, and again in 1997, the cadres whom he led and carried into politics with him would only grow in influence over the succeeding decades. Erdogan would be the most successful of these protégés, and his AKP the best of the MNP's offspring.

A mosque for all seasons

The Islamists who followed Erbakan into politics—including Erdogan, who would later name his first-born son, Necmettin Bilal, after his political idol—gained their distinct world view in part from membership of an immersive spiritual community. More than a few of the MSP's top politicians were members of the Iskenderpasa mosque in Istanbul's conservative Fatih district, led by the Sufi sheikh Mehmet Zahid Kotku. It was here that these men developed and refined their alternative vision for state and society in Turkey.[16] Their community's roots ran deep. Shunned by the Kemalist state, the Sufi community evolved to meet the new circumstances of the republic. After the Sufi lodges were shuttered, the sheikhs met with their communities informally, in mosque gardens or in private homes. Many took positions as state-appointed imams at mosques, quietly carrying on their Sufi role as well. Kotku, the imam of the Iskenderpasa mosque, came from just such a tradition. During Kotku's tenure, which began in 1952, the Iskenderpasa lodge was coming into its own as a place of fellowship for Imam Hatip-educated and other conservative professionals and businessmen, many of whom felt alienated in Istanbul's secular, European-influenced public life. In spite of his secular upbringing, Erbakan, for instance, was a deeply devout man with reservations about the West and secularism, and his attitude reflected that of a typical Islamic community member.

Sufi communities are traditionally founded upon the deep ties (*rabita*) that bind followers to a sheikh, whose authority is passed down through a line of teachers that ostensibly reaches all the way back to the Prophet Muhammad. The sheikh leads his community in interactive conversations to instruct them on matters of ethics and morality. Kotku's followers marveled at the incisiveness of the leader's conversation. Even outsiders praised Kotku for the cogent, unadorned style of his teachings, which were interwoven with practical messages. Kotku himself never expressed a desire to become overtly involved in politics. It is said that in the years leading up to his death in 1980, he admitted his regret at the extent to which his community had become embroiled in the political contests of the day. But Kotku's message was undeniably political: his teachings offered a depiction of a just society that implied clear prescriptions for political action. In these teachings, Islam provided a model for the organization of the country's economy. From Islamic principles, Kotku suggested, it is possible to derive answers on how to govern, even on fairly technical, economic matters.

Community members would come to Kotku for practical political advice as well: Turkish politician Korkut Ozal claims that his brother Turgut Ozal, who would later become the country's prime minister and president, first tried to enter the legislature on the Islamist MSP ticket in 1977 because Kotku advised him to do so.[17] As a young man Erdogan also attended the Iskenderpasa mosque, as did later AKP leaders such as Abdulkadir Aksu and Besir Atalay.[18]

National Outlook, or the roots of anti-Semitism among the Turkish Islamists

Today, the spiritual backgrounds of the AKP's leaders reach far beyond the Iskenderpasa community, which has declined in influence since Kotku's zenith. But during the 1970s—the heyday of radical politics in Turkey—the Iskenderpasa mosque was an important incubator for the Islamist National Outlook movement led by Erbakan and the alternative it presented to both Kemalist secularism and the leftists' concept of revolution. Erbakan's Islamists argued that nothing short of the complete transformation of society would save the masses from their misery. But for the National Outlook, this transformation would not be premised on a foreign, secular ideology, like communism. Turkey's salvation had to derive from the stock of traditions and ideas that had made the Turks great in past centuries—that is, from Islam.

Erbakan's depiction of Islam as an emancipatory alternative to capitalism was also irksome to conservatives, who labeled the Islamists "green socialists." Erbakan clung to this vision even after many of his closest followers had abandoned it for the doctrines of neoliberalism. In later years, some members of the Iskenderpasa community, including Ozal and Demirel, would embrace liberal capitalism. These men followed the economic doctrines of the International Monetary Fund (IMF), rather than those of Kotku or Erbakan. But in today's AKP, echoes of Erbakan's Islamist vision live on in Erdogan's appropriation of Islam as a justification for redistributionist policies.

Its darker side, too, has maintained a place in contemporary politics. Erbakan never grew tired of defining the world in terms of religious enmities, and until the end of his life he entertained the fantasy that a cabal of Jews controlled the West. In a 2007 television interview, he seethed when saying that "all infidel nations are one Zionist entity," and that this "Zionist bacteria" had been working to control the globe for more than 5,000 years.[19] Sadly, despite the AKP's globalism and pro-business stance, these same time-worn themes have worked their way into Erdogan's rhetoric. This ugly prejudice has resurfaced in recent years, a case in point being Erdogan's dark suggestion in 2012 of the existence of an "interest-rate lobby"—a poorly veiled code for Jews—that is conspiring to keep Turkey financially unstable for the "lobby's own benefit."[20] Understanding Erdogan requires understanding the pervasive intellectual influence imprinted on him by his predecessors, Erbakan and Kotku.

Erdogan meets Erbakan

Erdogan became a follower of Erbakan's National Outlook movement during his teenage years, when he joined the MTTB at Istanbul's Imam Hatip High School and attended Kotku's meetings at the Iskenderpasa lodge. In the late 1970s, like the MSP, the MTTB kept its distance from the fury of street politics, while also adopting a staunchly anti-communist stance. It would organize cultural events such as film showings, book clubs, and festivals to promote its cultural outlook and political views. It also published a weekly paper named *Milli Genclik Dergisi* (Journal of National Youth). Abdullah Gul, who would later assume several top posts in the AKP and the Turkish government, including the presidency of the nation, was involved in its publication.[21] In the writings and speeches of the MTTB, anti-communism was a common refrain: although they avoided the violent tactics of other youth associations of the period in step with Islamist organizations of the time, they were not afraid to take to the streets to oppose the spread of communist ideas among young people or to assert Turkish pride against foreign enemies. The association described its rallies as giving a voice to the genuine Turkish people, who were disgusted with the foreign ideologies of the radical leftists, which served only to desecrate Turkey's cherished institutions and values.[22]

Erdogan, loquacious from an early age, was a natural in this climate. He became president of the MTTB branch of his Imam Hatip school. From there, he joined the youth branch of the MSP, whose membership overlapped considerably with that of the MTTB. In 1976, three years after graduating from high school, he was chosen to be president of the MSP youth branch of the Beyoglu district in Istanbul, which included Erdogan's own Kasimpasa neighborhood. A year later, he became president of Istanbul's entire MSP youth branch. While attending a conservative youth conference, he met Emine Gulbaran. Like Erdogan, Gulbaran was a child of Anatolian immigrants to Istanbul and her parents had arrived in the city from Turkey's Arab–Kurdish Siirt Province in the conservative southeast of the country. Born in 1955, she studied at an all-girls high school and decided to don the hijab at the age of 15. Like her future husband, Gulbaran was enmeshed in Turkey's Islamist circles when the two met. They married on July 4, 1978.[23] But membership of the Islamist youth movement by this time entailed more than just romance or poetry readings. Erdogan became a leader in a movement under siege, threatened from both the left and the nationalist right, which saw the MTTB as a rival.[24]

1970s: the horrible decade

The 1970s will be forever remembered as the *decadus horribilis* in Turkey. The country's economic development model between 1960 and 1980, which was based on import substitution—using high tariff walls to nurture domestic industrial production—collapsed as oil prices skyrocketed in the late 1970s. Unable to afford oil and raw materials, industrial production came grinding to a halt: sugar, cooking oil, and margarine (which had replaced olive oil during the consumerist boom of the post-World War II years) had disappeared from store shelves by 1979. Sugar even appeared on the black market, a sign of complete economic collapse. To make things worse, political violence erupted on the country's streets. Even scant evidence of loyalty to one side, including something as simple as entering an area controlled by an opposing political faction, could provoke attacks from gangs of neighborhood militants. By the 1970s, this political radicalism had spread from the campuses across broad swaths of Turkey's urban landscape, as self-proclaimed, and competing, Marxist and other leftist guerrillas claimed control of entire neighborhoods in slums that spread across Istanbul, Ankara, and Izmir. The ultra-nationalists, too, attempted to take over neighborhoods. Meanwhile, in Anatolia's smaller, religiously mixed towns, ultra-nationalists and Islamists orchestrated massacres against the Alevis, a group of liberal Muslims despised by fundamentalists for their religious heterodoxy and social liberalism (as well as their support for socialist and communist ideas during this decade). During the 1970s, thousands of people died in these ideologically charged street clashes and pogroms.[25]

As the violence worsened, the toll on the Islamist youth movement mounted. Before the 1971 coup, one of Erdogan's closest friends, Mustafa Bilgi, was killed in the bombing of an MTTB office.[26] Erdogan also lost several other close associates during the uptick in violence that occurred later in the decade. Finally, when four Islamist youths were murdered in a period of days in April 1980, Erdogan and 400 of his followers took to the streets to protest peacefully against the attacks on their movement. In keeping with the group's rules of procedure, when the police intervened, the young Islamists did not fight back as the leftist radicals often did. Instead, they reportedly began to perform their ritual prayers. Erdogan and several of his friends were arrested during the demonstration, but they did not stay in detention for long.[27]

Fearing foreigners

The ability of the burgeoning Islamist movement to distance itself from the violence of the radical right- and left-wing student groups was perhaps its greatest strength. Given these groups' extensive preparations for violence, this distinction was not difficult to demonstrate: since the 1960s, Turkey's ultra-nationalists had been training in rural commando camps to fight leftists in the streets, and Turkey's leftist militants were making trips to guerrilla camps in Syria and Lebanon for training by Soviet-funded Marxist Palestinian groups. They returned with grim confidence in their ability to use violence as a political tool. Turkey's Islamists, in contrast, lacked any such paramilitary capability until 1978, when the MSP called on its youth branches to contribute to a force that might hold its own against the violent barrage it was suffering from the left and right.[28] Just as this project was maturing, in September 1980, during the formation of the MSP militia called the "Akincilar" (pioneers)—a name recalling the Ottoman advanced guard that raided the gates of Vienna in the seventeenth century—the TAF launched its most punishing crackdown yet. With a shattering blow, the military virtually wiped out the left in Turkey and placed the ultra-nationalists firmly under its thumb. While this would put an end to the age of left–right violence in Turkey, its memory has shaped conservative and Islamist discourse ever since. Those who lived in Turkey during the 1970s vividly remember the burning cars and midnight gunfire of that decade. Conservative politicians draw upon these poignant shared experiences to suggest that secular ideologies, divorced from Turkey's genuine roots, are bad for the country. The unfavorable comparison between the "snake oil" of Western thought and the "rich substance" of local conservative Islamic ideas is a common theme in this rhetoric. Rejecting capitalism and communism alike, and espousing a message of national sovereignty, Erdogan developed his populist side in the late 1970s. Reflecting on those years in 2012, he described them as a time when "symbols, slogans, and provocative actions eclipsed ideas."[29] For him, the people who actually rolled up their sleeves to help the common man had little concern with the fads of European political thought. It was the local boys, raised in the mosque, who were truly close to the people, and who had their best interests at heart.

Erdogan's musings on the period reflect what many conservatives in Turkey view as common sense. The protagonists in this tidy narrative of Turkey's recent history are the country's Muslim communities. These ordinary folk wanted nothing more than to lead a virtuous life, despite being constantly victimized by the Kemalist regime that denigrated them simply because they refused to turn their backs on Islam. These heroes were brought to television screens across the country in 2016 when Turkey's state broadcaster began airing a historical soap opera focusing on the MTTB during the 1970s. The series opens with a flashback: the lead, a handsome young MTTB leader, remembers painfully how a military officer murdered his father in cold blood because he protested against the ban on the Arabic call to prayer. The left appears in the next scene, in which the hero finds himself protecting a group of young boys on their way to a circumcision festival—a traditional rite of passage for Muslim boys—against a band of leftist radicals who are torching the car of an American diplomat. The impressionable leftist youngsters do not realize it, but they are being manipulated in a dirty game of cosmopolitan intrigue.

More than just prime-time entertainment, this nativist characterization of the left as a tool of international conspiracy has been commonplace among Islamists for decades. "For years, the West has been planning another military coup," one of Erbakan's followers, Sevki Yilmaz, said at a political gathering in 1991. "But the CIA, the American agents, in these past years they have been unable to find the right conditions to carry it out." The reason the West's plans had been thwarted, according to Yilmaz, is that Erbakan's Muslim youth were guarding the faithful. "The seeds that were planted in 1974 have borne fruit and now Imam Hatip students are in the universities," Yilmaz crowed. Since good Muslims, alert to the sinister intent of foreign ideas, now make up a sizable chunk of the student population, "anarchy has been prevented from entering the universities." Islam has fortified Turkey against the West's tireless attempts to sow discord in the country. And "the West is disturbed by this!"[30]

The same story is rerun in Turkey today. The almost axiomatic assumption that the West is constantly scheming to destabilize Turkey, mostly by using the leftists, appears frequently in the speeches of today's AKP leaders. And so does the assumption that conservative Islamists are the only social force in Turkey that can protect the country from another downward spiral of foreigner-led chaos, like the one that engulfed the country during the 1970s. Erdogan and Islamists view their movement as the true representative of the people. According to this nativist view, their detractors can only be representing foreign interests, acting as "proxies" for outside actors. Erdogan's ideological antecedents from the 1970s continue to shape him decades later, even as Turkey's most powerful leader. The 2013 Gezi Park rallies and 2016 coup attempt (both covered later in this book), though starkly different events (the first was led by a liberal civil-society movement and the second a nefarious plot by a would-be junta) were, for Erdogan, instances of the same phenomenon: conspiracies to topple the people's will that were backed by foreign powers.

4

The Generals Fashion a New Turkey

The Latin American-style coup (1980)

E vents during the 1980s unexpectedly strengthened the Islamists in Turkey. The TAF took power in a *coup d'état* in September 1980, and this time they were determined to end Turkey's paralyzing violence and change the course of its politics, once and for all. The military's crackdown in the aftermath largely achieved the former goal and fully achieved the latter, albeit at a cost. Though Erbakan, like leaders of other major parties, was arrested, the TAF's policies also inadvertently paved the way for the rise of political Islam in Turkey, a movement that would eventually decapitate the Turkish military, nullifying a major Islamist opponent.

The aftermath of the 1980 coup would be remembered as the most authoritarian period in Turkey since its first free and fair election in 1950. This coup was truly a Latin American affair, with the military taking over power directly and initiating a brutal crackdown on the whole of society, especially the left. Within a year, generals had arrested 122,600 people, a figure that would climb to nearly half a million before the military was finished.[1] Untold numbers were mutilated or killed in the torture chambers of state prisons. Overnight, the military outlawed virtually every civil-society organization in Turkey. More than 600 such associations were banned, and Turkey's major trade unions were shut down.[2] The right to collective bargaining was virtually eliminated.[3] Tens of thousands of militants, mostly from the left, fled the country. The coup traumatized the left, and accordingly many leftist thinkers developed a lingering grudge against the military. As a result of the actions of the military, the left entered a crippling decline from which it would not recover, leaving a void among the poor and working classes that the Islamists would fill in the 1990s.

The generals also arrogated to themselves the authority to screen political parties. Of the 17 parties that applied for participation in the first post-coup election of 1983, the TAF accepted only three, two of which were set up behind the scenes by the military itself.[4] On top of that, the military banned 700 politicians, the elite of Turkey's political class, from politics for up to ten years.[5] The generals wanted to punish these elites for the political gridlock of the late 1970s, when election law had allowed nearly a dozen parties to enter parliament because of Turkey's system of proportional representation. During that time of economic collapse, political polarization, and party inflation in the legislature, cooperation between the numerous factions in the legislature had ceased completely, and the resulting deadlock was the backdrop to civil war-like fighting on the streets. Among those condemned were Demirel, Ecevit, Erbakan, and Turkes, the four men who had dominated Turkish politics throughout the 1970s.[6]

On the eve of the coup, Erdogan was acting as the head of the Istanbul youth branch of Erbakan's MSP, completing his university education and playing semi-professional soccer. After playing for Kasimpasa's amateur team—Camialti Spor—Erdogan transferred to the semi-professional team organized by the Istanbul municipal government's utility and transportation company, Istanbul Electricity, Tramway, and Tunnel (IETT). This also meant he could be on the company's payroll as an employee.[7] When the MSP was shut down, Erdogan, too, took a temporary break from politics. He left IETT due to disagreements with the newly appointed management— thereby also leaving the soccer team—and took a private-sector job in the confectionery industry, beginning in a management position and then moving on to direct the company.[8] Though this ended Erdogan's formal soccer career, he has maintained his enthusiasm for the sport throughout his life. For example, in 2014 he donned a jersey and played in a symbolic inaugural match to announce the naming of a new stadium in Istanbul.[9] Shortly after entering the private sector, in 1982, Erdogan also began his mandatory military service—required of all Turkish males—in Istanbul.[10] Posted close to home, he maintained his political contacts even if he took a break from formal political life.

The demise of High Kemalism

By the 1980s, High Kemalism, hitherto official state doctrine, was declining in Turkey. Though everyone paid lip service to this dogma, its true believers were fast becoming a minority in the Turkish elite. If the archetypal Turkish civil servants of the early republic hailed from western Anatolia or the Balkans and spent their college years sipping coffee in Parisian or Swiss cafes, this breed of European-groomed public officer had become an endangered species by the 1970s. As Turkey developed and modernized, its bureaucracy opened its doors to young, ambitious Turks (mostly Sunnis, and a small number of Alevis, but never Jews, Greeks, or Armenians), who often hailed from central and eastern Anatolian towns.[11] Many of them spent their formative years far from the cosmopolitan luster of Europe. They were embedded instead in rural and religious community networks, which they brought with them when they entered public service. The more educated among them had received a technical education in the United States, but they had less admiration for the culture and political theory of Europe.

Kenan Evren: the general who (unknowingly) killed High Kemalism

For the rising class of Turkish politicians, the premium that Kemalism placed on strict secularism seemed badly out of touch with contemporary realities. Yet it was not a politician but a general, Kenan Evren, who would put the final nail in the coffin of High Kemalism.

Evren, the paternal figurehead of the 1980 coup, came from Alasehir (known in antiquity and the Middle Ages as Philadelphia), a town in the Aegean region's farming hinterland and the raisin capital of Turkey, where tradition and Islam were fixtures of everyday life. Thanks to his small-town upbringing, Evren was aware that most Turks who lived outside the large cities were comfortable with the idea of more religion in public life. Evren was also vehemently anti-leftist: he had carried out the 1980 coup to stamp out communism in Turkey, and now, with the Cold War in mind, he wanted to leave behind a country that would never have to worry about a threat from the left. He believed that injecting Islam into Turkish society and politics, though in violation of Ataturk's legacy, was the best way to inoculate it against future leftist movements and communism.

True to his small-town and agrarian roots, Evren also believed that the new glue binding Turkish society had to be something more adhesive than Westernization. The team of generals-turned-bureaucrats and politicians that he brought into power fashioned a new iteration of Kemalism. This new doctrine left intact High Kemalism's reverence for the state and authority, as well as continuing to foster the state's obsession with national security and, of course, with the icon of Ataturk. But it placed greater emphasis on the Islamic facet of Turkish identity. A set of opinion leaders calling themselves the "Intellectuals' Hearth" (Aydinlar Ocagi) figured prominently in this retooling of Turkey's official ideology. This movement began when a few dozen right-wing academics and professionals, sanctioned by the military, came together in abhorrence at the havoc that they believed the left was inflicting on public order and morality.[12] The movement's new theory, "Turkish–Islamic Synthesis," interpreted Islam not as a challenge to existing authorities, as Erbakan did, but as a means of restoring harmony under state authority.[13] Subsequently, the state openly embraced Sunni Islam: for instance, programs on Sunni Islam appeared on TRT, a publicly funded broadcaster and Turkey's only television network in the 1980s. The coup government also allowed Imam Hatip graduates to study within any university department, opening the door for the

Islamic schools to gain a status on a par with that of secular public high schools. Formally secular Turkey gradually became informally Sunni Islamic under the generals. The injection of Islamic codes into Turkey's body politic in the 1980s would culminate in the complete unraveling of secularism in Turkey in the first two decades of the twenty-first century under Erdogan.

Turgut Ozal's Janus face: economic liberalism and social conservatism

The generals and conservative elites who propagated the Turkish–Islamic Synthesis did not intend to strengthen Erbakan's Islamist movement, and in fact many of them saw Erbakan as dangerous. His Islam, wedded to political solidarity with Muslims overseas, seemed to them foreign and radical: imported from the battlefields of Afghanistan, it was not the folksy Anatolian Islam that they remembered from their childhoods. For his part, General Evren made little effort to hide his distaste for Erbakan. Indeed, the architects of the Turkish–Islamic Synthesis might have hoped that this new ideology would render Erbakan's more hard-edged political Islam unappealing, something that was apparently demonstrated when, in the 1984 local election—the first election in which Erbakan's party was permitted to compete—RP, which Erbakan established behind the scenes due to his political ban, won a mere 4.5 percent of the vote.[14] With Erbakan still banned from politics and his party still reeling from the 1980 coup, the Islamists were unable to make a strong showing. At least momentarily, the political center that the generals had imposed was keeping Erbakan at bay. But events in the aftermath of the coup also demonstrated a cardinal lesson of Turkish politics: Turks may acquiesce in military rule, but at the ballot box they will not support military-backed candidates. In the general election of November 1983, the Nationalist Democracy Party (MDP), led by former general Turgut Sunalp and endorsed by the military, lost in a landslide to Turgut Ozal, a political neophyte, a World Bank economist, and the undersecretary of the Turkish State Planning Organization (DPT)—the powerful body responsible for overseeing the government's economic-development policies until the 1980s. As prime minister, Ozal, leading his newly founded Motherland Party (ANAP), subsequently came to represent this new political center.

Ozal dominated the political scene in Turkey throughout the 1980s, ushering in sweeping economic liberalization, paving the way for a period of growth, but also a more open attitude toward Islam in politics. Turkey witnessed the emergence of a middle class (and the olive oil made a comeback to satisfy the tastes of the new bourgeoisie). Propelled by the rising numbers of urban and middle-class voters, Ozal subsequently won successive elections in the same decade.

In the long term, however, the political climate that the general and Ozal fostered during the 1980s helped create new possibilities for Erbakan and his Islamist movement.[15] Firstly, the Turkish–Islamic Synthesis made public Islam acceptable for the mainstream, a far cry from Ataturk's model of *laïcité*. Turkey has long had legal and customary proscriptions on the mixing of religion and politics that are much stricter than those, say, in the United States. But these constraints eased as the Turkish–Islamic Synthesis promoted a more lenient understanding of which sorts of religious reference were taboo and which ones were merely harmless expressions of shared culture. Using religious imagery and quoting chapter and verse from the Qur'an no longer placed one far from the main line of Turkish politics. To normalize public Islam further, Ozal also increased funding for Imam Hatip schools, raising the caliber of education in such institutions to rival that of public secular schools. Existing Imam Hatip schools opened elite-level institutions providing education in English, which attracted top-performing students from conservative families in rural Anatolia. During these years, the military authorities also supported mandatory courses on religion in all public schools. The Turkish military had changed its mind on religious education in less than a decade: teaching religion at a young age, they now thought, would inoculate the youth against the dangerous ideology of communism that had corrupted a generation and plunged Turkey into chaos during the late 1970s.[16] General Evren himself often sprinkled Qur'anic verbiage into his own policy speeches. Following suit, Ozal openly expressed his religious leanings, even making them part of everyday state rituals in Turkey. Tellingly, members of the more conservative-oriented flank of Ozal's centrist ANAP often oscillated to and from the Islamist wing of the party, whose members had left Erbakan's MSP to join the ANAP.

Ozal's conservative side would have become more dominant had it not been for his wife Semra, a cigar-smoker who championed a less conservative vision of Turkey than did her husband, often pulling him toward the center. Under Ozal, who was half Kurdish, the country became more liberal in its politics, though his era also saw the beginning of a multi-decade fight against the PKK. Although it was established in 1978, the PKK was not a key player in the civil war-like fighting in the streets in that decade. Rather, the organization launched itself onto the national stage in 1984 when it sent its fighters to raid two Kurdish towns in Turkey's southeast. Ozal's reaction to the group's surge was to deploy full military force against it. This reaction led to further PKK attacks, and Turkey entered a cycle of violence that continues to this day, with occasional PKK "ceasefires."

Of course, the Ozal years also left a positive legacy, a very significant one. Though a conservative Muslim, Ozal saw Turkey's place in the West, and thanks to him the country not only embraced free-market economics, but also moved even closer to Europe and the United States. In 1987, he awakened Turkey's quiescent EU-accession process by reapplying to join the union's predecessor, the European Communities (EC). He also strengthened ties with the United States: when Saddam Hussein invaded Kuwait in 1990, Ozal was one of the first leaders to come out in support of the United States, and Turkey later provided significant logistical assistance to Washington in the First Gulf War of 1991. As a conservative Muslim who saw himself as a Westerner and an avid believer in the free-market economy, Ozal left behind a transformed country.

Erdogan enters politics...

But Erbakan did not entirely leave it to Ozal to create a new Turkey. By 1985, Erbakan was flagrantly defying the ban on politics that the military authorities had imposed on him. In the conservative central-Anatolian stronghold of Konya, he was addressing rallies of ecstatic followers and traveling to Istanbul to endorse party candidates.[17] The other banned political figures from the 1970s had begun doing the same. Ozal relented, and the political ban on these politicians was lifted in 1987 after the passing of a referendum. The political elite that had nearly brought Turkey to ruin in the 1970s returned to politics. It would take them and their successors just over a decade to lead the country into ruin again, preparing the path for Erdogan's rise in 2002.

In 1987, Erbakan led the charge in a general election in which his RP narrowly missed the 10 percent national electoral threshold that the authorities had put in place to keep marginal parties out of parliament following the 1980 coup. Two years later, in 1989, the RP doubled its 1984 vote in local elections and took control of a handful of important municipalities. It had benefitted from the implosion of the left, in particular the unions in working-class districts in the aftermath of the 1980 coup. The Islamists were at the gates.

Erdogan was entering his career in professional politics just as the RP was beginning to hit its stride in post-coup Turkey. After completing his military service, Erdogan went back to work for Erbakan.[18] It was rumored that Ozal's center-right ANAP, open to the Islamist-right brand of politics, had offered Erdogan an enticing position, but Erdogan stayed by his mentor's side and quickly rose through the party ranks. He was promoted from the youth branch into the big leagues in 1984, when he was made chairman of the RP branch for the Beyoglu district.[19] Within a year, he became chairman of the party for the entire city of Istanbul. Soon after, he was elected to the party's executive board, the body responsible for running day-to-day affairs across the country.[20] Although Erdogan had not yet entered the public eye, within the Islamic movement he was gaining recognition as a rising star.

...and runs to become mayor in his old neighborhood, but loses

In September 1986, Turkey held a special election to fill 11 vacant seats in the parliament. One of these seats was in Istanbul. With every party competing for this single seat, the RP had no realistic chance at victory, as Islamists were still a small force, despite Erdogan's confident declarations that nobody would stand a chance against it.[21] With little at stake, the party put Erdogan on the ticket in what was essentially a dress rehearsal for electoral politics. Erdogan lost, but his campaign demonstrated the extent to which he had won the loyalty of the RP grassroots during his years as an organizer in Istanbul. Under him, RP's Istanbul branch spent the 1980s meticulously organizing in working-class districts of Turkey's largest city, filling the void vacated by the left and the unions, who had been decimated by the 1980 coup—and they would eventually be rewarded for this work.

The real show began when Erdogan ran for mayor of Beyoglu in 1989. The campaign was a sensation. For years, younger members in the party had been urging the RP to reach out beyond the pious and conservative communities that were the backbone of Erbakan's movement. Initially, Erdogan had been resistant to anything that might sully the party's essence, but in the election for Beyoglu, encompassing poor areas, such as Kasimpasa, as well as bohemian neighborhoods overlooking the Bosphorus, he put this new approach to work more successfully than ever before. He took photo opportunities at *meyhanes*—tavern-style Turkish restaurants where alcohol flows freely—and he even pulled publicity stunts by visiting Istanbul's legal brothels.[22] Standing among the gobsmacked sex workers, he insisted that most of them would support the RP and its conservative mission, since it was the only party that would rescue them from their trade.[23]

In his mid-thirties, then, Erdogan became the face of the rising generation in the RP. For many, he looked nothing like the stereotypical Islamist so often caricatured in the secular press. Tall and athletically built, with a neatly trimmed mustache, he charged through his childhood stomping grounds in a suit. Paying visits to the living rooms of countless local families, he conversed about everyday problems, and he blamed the elitist politicians for neglecting the common man. Surrounded by his electrified followers, it seemed that Erdogan could not lose. But he did. When the results came in, he came up short by a razor-thin margin. Joined by his supporters, he cried foul, and then locked horns with the judge overseeing the vote count. In an outburst, Erdogan accused the judge of being drunk, and the authorities quickly detained him.[24] But even as he served his week-long stint in confinement, he must have seen that this loss came with a glimmering silver lining. With this campaign, Erdogan proved his mettle to a legion of grassroots followers. Nationwide, he had become the face of the RP's initiative to rebrand itself as a party for the ordinary Turk. The slogan he used said it all: Erdogan is "one of us," his canvassers chanted, a motto implying that, unlike the other candidates, he had grown up on the very streets where he campaigned. Another of his key accomplishments was the decision to put women in charge of canvassing the electorate, a revolutionary step for a conservative movement.

He knew the people and their problems, and he shared their values. As for his overt Islamic rhetoric, well, this was merely a reflection of his being raised in a household where values mattered. His was a common-sense Islam, the same kind that "real" Turks cherished.

The Turkish center-right commits hara-kiri

But what helped Erdogan and the Islamists most was the collapse of the dominant center-right pillar of Turkish politics in the 1990s. When Turkey switched from military rule in 1983, center-right voters flocked to Ozal's ANAP, a newcomer. Once he took office, Ozal cultivated for himself a reputation as a competent techno-crat, determined to trim the red tape that was stifling the Turkish economy. To be sure, his liberal reforms brought increased effi-ciency to Turkey's economy, and his emphasis on infrastructure provided access to basic services, such as electricity, landlines, and water, for many who had never enjoyed them before. But economic liberalization also brought more visible inequalities. Even worse, the Ozal administration became mired in corruption scandals. The prime minister surrounded himself with family and friends, who had a hearty appetite for the material rewards that public office could bring, and seemed unable to stop his kith and kin from abusing their newfound privileges. More than ever before, the political road was paved with personal relationships, favors, and bribes.

Ozal moved from the prime minister's office to the presidency in 1989, elevated by a vote in parliament, where his party held a majority. At this time, Ozal left the ANAP—in accordance with the Turkish constitution, which stipulates that the president be a non-partisan figure. While still subject to the generals' political ban, Demirel had from behind the scenes established his own center-right movement, the True Path Party (DYP), before being permitted to re-enter politics following the 1987 referendum. With Demirel, the DYP won the 1991 general election against the ANAP, now led by new party chief and prime minister Mesut Yilmaz. The generals had unintentionally riven Turkey's dominant political bloc in two, and its leaders did very little to unite the two halves. While ideological differences between the two parties were minimal, competition between Demirel and Ozal, and then their successors, Tansu Ciller, a US-trained economist, and Yilmaz, a German-trained economist, respectively, was rancorous. Ultimately, feuding between the center-right parties and their leaders destroyed Turkey's dominant political bloc, with grave repercussions for the country's democracy.

After Ozal's death in 1993, Turkey began to slide into full-blown crisis. Demirel vacated his seat as prime minister to take over as president. This made room for Ciller to be elected DYP party chief and to take over as prime minister. A professor of economics at

Istanbul's prestigious Bosphorus University, Ciller had been brought into Demirel's DYP only two years before in a bid to garnish the party's image as forward-thinking and modern. At first, many hoped that she would invigorate the party, but her government turned out to be a disaster. Less than a year into her term, the economy was spinning out of control, with interest rates and inflation soaring.[25] Bank lending rates reached 1,000 percent and inflation peaked at 100 percent.[26] Turkey's major businesses battened down the hatches: Koc Holding, one of Turkey's largest conglomerates, halted its production of automobiles and refrigerators.[27] Unemployment was rising, and the situation of those who did manage to hold down jobs was growing worse: Ciller's attempt to set things right with a sharp devaluation of the currency cut in half the purchasing power of salaried employees.[28] All told, the liberalization agenda set in motion by Ozal and continued under Ciller laid the ground for a new era of economic growth in Turkey. But for the ordinary Turk in the thick of such difficult times, reassurances about the future provided cold comfort.

Ciller's performance would have been politically costly under any circumstances. But insult truly became injury when allegations began to emerge that she was growing rich from the spoils of her office, and that her husband, Ozer Ciller, had long been using the couple's political connections to make money. The dramatic increase in Ciller's wealth since her entry into politics became a topic of unending speculation. The picture was ugly indeed. While ordinary Turks were tightening their belts, those at the top were making a killing, or at least so it seemed. In the midst of these events, *Milliyet*—a newspaper close to Turkey's secular estab-lishment at the time—published a poll showing that 69 percent of respondents rated the government poorly and 70 percent did not trust Ciller.[29] At this time allegations emerged that Ciller's opponent and the ANAP leader, Yilmaz, was also corrupt. Instead of being a political race, the DYP–ANAP competition turned into a personal spat about who was more corrupt and who had alleg-edly embezzled more money. The feud blighted the center-right, which appeared detached from the man on the street as Turkey went through three major economic crises in less than a decade under successive Ciller and Yilmaz governments. As Erdogan had stated plainly two years before the *Milliyet* poll was conducted: "Our people can see that the current system in Turkey has gone bankrupt."[30]

5

Erdogan's Meteoric Rise as Istanbul's Mayor

The Just Order campaign

For Erbakan's RP and Erdogan, the failures of the center-right presented a golden opportunity. Capitalizing on popular frustration, the RP began to reframe its message in the early 1990s. Erbakan proclaimed that Turkey's problems went deeper than the individual venality of Ciller or Yilmaz. The entire system was corrupt to its core, the RP insisted, and nothing short of a total remaking of the country's socio-economic system could bring an end to the misery of the ordinary Turk. Erbakan called this new ideal society the "Just Order" (Adil Duzen). Under this order (predicated on the tenets of "Islam"), politicians would cease to be corrupt, while peasants and working people would cease to be exploited. Turkey, finally, would escape from its century of subjugation to the West. As things stood, the country's participation in the modern world system had dragged it into the "order of slavery," in which "imperialists" and "Zionists" dominated the once mighty Turkish people.[1] This was why its politicians could get away with such corruption; this was why interest rates could not be tamed and unemployment was rising.

The Just Order campaign was essentially a repackaging of the same ideas that Erbakan had been propounding since his days with Kotku in the 1970s with the National Outlook movement, albeit with a shift in emphasis and tone. In the rhetoric of the new RP, condemning Turks for their wayward lifestyles took a backseat to castigating the establishment and the West for Turkey's ills. By shifting the blame this way, Erbakan hoped to reach audiences that previously had been put off by the Islamists' accusatory jeremiads. This new message also came with new optics: RP television ads began to feature people who seemed to come from all walks of life, and who evinced varying levels of piety.[2] Even uncovered women went on display. Filiz Ergun, a dentist and council member in the Istanbul district of Gungoren who became one of the faces of the new RP, did not cover her hair, and she insisted that the party embrace modern professional women like her.[3] A bigger stir was made when Gulay Pinarbasi, a fashion model and actress, joined the party in 1993. She began covering her hair, and pledged to live a completely different life in line with the teachings of "Islam."[4]

Islamists build strength through grassroots politics

As the party refurbished its image, it also built up its ability to increase voter turnout. Party rolls grew precipitously during the early 1990s, from fewer than 200,000 in 1991 to more than 1 million in 1993, and then to over 4 million by 1995.[5] That year, in Istanbul alone, the RP claimed to have more than 300,000 members in its women's branch.[6] But numbers alone fail to capture the effectiveness of the RP political machine. Erbakan was fond of saying, "Other parties have members, we have believers."[7] And truly, the RP's levels of supporter commitment and organization were the envy of every other party in Turkey. Being an RP member meant much more than paying annual dues and attending the occasional party congress. Members pounded the pavement daily, sometimes months before polling day.[8] By the middle of the 1990s, the RP had Turkey's premier voter database: a completely computerized record of the country's voters, something that none of the other parties possessed—and a rarity even among parties globally—which would help Erdogan take the country's helm in 2002.

The RP cadres worked within a dense hierarchy that stretched all the way down to the individual street, and often to the individual apartment building. This legion of activists was organized and determined to reach outside the religious networks that had previously confined their party.[9] Topping Erdogan's list of commands to his army of canvassers was an admonition: "Don't act holier than thou. Don't judge. Smile."[10] By the early 1990s, this remodeling had begun to pay dividends. The results of the 1991 general election carried Erbakan and his party into parliament for the first time since the 1980 coup.[11] Afraid of once again falling below the 10 percent threshold, the RP ran in partnership with the Nationalist Work Party (MCP), the latest iteration of Turkes' never-dying far-right movement, and the Reformist Democracy Party (IDP), a small ultra-nationalist and hard-line Islamist faction with localized support among Turks and Circassians in east-central Anatolia. This political partnership won 16.9 percent of the vote, granting them 62 seats in the 450-member parliament. Although far from a revolution, the RP once again had a voice on the national stage. After more than a decade, Erbakan was allowed back on the parliamentary floor, where he immediately took up his old pastime of cleverly ribbing his centrist rivals for their failures and declaring that nothing short of an RP government could save Turkey.

The Turkish left dies in Istanbul

Erdogan again narrowly missed entering parliament in the 1991 election. But in retrospect this was only a minor setback, since he would win his next election, and this victory would come with a more coveted prize: the keys to the Istanbul Metropolitan Municipality. Becoming mayor of Turkey's largest and most eclectic city more closely suited Erdogan's attraction to the limelight. Indeed, it made him the protagonist in a drama that seemed to encapsulate Turkey's nationwide predicament during those years: the massive growth of administrative problems facing the country and the glaring lack of leadership needed to tackle them. On the eve of the 1994 mayoral elections, Istanbul appeared to be at the center of this dysfunction. Like developing cities across the world, it was grappling desperately with the mammoth challenge of explosive demographic growth: during the 1980s the city's population increased by 54 percent, and this massive influx continued throughout the 1990s.[12] The bulk of these recent arrivals were poor individuals with little education. If they were not fleeing poverty in the Anatolian interior, they were fleeing the brutal war in the country's Kurdish southeast between the Turkish military and the PKK.[13]

In the 1989 local elections, the ANAP suffered a nationwide rout in what many saw as a referendum on the Ozal administration. Nurettin Sozen, a medical doctor from the center-left Social Democratic People's Party (SHP)—the 1990s incarnation of the secularist CHP—became Istanbul's mayor, creating hopes for the left's nationwide rise. With its platform focused on clean government and anti-corruption, the SHP promised a break from the past. But under the new administration, things only appeared to get worse. For one thing, Istanbul saw its population nearly double in the 1990s, creating massive demand for public services, a gargantuan task for any administrator. Just as Ciller's and Yilmaz's center-right was losing its grip on the country, the center-left proved to be a bitter disappointment in Istanbul. The left's tenure began on a sour note when Sozen found himself at loggerheads with the city's sanitation workers over a pay dispute. Their demands unmet after a seemingly interminable period of negotiation, the sanitation workers went on strike, allowing entire sections of Istanbul to become putrefying wastelands. The problem reached an unimaginable level of morbid absurdity when one of the trash heaps that were slowly engulfing a slum neighborhood exploded. Methane gas had built up beneath the filth, finally igniting and causing an avalanche that killed 27 of the hapless poor.[14] As if to complete the hellish tableau, that winter the air filled with soot from the millions of coal-burning ovens that families were using to heat their homes. Many began wearing surgical masks before venturing outside.[15]

But it was water that ultimately turned the public resolutely against the Sozen administration. Just as he took office, Istanbul fell into a severe drought. Annual rainfall between 1992 and 1994 dropped 18.5 percent from its long-term average.[16] For an expanding city located on two peninsulas where fresh water had always been a precious commodity, this was a calamity. Years later, Sozen recalled how he would leap out of bed in the middle of the night overjoyed at the sound of rain, only to realize it was just the sound of rustling leaves.[17] Those who lived in Istanbul during those days remember keeping large containers of water in their bathrooms and kitchens as preparation for the inevitable cut-offs that had become part of life in the city.

Three years into Sozen's term, as Turkey neared its next local elections, this daily frustration found its outlet. Ergun Goknel, a Sozen appointee who ran the Istanbul Water and Sewerage Administration (ISKI), appeared on the national stage as the main character in a scandal. Goknel had divorced his wife in 1992 to marry his new flame, an ISKI employee three decades his junior, offering his wife a divorce settlement valued in the hundreds of thousands of dollars.[18] But his jilted wife was not content to console herself quietly with her new fortune. She went to the press to declare the size of the settlement—which was far too large for a public servant to afford—and to voice her suspicions about her husband's alleged illicit dealings. This triggered a flurry of speculation in the press about corruption in ISKI and the SHP, and Turkey's prosecutors sprang into action, preparing a handful of high-profile cases against leftist leaders.[19] While ISKI burned, Goknel married his new wife at the Istanbul Hilton, the city's first American-built deluxe hotel. Mayor Sozen, infuriated, removed Goknel from his post and declared that he would support the harshest disciplinary action against any corrupt dealings uncovered in a criminal investigation.[20] It was a buck too short, a day too late: the Turkish left, already weakened due to anti-leftist measures implemented in the aftermath of the 1980 coup, died in Istanbul in 1994.

Across the country, too, the left faced a challenge: like the center-right, the center-left was also divided as a result of the military's 1980s ban on politicians. CHP leader Ecevit, barred from politics, set up his own movement behind the scenes: the Democratic Left

Party (DSP). In the meantime, much of the center-left rank and file gradually re-formed the CHP (after setting up many leftist parties, such as the SHP, which united, fought, split up, and reunited in the good old fashion of garrulous leftist politics). Despite the fact that there were few ideological differences between the CHP and DSP, the two parties entered into a visceral and debilitating fight in the 1990s. Although Ecevit would become prime minister as head of an unwieldy coalition from 1999 to 2002, the left would not regain the popularity it had enjoyed in the 1970s.

Erdogan becomes a household name: the 1994 Istanbul mayoral race

This scandal that brought down the left in Istanbul could not have been juicier had it been penned by the writers of Turkey's famous soap operas. It was unfolding during the peak of the local-elections season, and with every sordid detail it seemed to prove what Erbakan and his party had been saying all along: that the people were suffering because they were governed by elites whose moral fiber had been rotted by Western ways. Turkey's leaders were too busy fleecing the public and having affairs with each other to bother themselves with the problems of the suffering masses. Maybe a shock of good old-fashioned Islamic morality really was what the country needed.

Indeed, Erdogan's 1994 campaign played upon these themes with tremendous virtuosity. He called the RP the "voice of the silent masses."[21] Like the DP of the 1950s, Erdogan cast his party as the only true representative of the innumerable ordinary Turks who had been abandoned by an apathetic and corrupt elite. Because a major source of Istanbul's misfortunes was the venality of its guardians, piety became a practical solution. Moreover, in contrast to Erbakan's abstract manifesto, Erdogan developed concrete proposals to tackle the city's problems. In his famous "emergency action plans," he detailed exactly how he would address the municipality's garbage, water, pollution, and housing issues.[22] While other parties lacked the grassroots infrastructure to communicate directly with the residents of Istanbul's shanty towns, the RP machine could interact with them at a highly granular level, thanks to its vast database.[23] Populism, too, helped the RP's cause. The party pledged to keep bread prices low through municipally subsidized bread factories, and RP representatives handed out coal and groceries in poor neighborhoods, once again taking advantage of their computerized database. It was said that one RP lieutenant even handed out gold coins to prospective voters.[24]

The 1994 nationwide local elections were no landslide, despite the public rancor at the centrist parties and the RP's new political initiative. If anything, it showed that the vast majority of the voting public was still not comfortable with the Islamist RP alternative, even when the establishment parties were at their worst. Erdogan's claim to be the people's voice has always been belied by the reality that, as this book goes to print, his party has never secured the support of more than the slimmest majority of the Turkish population. In 1994, Erdogan's supporters were a minority indeed: he took only 25.2 percent of the vote in Istanbul. But since the other parties on both the left and the right were deeply divided, a quarter of the vote was enough to deliver the Istanbul Metropolitan Municipality into his hands.

The RP also ensured that the wind was at Erdogan's back. Across the country, the RP was performing better than ever. It garnered 19 percent of the vote nationally, doubling its share from the previous local elections, in 1989. With this result, the party took charge of 28 of the 76 mayoral seats in provincial capitals.[25] For the first time, political Islamists had become a major factor in everyday life for citizens across vast swaths of Turkey.

Istanbul is Erdogan's stage

Shortly after his 1994 election victory, Erdogan chastised a journalist. "Why do you always ask me about closing bars and brothels?" he bristled. "Why don't you ask me about buses, rubbish collection, pollution, or water?"[26] He knew that these were the matters that would make or break his reputation in public office. Luckily for him, the leftists were not a hard act to follow, and Erdogan was a competent and energetic administrator. Even his opponents had to admit that, under his leadership, Istanbul's residents saw the quality of basic services improve. Residents saw new amenities under Erdogan, such as new hospitals and schools, and the expansion of the city's bus system. Judas trees, native to Istanbul, emerged again along the city's boulevards with their signature deep-pink blossom. Erdogan also carried to fruition numerous improvements to Istanbul's metro system that had begun under his predecessors' tenures.[27] His administration visibly improved Istanbul's smog problem by expanding the city's natural-gas distribution system as a replacement for dirty coal-burning heaters, a development that would eventually create a Turkish reliance on gas imports from Russia.[28] Erdogan also tackled Istanbul's water crisis. He replaced the leftist political appointees with a team of respected academics and technicians who completed several important water-treatment projects begun under Sozen and his other predecessors. In 1994, less than 15 percent of Istanbul residents had access to waste-water treatment. By 1998 this figure had climbed to roughly 65 percent.[29] ISKI also presided over the infusion of about half a billion dollars to complete a long-term plan to clean up the Golden Horn, which was started under Bedrettin Dalan, Istanbul's mayor from the ANAP in the 1980s.[30] Erdogan demonstrated that the Islamists could not only govern but also do it well.

But, of course, the most direct beneficiary of Erdogan's tenure was his core constituency—the poor and the pious. He launched a policy of renovating slum neighborhoods with purpose-built housing for Istanbul's millions.[31] This initiative (which would be greatly expanded under the AKP) helped integrate poor migrants—as Erdogan's father had been—into the city. Erdogan also made an effort to develop these areas into livable spaces. They offered free or highly subsidized community services, such as sewing courses and computer classes.

Although Erdogan promised to create a new Istanbul, some things never seem to change in local government. One sordid aspect of politics that the Erdogan administration did uphold was the patronage and favoritism that has long been part of Turkey's political culture. A month and a half into his term, Erdogan declared that his administration had made important shake-ups in the municipality's ranks, and that "from now on you will not hear of municipality employees becoming involved in corruption and exploitation."[32] But the reality was somewhat less pristine. Although the RP had gained a reputation for clamping down on bribery and other forms of corruption, it was no stranger to using public office to its own advantage. In the Eminonu district of Istanbul, the RP promptly replaced 200 municipal workers with their own loyalists, and RP leaders found creative ways of pushing out civil servants whom they did not have the authority to dismiss. The months after the RP victory saw a spate of stories detailing the assignment of expert civil servants to absurd duties like counting the number of cars or dogs in a neighborhood.[33] Admittedly, Erdogan needed to appease the grassroots: this victory belonged to the party, just as much as it did to him, and the RP was determined to reap the rewards of its new authority. Before long, allegations were raised that contractors had to pay donations to RP "charities" in order to bid on big-budget municipal projects.[34] Today, it is rumored that a very similar system funnels money into the coffers of the AKP.

But regardless of these shortcomings in his bureaucracy, Erdogan ran Istanbul successfully, proving himself to be a capable administrator and politician whom common Turks could trust. All he needed was a perfect storm to carry him into power.

6

The Perfect Storm

The Islamists come to power

Although the RP won a plurality of the vote in the winter 1995 general election, it lacked sufficient seats to form a government. In fact, votes were so evenly split among the top parties that no two held enough seats to form an absolute majority in parliament. As leader of the RP, Erbakan unsuccessfully tried to form a coalition government. But he was unable to garner enough support, and other party leaders took the initiative. Ismail Karadayi, the head of the TAF, which considered itself to be "the guardian of secularism," reportedly pressured other parties to form a coalition without the RP, expressing his unease at the idea of RP rule: "If this coalition is formed, I fear ensuing events will upset us all. If there is a way to prevent this, do what you must."[1] The DYP and the ANAP, having earned 19.2 and 19.6 percent of the vote respectively, just below the RP's 21.4 percent, formed a coalition government to be headed first by Yilmaz, and later by Ciller. The DYP–ANAP coalition won a parliamentary vote of confidence, with 257 of the 550 deputies voting in favor. However, Turkey's Constitutional Court ruled the vote of confidence to be invalid because the government had failed to secure majority support (273 votes) of the legislative quorum. Ciller dissolved the government. She instead formed an alliance with the RP, agreeing to make Erbakan the first Islamist prime minister of Turkey in return for the position of deputy under him. In July 1996, their coalition narrowly won an absolute majority and formed a government. For the first time in Turkey's history, the Islamists were officially in charge as the leading party in the government.

The RP–DYP coalition government received criticism for Erbakan's foreign policy. When Erbakan went on an African tour, visiting Egypt, Nigeria, and Libya, his obsequiousness toward the Libyan leader, Muammar Gaddafi, angered even his own constituents back home. Erbakan appeared passive in the face of Gaddafi's reprimands that Turkey's Israel-friendly foreign policy was proof that the imperialist powers had placed it "under occupation" and that Turks had lost their "national will." Gaddafi also lambasted Turkey for its Kurdish policy during his joint press conference with Erbakan, greatly embarrassing the Turkish prime minister.[2] This public browbeating did not play well at home. Despite these reactions, Erbakan maintained his pro-Islamist foreign-policy focus, hewing to his National Outlook origins. He proposed new international allegiances, such as a "D-8" (the "D" standing for "Developing"), composed of the eight most populous Muslim nations, to compete with the G7. Erbakan also suggested an Islamic security organization to rival NATO, as well as an Islamic currency called the dinar. Deeply alarmed, the military established an initiative called the "Western Working Group," tasked with monitoring all RP activities.

Buoyed by Erbakan's electoral victory, RP members exhibited local outbursts of Islamist sentiment as well. On November 10, 1996—the anniversary of Ataturk's death in 1938 and a national holiday—Sukru Karatepe, the RP mayor of the east-central Anatolian city of Kayseri, made remarks against the secular state that landed him with a jail sentence: "Even if I were left alone in this world as the only member of the RP, this repressive order must change," he declared. "This antiquated order that sees people as slaves must change. Muslims, don't you ever let go of this drive, this bitterness, this hate, and this faith. This is our duty."[3] For this outburst, Karatepe was arraigned on charges of "religious incitement," and the courts sentenced him to one year in prison.

The 1997 "soft coup" against the Islamists

A few months later, on January 31, 1997, Bekir Yildiz, RP district head of Ankara's outlying Sincan district, delivered a dramatic speech, threatening that Muslims who believed in the hijab would target secular people who "had fallen ill with their own mistakes," forcefully "injecting sharia into their arms."[4] Once more, there were legal consequences: the courts slapped a four-year jail sentence on Yildiz for these statements. Then the military took matters into its own hands: the TAF sent a contingent of 20 tanks and 15 armored vehicles through Sincan as a symbolic warning against the RP-led borough government. Deputy chief of general staff Cevik Bir characterized this as an act of "recalibrating" democracy.[5] The rolling of tanks through Sincan would trigger a set of events, later dubbed the "soft coup," which culminated in the RP's fall from power.

Though the government protested these threats from the military, a week later tens of thousands of women in Ankara held a demonstration against Islamists called the "Women's March against Sharia," aligning many civil-society groups and opposition-party leaders with the secular military. As tensions between the TAF and the government continued to escalate, on February 28 the military-dominated Turkish National Security Council (MGK) held a meeting to discuss the issue of *irtica* (reactionism), a code word for Islamism since the late days of the Ottoman Empire. Following this meeting, the MGK issued a list of 18 policy recommendations, making it clear that failure to comply with these recommendations would result in serious sanctions. One of the most important MGK "recommendations" was the imposition of eight years' mandatory secular schooling, which would force the closure of Imam Hatip middle schools. A year later, the Higher Education Council (YOK), a government regulatory body responsible for the university system, put in place a penalty that made it difficult once more for Imam Hatip students to attain high scores on university entrance exams. Erdogan, at the time mayor of Istanbul, railed against the legislation, citing it as proof of the enduring mission of the Kemalist few to marginalize the pious masses.[6] Watching the events unfold from Istanbul as the city's mayor from the RP, Erdogan must have felt aggrieved to hear his alma mater accused of being an insidious institution.

For his own part, once presented with a memorandum from the military, Erbakan initially refused to sign it unless the terms were softened, and he scrambled for parliamentary support from other parties. He was eventually forced to sign, but tried to impede its enforcement by instigating parliamentary debate on the recommendations. Mustafa Kalemli, speaker of the parliament and a member of the ANAP, refused, insisting: "The government is the guardian of the [MGK's] decisions."[7] Like Kalemli, labor and employer unions and much of the media announced their support for the MGK memorandum, aligning civil-society groups with the secular state once more.

Other secular forces began mounting so much pressure on the RP that the party's power started to unravel. Eventually, faced with growing demonstrations by secular NGOs, fierce criticism from the media, rebukes from many members of the Turkish Industry and Business Association (TUSIAD)—Turkey's club of Fortune 500 billionaires—and, last but not least, the looming threat of a military coup, the RP relinquished power and the RP–DYP government was dissolved on June 18, 1997.[8]

Washington acquiesced in the "soft coup," if tacitly. US secretary of state Madeleine Albright explained on July 11, 1997 that while military intervention was not necessarily "a silver bullet" to Turkey's problems, the United States had "made very clear that it is essential that Turkey continue in a secular, democratic way."[9] The EU also put its tacit blessing behind the coup, saying that while it was "concerned at the implications for democratic pluralism and freedom of expression," "this decision [the coup] is in accordance with the provisions of the Turkish Constitution."[10]

On June 30, a new government was formed with the ANAP, Ecevit's DSP, and the smaller center-right Democrat Turkey Party (DTP) on board, excluding the RP. The secularists had won, but the Islamists, including Erdogan, would hold a deep grudge against them, singling out the TAF for its role behind the scenes in bringing down the Erbakan government. For his own part, Erdogan, meticulously patient and a political gradualist, drew valuable lessons from the "soft coup." When he came into office, he would move forward very slowly to consolidate power. To achieve all this, though, first he had to come to power—on a non-Islamist platform.

But for now, using his strongest virtue, patience, Erdogan focused on what he did best at that time: governing Istanbul. While the national elite was bogged down by Turkey's political wars, Erdogan was busy diligently improving the city's governance and services and thus slowly raising his national profile. Erbakan's star was falling, and Erdogan's was rising. Thus Erbakan's ouster as prime minister left Erdogan as the most powerful and most popular elected RP official in the country. Watching developments, Erdogan drew another conclusion: Erbakan was a failure and at some point he would need to be dropped.

The Turkish high court bans the Islamist RP and its successor

For his own part, Erbakan's downward spiral in Ankara only continued. On May 21, 1997, the prosecutor for the Turkish Constitutional Court, Vural Savas, launched a case to shut down the RP for "acting as the focal point for acts against the secular republic."[11] The case was closed on January 16, 1998, and the RP was shut down by the country's high court. Prominent RP politicians, including Erbakan, were banned from politics for five years. At this time, those RP members not banned from politics, including Erdogan, formed a new political movement, the Virtue Party (FP). This organization followed a slightly more moderate line compared to the RP. But it too was eventually shut down by the Turkish high court in 2001 since its leadership largely identified with Erbakan and his policies. At the time, RP leaders took their case to the European Court of Human Rights (ECHR) in Strasbourg, which upheld the Turkish court's decision in its judgment entitled "Case of Refah Partisi (the Welfare Party) and others v. Turkey."[12] When the Turkish high court also shut down the FP in 2001, the ECHR did not signal that it would make a different decision.

The Turkish Islamists choose moderation over violence

These developments left the Turkish Islamists with two possible trajectories: radicalization or moderation. The former, an unsavory option, would be to follow the "Algeria model." In 1992, the Islamic Salvation Front (FIS) won the Algerian general election. Following this victory, the military executed a *coup d'état*, annulled the election, and shut down the Islamist party. In response, Islamists launched a violent campaign against the country's military and secularist institutions. In the ensuing events, around 200,000 people died as a result of the gruesome acts committed by the Islamists and the military's reaction to them. Algeria went through a decade of horrific violence.[13]

Thankfully, the Turkish Islamists picked the alternative: moderation. At that time, Erdogan was banned from politics due to his conviction in 1998 by a court for reading an allegedly incendiary poem, which the courts said undermined Turkey's secular constitution. And a demoralizing reality became apparent to Erdogan: he could establish yet another Islamist party, acting behind the scenes, but that party, too, would be shut down by the high court. In all likelihood, the ECHR would again uphold the decision, and this process would be repeated over and again. Wisely, Erdogan adapted. He stood up to his former mentor, Erbakan. This schism became apparent to the public at the FP's May 2000 convention when Erbakan's hand-picked successor, Recai Kutan, received 633 votes from the delegates and became the party's chair. However, Abdullah Gul, who had served as minister of state in the Erbakan–Ciller cabinet in 1996–7, and was now an Erdogan ally representing the reform branch within the FP, came close, winning 521 votes. The writing was on the wall: the Turkish Islamists were splitting into two camps.

The first group, a doctrinaire minority led by Erbakan's protégés (Erbakan himself was still banned from politics), established the Felicity Party (SP) and remained a hard-line group. The second group, led by Erdogan, formally abandoned the National Outlook philosophy and set up the AKP in August 2001 with many prominent rank-and-file RP members, including Gul. The inclusion of Gul, an economist by training who had completed graduate work in the UK, earned a Ph.D. from Istanbul University, and worked for the Islamic Development Bank in Jeddah, Saudi Arabia, added a special cachet to the AKP. Many key names from the center-right ANAP and DYP, too, joined the AKP. Erdogan declared his party to be a conservative democratic force, renouncing his Islamist antecedents.

The AKP comes to power

By moderating his new party's platform away from the National Outlook and embracing the tenets of the center-right brand of Turkish politics (democracy, a pro-Western foreign policy, free-market economics, and "soft-secularism"), Erdogan was able to appeal to a much wider range of people than Erbakan ever had. Compared to the RP's 21.4 percent vote share under Erbakan in 1995, the AKP won 34.4 percent of the vote in the November 2002 election. Advocating the increased distancing of Turkey from the West and realigning the country's foreign policy with Muslim countries in the Middle East, the RP had almost exclusively attracted Islamist supporters. In contrast, with its platform of advancing Turkey's EU membership bid and a legitimacy-building alliance with center-right politicians, the AKP was able to attract moderate middle-class voters who did not necessarily share the party's political–religious concerns in foreign policy, but were nonetheless frustrated with Turkey's economic conditions and the performance of the established parties. In domestic politics, too, the AKP had the capacity to engage a wide coalition—embracing traditionally left-leaning working-class, center-right middle-class, rural nationalist, and urban Islamist voters alike—thereby attracting an electoral support base far broader than the RP's loyal Islamists.

Economic slump helps Erdogan's victory

Erdogan's step in forming the AKP as a new movement and branding it as a conservative democratic force could not have come at a better time for him. Just as the new party was coming together in 2001, Turkey experienced its worst economic crisis since World War II. This crash destroyed what was left of the country's traditional parties, allowing the AKP to supplant them as the party representing the country's dominant center-right pillar.

The roots of Turkey's 2001 economic crisis lie in the 1990s. During that period, the country suffered a full-blown PKK insurgency, which killed thousands and caused humanitarian suffering for the country's Kurdish community, which was caught in the fighting between the PKK and Turkish security forces. The conflict cost the country's economy billions of dollars, also scaring away investors. On the economic front, triple-digit interest and inflation rates, large government deficits, volatile financial markets, a frail banking system, capital flight, and a weak currency throughout the decade pummeled Turkey. As mentioned previously, corruption in the two dominant center-right parties and infighting between their leaders only added to the sense of chaos. Accordingly, the country experienced three major economic crises in quick succession—in 1994, 1998, and 1999—as well as a number of other slumps. For the average Turk, the 1990s felt like hell. Economic growth was extremely volatile during this period, swinging from −5.5 percent to 9.3 percent.[14] The chronically high inflation rate reached more than 120 percent in 1994 and never dropped below 60 percent.[15] This volatility made Turkey seem a risky bet for international capital, and it lost badly needed foreign currency. Attempts to reverse this dangerous slide into crisis, such as international assistance and government reforms, proved ineffective, and the economic chaos reached a crescendo with the 2001 crisis.

The trigger of this crisis, the worst downturn to date, was a personal spat between the prime minister, Bulent Ecevit, and the president, Ahmet Necdet Sezer—the latter reportedly throwing a copy of the Turkish Constitution at Ecevit during a meeting of the MGK in 2001. This gesture was enough to cause the teetering house of cards to collapse: the country's economy simply went into meltdown; the Borsa Istanbul (stock market) crashed, and the Turkish lira tumbled to historic lows. The IMF and a cooperative DSP–ANAP–MHP coalition instituted brutal austerity measures, freezing salaries and shearing Turkey of what little welfare state it had.

The suffering caused by the decade of distress, culminating in the 2001 crisis and the painful austerity measures, is seared on the public memory. The Turkish electorate would not forgive the three parties in the coalition government (the DSP, the ANAP, and the MHP) or the DYP, each of which bore its share of the blame for the economic crises since 1990. Having witnessed five governments in six years and exhausted by successive economic crises, corruption, and infighting among their elites, the public voted out the country's entire cadre of political leaders in the November 2002 election. The driver of the AKP's dramatic victory at the turn of the twenty-first century was simple: the public wanted to wipe the slate clean of the twentieth.

Erdogan creates the "AK" brand...

Erdogan and his party capitalized astutely on the void left by the implosion of Turkey's political center. The party's initials translate as "white" in Turkish, a metaphor for cleanliness, newness, and purity. This imagery underlined that the AKP was untainted by the cataclysmic 2001 crisis, and the many crises and corruption scandals of the 1990s. Instead, the party presented a new political agenda to the voters, advertising itself as a socially conservative and economically liberal organization, far different from the RP or the FP. The AKP also adopted an unabashedly pro-market stance, setting itself apart significantly from Kotku, Erbakan, and the RP–FP, who rejected capitalism.

The AKP's willingness to avoid repeating the RP–FP's controversial style and politics was also evident in the organization's foreign policy. On Iraq, for example, the party adhered to Ankara's traditional tenets of working and consulting with the United States. When interviewed on the matter in 2002, the AKP's second man, Gul, declared that his party would follow the existing Turkish foreign-policy orientation in the event of US action in Iraq. As long as the planning and execution of a campaign in Iraq satisfied Ankara's concerns, the AKP would pursue a policy of cautious and qualified support with an eye to Turkish security.

...and embraces Europe

More important than its Middle East policy, the AKP's dramatic foreign-policy shift away from the RP platform and toward embracing EU accession helped it to project itself as a mainstream, center-right political party. Turkey's EU accession became a realistic possibility, one within reach, just as Erdogan was setting up the AKP as a moderate force. Turkey had not become a candidate country for EU accession talks until 1999. As a result, in 2001, when the AKP was founded, the idea of gaining entry into the EU became a legitimate possibility for Turkey.

The major obstacle to Turkey's EU bid was the death penalty. Although Turkey already had a moratorium on capital punishment, Brussels wanted Ankara to eliminate it before it would consider Turkey for membership. This was a heavy load to lift. Abolishing capital punishment would mean allowing the jailed PKK leader Abdullah Ocalan, caught by Turkish forces in 1999 and sentenced to death that same year, to live. Nevertheless, in August 2002 the outgoing DSP–ANAP–MHP government met the EU's condition, suggesting how seriously the Turks took EU accession. The heavy lifting was done, and Erdogan did not renege on this pledge.

Indeed, when Erdogan voiced his support for EU accession in the 2002 general election, his rhetoric did not mark a shift in the nation's policy, but rather solidified his self-declared moderate stance. At the time, EU accession had wide public support: in a 2002 poll, 64 percent of respondents said they wanted Turkey to join the EU, while only 30 percent said they did not.[16] By favoring EU programs in public, Erdogan articulated a convincing case for moderation, which succeeded in appealing to the masses. His message was simple: the AKP could not be considered an Islamist party, for it, too, sought to embrace Western values, the proof of which was its support for the country's EU vocation. Proving his moderate bona fides was enough to win over more supporters than the RP ever had. But it was Turkey's steep electoral threshold that would deliver the AKP with a solid majority in the country's legislature, despite its winning only 34.4 percent of the vote in the 2002 parliamentary election.

The gift of the electoral threshold

Turkey has an extremely high national electoral threshold necessary for parties to enter parliament. In order to gain any seats, a party must first win 10 percent of the national vote. Legislative seats are then allocated in proportion to the share of the vote each party received. In the event that a party falls below the threshold, the seats that it would have received are instead awarded to other parties, with preference given to the party with the highest number of votes. This threshold was put in place following the 1980 coup to prevent a proliferation of political parties in parliament and the ensuing deadlock, as seen in the late 1970s. As the party system stabilized in the late 1980s around large parties, a debate emerged about lowering the threshold—Turkey possessing the highest electoral threshold among Western-style democracies. But the DYP and the ANAP, which ran the country for most of the period between 1983 and 2002, shied away from making this change, and by the 1990s the threshold had gained a new, unspoken function: blocking Kurdish-nationalist parties from entering parliament.[17] Whereas most countries with an electoral threshold set it between 1 and 5 percent, such a figure didn't seem enough to thwart Kurdish parties, which typically polled around 6 to 7 percent in elections. Accordingly, Turkey's dominant parties kept the 10 percent threshold to be on the safe side. But in the end, this fateful decision would backfire in the most unexpected way.

In the 2002 election, the threshold kept the country's key center-right (and center-left) parties out of parliament. In fact, all four major parties in the outgoing legislature, namely the DYP, ANAP, DSP, and MHP, fell below the 10 percent threshold. The electorate punished them for the 2001 crisis so fiercely that the ANAP received just 5.1 percent, down from 13.2 percent in 1999. The DSP dropped from 22.2 percent to 1.2 percent, and the MHP from 18 to 8.4 percent in the same period. Other than the AKP, only the CHP was able to enter the Turkish legislature, receiving 19.4 percent of the vote and 177 seats, up from 8.7 percent in 1999, when it had failed to enter parliament due to the threshold. (That the CHP was not in the outgoing parliament allowed it to escape stigma in the eyes of the angry electorate.) A few Kurdish nationalists, too, entered parliament as independents, thus circumventing the threshold.[18] Turkey's political bosses on the center-right would never enter parliament again. And, ironically, they were replaced in part by the Kurds.

The AKP picked up most of the seats that the DYP and the ANAP would have received had the threshold not blocked them. As a result, though the AKP only won just over one-third of the votes, it gained 67 percent of seats: 365 members of the party entered the 550-seat parliament. This solid majority was unexpected—even for Erdogan. Polls had been showing that the DYP would enter parliament.

Backed by one-third of the popular vote but enjoying two-thirds support in the legislature, the AKP suddenly found itself in full control of the country's parliament. The man from the other side of the tracks had just crossed over and, now, everybody was waiting to see what he would do next.

7

Erdogan in Power: The Good Years

F ollowing the dark days of the 1990s, the first term of the AKP
government, between 2002 and 2007, ushered in an unprec-
edented period of economic growth and political stability.
The electorate would repeatedly and generously reward Erdogan
for this accomplishment.

During his ascent to power, Erdogan was careful to remember the
many lessons he learned from watching Erbakan and the Islamists
who came before him. His astuteness and caution were critical,
since his path to dominance over Turkey's political system was
not smooth, even after the AKP won the November 2002 general
election. Erdogan had to wait five months to become prime minister after the AKP victory, until his political ban, which had been
imposed following his prison sentence, was reversed. It was not
until March 2003, when the country's AKP-dominated parliament
allowed Erdogan to run in a by-election, that he could take the
office of prime minister, as the constitution required that the prime
minister also be a member of parliament. Gul, who had taken office
as prime minister in November 2002 following the AKP victory,
simply gave up his job for Erdogan, establishing a precedent in the
relationship between the two AKP leaders in which Erdogan would
always be dominant, and Gul deferential.

Once elected, though, Erdogan knew that he had to tread
carefully and maintain his center-right appeal. Though he would
abandon this platform over time, what mattered to him most
during these early days was political survival. And with a still-
powerful military, bureaucratic and civil-society elite, and the

Constitutional Court watching him closely, this made tactical moderation and the embracing of center-right political values essential.

Erdogan's bright side: Turkish **Wirtschaftswunder**

Erdogan did, however, borrow one characteristic from the center-right of Turkish politics which he has retained up to the present day: a commitment to a free-market economy. This policy brought Turkey economic growth and higher living standards, and made Erdogan more popular than his predecessors in the 1990s had ever been.

A few factors helped Erdogan achieve this successful economic performance. First, he was lucky to reap the economic benefits of the austerity measures implemented by the DSP–ANAP–MHP government in the aftermath of the 2001 crisis (without having to suffer the political consequences of putting them in place). The year following the program had been painful for ordinary Turks, as the government slashed expenditure and froze salaries to balance its books. With growth returning, economic indicators started to stabilize just as the AKP won the 2002 election. The inflation rate dropped from 53.5 percent in 2001 to 47.2 percent in 2002 and 21.9 percent in 2003. As it stabilized to around 7 to 9 percent and the economy started to recover, Erdogan slashed six zeros from the currency. Turkish banknotes were no longer required to reach the millions and billions. For the Turks, this signaled a tangible return to economic stability: a cup of coffee no longer cost millions of lira.

In turn, the AKP took credit for liberating the lira from high and chronic inflation. Indeed, to date, the transition is hailed as a key AKP economic success by both large sections of the electorate and the international markets. Furthermore, correlating with Erdogan's early rule, a general sense of optimism permeated the public, driven by the conviction that the period of political crises was finally over.

91

Foreign investors, too, saw Turkey, with its recent liberal initiatives aimed at accelerating its EU accession, as stable. Erdogan's economic performance was facilitated by the continued confidence that investors held in the AKP at that time: foreign direct investment (FDI) in Turkey reached its apex of $22 billion in 2007.[1]

Although Gul's economic team, headed by the minister of economic affairs, Ali Babacan, led Turkey's *Wirtschaftswunder*—a period of unexpected economic growth and stability—it did not mastermind it independently. Rather, it faithfully executed reforms initiated by minister of economic affairs Kemal Dervis in the outgoing DSP–ANAP–MHP government. Nevertheless, the public perception was that the AKP was both single-handedly saving the economy and effectively governing the nation.

Even more importantly, Erdogan gave more people a slice of the country's economic pie. He restructured Turkey's small and malfunctioning welfare system, placing free health care and better education within reach of millions of people. Previously, poor Turks seeking medical care would have to arrive at public hospitals at 5 a.m. in order to avoid lines. Those who were not seriously ill would usually find themselves turned away, forced to try their luck the next day, sometimes waiting weeks and months before seeing a doctor. Erdogan not only improved the quality of health care across the country, but also launched an online and phone appointment system whereby his citizens could book appointments with their doctors, which is still used to this day. As a result of Erdogan's reforms, life expectancy at birth jumped from 70 years in 2000 to 75.3 years in 2014, and the infant-mortality rate dropped from 33.7 per thousand live births in 2000 to 16.5 in 2013.[2] In 2011, Turkey joined the rank of "high human development" countries according to the United Nations Development Programme's (UNDP) Human Development Index (HDI).

One of Erdogan's key achievements was the delivery of a mortgage system. (Indeed, emblematic of the recent arrival of this form of credit in the country is the fact that the Turkish word for mortgage is *mortgage*.) Prior to Erdogan, most Turks could buy homes or cars only with cash, which meant that only the upper classes could afford such purchases on their own. But thanks to Erdogan's reduction of the inflation rate, mortgages suddenly became available, giving millions of middle- and working-class Turks access to credit, endowing them with the ability to buy their first homes.

The sudden spread of wealth in the 2000s was the gift that kept giving at the ballot box: Erdogan won the next two elections, in 2007 and 2011, with increased majorities. Thanks to the threshold, Erdogan's AKP continued to receive sweeping majorities in the legislature, though his party has never received more than 50 percent of the vote. The AKP's strength in the legislature was disproportionate to its mandate as expressed by the electorate, and this created a fundamental disconnect between governance and representation that would continue to color Erdogan's leadership style for the coming decade.

Erdogan goes to Brussels

Even if his domestic mandate was limited, Erdogan had a clear and unquestioned mandate in foreign policy for EU accession. In the general election of November 2002, 83 percent of votes were cast for parties with clear pro-EU platforms. As a result, Erdogan decided it was time for him to embrace Brussels and execute Turkey's EU aspirations. For a long time, there had been an implicit understanding that Turkey's lackluster performance on human rights impeded EU accession. Now an opportunity emerged to push simultaneously for accession to the EU and improvement in human rights. Indeed, there was tangible evidence of his aggressive expansion of civil rights and liberties early in his leadership. From 2002 to 2007, democratic freedoms improved across various sectors. In 2002, the US-based NGO Freedom House gave Turkey 4.5 out of 7 on its "Freedom in the World" index, where 1 indicates "free" and 7 "not free." By 2007, its score had jumped to 3. In the same period, Turkey's "press freedom" score improved from 58 to 49 (on a scale of 0 to 100, 100 being "least free"), its "legal environment" score improved from 26 to 19 (on a scale of 0 to 30), and its "political environment" score improved from 23 to 19 (on a scale of 0 to 40).[3] Impressed by these indices, outside observers congratulated Erdogan and the AKP for their commitment to improving Turkey's democratic institutions.

The EU allows him to curb the military's powers...

Erdogan's democratic reforms went in tandem with his vision of curbing the military's formal political powers, something that was required in order for Turkey to qualify for accession talks with the EU. Thus, in 2003, shortly after coming to power, Erdogan placed the military's influence over governmental affairs on the chopping block as part of harmonization reforms for EU membership negotiations. In particular, he considerably reshaped the responsibilities of the Turkish National Security Council (MGK), which was headed by the military and had sole responsibility for drafting Turkey's national-security and foreign-policy doctrines, which it passed to the government for implementation. New government reforms demoted the MGK to an advisory council without real executive power, as well as increasing civilian presence in the institution. An army general had previously filled the position of MGK secretary general, but now this position could be held by a civilian, whom the president was to appoint from a list of candidates selected by the prime minister. Further restructuring subjected the MGK to executive authority. Prior to the reforms, the MGK met monthly and communicated policy to the cabinet, thereby setting the political tempo for Ankara. But now the MGK would convene only every other month and report to the deputy prime minister. Thus, thanks to the goal of EU accession, Erdogan was able to curb the military's control over civilian government. The next step was eliminating the military's actual power in politics, but Erdogan knew he would have to remain patient in order to avoid suffering the same fate that befell Erbakan.

...but not Turkish (and European) secularism

Despite his reforms to the military, shortly after coming to power Erdogan became disillusioned with the EU, as a series of ECHR decisions rolled in against his vision of diluting, and eventually dismantling, Turkey's brand of secularism: *laïcité*.

Although mentioned in earlier chapters, *laïcité* warrants a more detailed explanation. Practiced in France (from where Ataturk borrowed it) and other European countries, *laïcité* is distinct from American secularism. While the United States is secular, providing freedom *of* religion in education and politics, many European societies are *laïque*, providing freedom *from* religion in education and politics. American secularism has been shaped by the American experience: the United States was founded primarily by people, often themselves devoutly religious—including Puritans, Huguenots, Catholics, and Jews—who escaped religious persecution and established a form of secularism that permitted adherents of varying religions to practice their faiths freely and provided them with equal access to politics and education. Thus, American secularism is essentially not anti-religious. Rather, the country's founders wanted to create a pluralistic religious environment to get away from the tradition of a state religion that banned all others.

Conversely, European secularism emerged in single-faith environments in which one religion, and often one sect of a particular religion, dominated politics and education. The Catholic Church, for instance, wielded absolute political and pedagogical power in France, and enjoyed similar sway in other southern and central-European countries. In northern Europe, Lutheran Churches had similar authority, while the Orthodox Church dominated southeastern Europe. In the age of the Enlightenment, European societies reacted to the huge role of religion by limiting the absolute power of one faith over the state. Thus, *laïcité* was born, ensuring that religion would be, at least in principle, entirely separate from education and government, with the idea that it would eventually become an entirely private matter. After an arduous process and much contestation, France became officially *laïque* in 1905. Other European countries followed suit. Though not to the same level of strictness, Ataturk established Turkey in the 1920s in the mold of contemporary France—the model country of *fin de siècle* Europe—and thus adopted this pattern of *laïcité*, providing freedom *from* religion in education and government. The bottom-line difference between US-style secularism and *laïcité* is that the former is neutral toward religion whereas the latter—which Ataturk's Turkey firmly embraced—seeks to control it, and relegate it to the private sphere.

Turkish secularism faced its first serious challenge in the aftermath of the 1979 Islamist revolution in Iran when the wearing of the hijab spread all over the Middle East. In the 1980s, Turkey banned the hijab for women on college campuses and schools, and also for those working as public employees. This ban was based on the idea that the hijab was a religious symbol and had no place in a *laïque* society, as schools and government buildings were considered public spaces.[4] Turkish college students who wore the hijab led a campaign against this ruling, taking their cases to the Turkish courts, which upheld the ban. In 2004, after being subject to disciplinary measures for wearing a hijab on college campus six years earlier, a female Turkish student appealed the decision in the ECHR, but the court decided to uphold Turkey's ban on wearing hijabs in universities. In 1998, Hayrunnisa Gul, the wife of Abdullah Gul, also took the ban to the ECHR, but withdrew her case in 2004, the same year the court reaffirmed the constitutionality of the headscarf ban.[5]

Erdogan has always wanted to take down Ataturk's *laïcité*. These decisions were critical agents in convincing him that, in the long term, the EU would not be his ally in helping him recalibrate the relationship between politics and society in Turkey. Thus, Erdogan's appetite for EU accession soon fizzled away. Tellingly, in November 2005 he chided the ECHR, also putting a nail in the coffin of Turkey's EU vocation, stating that the decision on the hijab lay not with the European court, but with Muslim jurists (*ulema*).[6]

Turkey's (sad) EU-accession story

Of course, Turkey's EU accession was not stalled just because of Erdogan. It takes two to tango: key European nations, namely France and Germany, didn't commit themselves to Turkey's EU membership even in principle, especially after respective leaders Nicolas Sarkozy and Angela Merkel came to power. The EU appeared an unwilling partner in the negotiations almost from the very start.

In December 1997, the EU had rejected Ankara's application for membership. In the words of Jean-Claude Juncker, then prime minister of Luxembourg, which in that year held the presidency of the European Council, "It cannot be that the representatives of a country in which torture is still going on can sit at the table of the European Union."[7] This attitude generated widespread Turkish consternation toward the union. Then, in December 1999, the EU dramatically changed its position. And following some US lobbying on behalf of Ankara, Brussels reluctantly accepted Turkish candidacy and promised to treat its application in the same manner as applications from other candidate states.

However, many EU member states' opposition to Turkey's membership continued unabated. Accordingly, in 2005 Brussels explicitly decoupled Turkey's accession process from that undergone by former candidates, with substantive new bureaucratic hurdles applied to Ankara (and other incoming countries at the time, such as Croatia). The EU subjected Turkey to modified negotiations: talks that for other accession countries had consisted of one round were broken down into 35 "chapters" of policy issues to be addressed during membership discussions with Turkey—discussions in which the 27 different member countries each had a veto on both opening and closing each chapter. This meant that Turkey effectively faced 1,890 potential vetoes in 2005 just as it entered accession talks with the EU. Not unexpectedly, no substantial progress has been made in Turkey's EU negotiations, whereas Croatia did (deservedly) become a member in 2013.

How many people died in World War I, and what are their names?

The EU created unfair hurdles and absurd hoops for Turkey to have to jump through in order to be granted membership, undoubtedly frustrating Erdogan and undermining his willingness to shape his country in Europe's image. A joke about Turkey's EU accession, as told by Turkish political scientist Soli Ozel, encapsulates the disappointment Erdogan and others felt when the EU refused to treat Turkey's accession equally alongside other candidate countries' membership talks. The joke is that after dealing with a number of accession countries for a number of years, the EU becomes sick and tired of the arduous talks, and calls in candidate countries Serbia, Montenegro, and Turkey for a test on European history. The EU tells the three countries that they will be asked one question. If they know the answer, they can join the EU, otherwise they will be rejected. The Serbs are offered the question, "When did World War I begin?" This is an easy question. "The answer is 1914." The doors open, bells ring, and Serbia joins the EU. Then the Montenegrins are asked, "When did World War I end?" This, too, is an easy question. "The answer is 1918." The doors open, bells ring, and Montenegro joins the EU. Finally, the Turks are asked: "How many people died in World War I, and what are their names?"

The EU's reluctance toward Ankara has permitted Erdogan to turn hostile toward the negotiations, which, in turn, has allowed him to dismiss any retaliation from the EU—measures that would otherwise have hampered his authoritarian tilt. Europe ought to take partial blame for its shortsightedness in dropping the ball on Turkey's accession after it helped Erdogan put the secular military under government control. The formal exit of the military effectively made the EU the grand arbiter of Turkish democracy, a role Europe was not and is not interested in playing. This also gave the AKP grounds to solidify its spurious approach toward Europe: it paid lip service to EU accession to eliminate the military's formal political power and maintained good ties with Europe, while nurturing anti-Western sentiments at home.

Shifting foreign policy to the Muslim sphere

Looking at Turkey's foreign-policy changes under Erdogan indicates the tactical nature of his commitment to building relations with the West and continuing the EU accession process. Superficially, the Turkish government carried out significant economic and political reforms, trying to improve its human-rights records to gain EU membership. But, under the surface, Ankara has also cultivated relationships with nations more worrisome to the West. Before the AKP, Turks looked to the West for political and economic cues, but during Erdogan's first decade in government Turkey became a close friend of regimes such as that of Syria, and drew closer to Iran than it has been since the era of the shahs. Israel was no longer Turkey's only regional partner.

The change in Turkish–Syrian ties under the first Erdogan administration is telling. As recently as 1999, three years before the AKP's election, Turkey and Syria had come to the brink of war, due to the latter's support of the PKK in battling the Ankara government. It had become known by the 1990s that PKK leader Ocalan lived in Syria and the PKK received training inside both that country and Syrian-occupied Lebanon. In fact, Ocalan was so comfortable in his Damascus home that he gave an on-site interview to a Washington-based journal in early 1998.[8] Nevertheless, Damascus repeatedly denied Ocalan's presence, and only when Turkey finally threatened Syria with war, and massed troops along the Syrian border in late September 1998, did it respond. In the end, the Assad regime, accepting the seriousness of the Turkish threat, expelled Ocalan from Damascus. The PKK's leader tried in vain to find a country that would host him, and ended up in Kenya, where he was captured in 1999. He was brought to Turkey and sentenced to death. After the abolition of capital punishment in 2002, his sentence was commuted

99

to life in jail.[9] He has since been serving his term in solitary confinement on Imrali Island, off the coast of Istanbul, a remote and wuthering rocky outcrop.

When Erdogan came to power in 2002, Turkish–Syrian ties had admittedly improved a little since Ocalan had been sent to Imrali. Nevertheless, Erdogan launched an initiative to boost relations, which improved dramatically through well-publicized bilateral visits. Within the first two years after the AKP was elected, there were more than 30 ministerial-level visits, including Assad's January 2004 trip to Ankara. This visit marked the first Syrian presidential sojourn in Turkey in 57 years, and Assad and his wife were showered with media praise.[10] The two nations also signed cooperation agreements in areas ranging from oil and gas to security affairs. As a result, the trade volume between the two countries, which stood at $241 million in 1999, jumped to $910 million in 2003.

With Tehran, a similar rapprochement took place. For instance, the two countries signed a treaty of educational cooperation in December 2002, paving the way for an exchange of students and curricula, an ironic agreement between a formally secular state and a theocracy. Trade between the two countries boomed, growing from $1.2 billion in 2002 to $2.3 billion in the first eight months of 2004 alone.[11] Erdogan visited Tehran to discuss deeper economic, political, and security ties, and later the two countries signed a 25-year contract for the sale of Iranian natural gas.[12]

One of the most important agents in cementing the AKP's desire to woo Muslim states was Ahmet Davutoglu, born in rural central Turkey in 1959. The son of a conservative businessman, Davutoglu studied at Istanbul's liberal Boys' High School, then completed his undergraduate studies and Ph.D. in international relations at Bosphorus University, another educational institution known for its liberal values. After working as a professor at the International Islamic University in Malaysia, Davutoglu became an advisor to Gul, then foreign minister in the AKP cabinet. Eventually, Davutoglu moved to become an advisor to Erdogan, then prime minister, during the first AKP government. Davutoglu took office as Erdogan's foreign minister in 2009 during his second term and, finally rising to the top, became prime minister in 2014 during Erdogan's third term. In what he called a "zero problems with neighbors" policy, Davutoglu argued that Turkey could become a powerful country only if it utilized the full "strategic depth" of its neighborhood and adjacent areas, developing better ties especially with those Muslim neighbors with whom it shared cultural affinity.[13] Turkey is surrounded by several areas that he termed "land basins" (southeastern Europe, southwest Asia, and the Middle East/North Africa) and "sea basins" (the Mediterranean, Black Sea, and Aegean), and, he wrote, must closely follow and manage developments in those basins—and Islam was perhaps the key factor to cementing ties of trade diplomacy. Close links with Israel and focusing foreign policy on the West prevented Ankara from fully utilizing the strategic advantages available through good relations with its Muslim neighbors. Hence, Turkey's future power depended on improving ties with the largely Muslim nations of the east, including nearby Iran and Syria.[14]

Even more perturbing than the AKP's pursuit of better relations with Syria and Iran was the blatantly anti-Western rhetoric the party began to espouse. The AKP demonized the EU and the United States, while maintaining good ties with both. Some dismissed such rhetoric as harmless domestic politicking.[15] In reality, it had devastating consequences: a decade into the AKP's tenure, few in Turkey cared for the West, many people opposed EU accession, and most actually hated America. Indeed, by the end of the first decade of the twenty-first century, the United States and the EU would have little leverage and few allies left in Turkey.

The Iraq War

Although Erdogan's double-edged commitment to the West must have been a factor in the deterioration of their relationship, it is also important to acknowledge the crippling effect the war in Iraq had on US–Turkish relations during the first Erdogan government.

In early 2003, Turkey was under significant pressure from the United States to provide cooperation in case of an American attack on Iraq. But when US vice president Dick Cheney visited Turkey in 2002 asking for Turkish permission to open a northern front against Saddam Hussein from Turkey, the prime minister, Bulent Ecevit, rebuffed him. Washington was, therefore, elated when the AKP won the November 2002 election. By February 5, the new prime minister, Abdullah Gul, had declared Turkish support for military action in Iraq and committed to asking the country's parliament to open Turkish military bases to American troops.

In the end, however, in a departure from the tradition of "whipping" in parliamentary democracies—in which parties enforce factional discipline in legislative votes—the AKP leadership decided to allow its members to vote with their consciences on the legislative motion to allow US troops to open a northern front against Saddam Hussein from Turkey.[16] In a historic vote on March 1, 2003, 264 voted in favor and 250 voted against, with many AKP deputies in the latter camp, alongside the opposition CHP, and 19 deputies abstaining. But the Turkish law regarding the deployment of foreign troops inside the country, as interpreted by the Constitutional Court, requires a majority of all members present to vote for such a motion. Subsequently, the motion was rejected, as it failed to garner the required 267 votes of the 533 deputies present. Though it had initially raised hopes in Washington, the new AKP government ended up refusing to aid the United States in the Iraq War. The AKP avoided the messy entanglement and burden of the war by somehow inadvertently letting the ball drop in the parliament. Erdogan discovered that he could have his cake and eat it with Washington. This conclusion would guide his policies regarding the United States in the future.

The Iraq War vote nevertheless strained US–Turkish relations more than any other military conflict to date. Many in Washington took a hostile view of Turkey for not supporting the United States in the war, some even unfairly blaming the country for the 2005 Iraqi insurgency.[17] In July 2003, in what was perceived to be a retaliatory act, US troops detained and hooded a group of Turkish special forces in the Iraqi city of Sulaymaniyah, an event depicted in the Turkish film *Valley of the Wolves: Iraq*, which became an all-time hit in Turkey. Anti-American views spread in Turkey like brush fires, often fueled by pro-government media. Another film, entitled *Metal Storm*, a thriller adapted from a novel, alleged that the Iraq War was a US-led organ-harvesting operation benefitting Jews and Israel, and became a box-office smash. Erdogan's wife Emine Erdogan attended the movie's premiere, after which she expressed being proud of the movie.[18] These sentiments built on resentment lingering from the 1991 Gulf War, during which Turkey offered full support to the United States only to be left with economic losses in the billions of dollars.[19] Eventually, Erdogan allowed the United States to have fly-over rights across Turkish airspace, establishing a de facto northern front in Iraq, though his government maintained its hostility toward Washington's Iraq War.

Although there was a slight improvement in US–Turkish relations when US national-security advisor Condoleezza Rice visited Turkey in 2005, relations did not really pick up until 2007, when US president George W. Bush pledged to increase intelligence cooperation to aid Turkey in its fight against the PKK camps inside northern Iraq. Nevertheless, anger toward American involvement in Iraq would eventually provide fuel for the AKP's anti-Western rhetoric, allowing it to catch fire in Turkey.

Erdogan's first report card

Regardless, Erdogan was able to convince Turkish business interests, the media, and civil society at home, as well as the EU and the United States abroad, of his commitment to genuine moderation and his conservative democratic credentials. His supporters encouraged people to look at his policies and ignore his anti-Western rhetoric. It was indeed difficult for many analysts to get a clear hold on

Erdogan's politics in the beginning. The AKP's success in the 2002 general election in winning nearly a third of the vote was mainly due to its ability to attract center-right ANAP and DYP voters and the rank and file of these parties. The folding of the center-right under Erdogan's Islamist movement meant that, in the beginning, the AKP would have an awkward pendulum-like political identity: the party would be pro-Western and anti-Western, pro-"soft secularism" and anti-secularist, all at the same time. Only after the 2013 Gezi Park rallies, when Erdogan viciously cracked down on liberal, pro-democracy demonstrators, would most observers concede that the illiberal legacy that the AKP had inherited from the Islamist wing of Turkish politics was deeply ingrained in its political philosophy. By that time, it was too late to warn about Erdogan's Islamist pedigree and goals for Turkey. His illiberal side had already overpowered the moderate characteristics the AKP had borrowed from the center-right, which was long dead.

The final gasp of the center-right

As Erdogan and his AKP continued to accumulate power and support, secularists and the military tried to undercut the party's access to the executive branch of government by opposing Gul's presidential bid when the secularist president, Ahmet Necdet Sezer, was getting ready to step down in August 2007.[20] Faced with this challenge, the AKP brought forward the date of the scheduled November 2007 general election to July 22 in order that it might function as a referendum on the AKP's governance.[21] Although the center-right Democrat Party (DP)—a reincarnation of the DYP, now somewhat wishfully adopting the name of the mother of all Turkish center-right parties—entered the election, they won less than 6 percent of the vote and thus could not enter parliament. After a failed merger with the DP, demonstrating further the incompetence of the center-right, the ANAP did not even compete in the election. Turkey's center-right parties, which had run the country in almost unbroken succession between 1950 and 2002, were dead. The AKP, on the other hand, won 47 percent of the vote, cementing its status as Turkey's new right-wing political option and proving its democratic credentials to domestic and international observers. The stage was set for Erdogan's ascent to true power.

8

The Silent Revolution

Murder in Istanbul

An alleged coup plot orchestrated by the secularist military and its allies against the government, which came to be known as the Ergenekon case, was the turning point in Erdogan's consolidation of power. The opening act was a gruesome murder in downtown Istanbul on a cold winter's day. At around three o'clock in the afternoon of January 19, 2007, a Turkish-nationalist youth shot Turkish Armenian journalist Hrant Dink in the back of the head three times in broad daylight outside the Istanbul offices of *Agos*—the Turkish Armenian bilingual newspaper that Dink had founded 11 years earlier. Dink was one of Turkey's most vocal proponents of Armenian cultural rights. He had attracted heavy criticism for acknowledging the Ottoman Empire's 1915 killing of Armenians as genocide, despite his firm insistence that this was an issue to be discussed among the Turkish and Armenian people without outside arbitrators who tried to use allegations of genocide as a weapon against Turkey. He declared: "My only desire is having the ability to freely and thoroughly discuss our common history with my dear Turkish friends without extracting any animosity from said history." Dink was an inspiring Turkish citizen. When I met him a few years before he was shot, I asked him about the meaning of the word *agos*. He told me that it was an Anatolian Armenian word that described the earthen channel created as a result of plowing: "This is how water finds its way to earth, and this is how Turkish Armenians are"—referring to their persecution and dislocation in

Ottoman Turkey. "We are looking for the channel through which to return to our earth."[1]

In 2006, the Turkish courts charged Dink with the crime of "insulting Turkishness" due to his views on Turkish history, particularly his statements concerning genocide. Not clearly defined in the Turkish penal code, the article that outlaws "insulting Turkishness" is commonly employed to silence critics of the government. Prior to his murder, Dink had received numerous death threats from hard-line nationalists and had lamented the security forces' failure to provide him with police protection.[2] What is more, he was invited to the office of Istanbul's government-appointed mayor and warned about his activities. In an article published the day he died, he ominously wrote: "Are these threats genuine or not? To be honest it is impossible to know. For me [...] what is really unbearable is the psychological torture I am experiencing."[3]

Enter the Deep State

Dink's death sparked protests by Turkey's liberals, who accused the state of collusion in his murder. Dink's 17-year-old killer had traveled to Istanbul from faraway Trabzon (the unofficial capital of Turkey's conservative and nationalist eastern Black Sea littoral) to spend days surveilling Dink around the *Agos* offices before committing the murder. This set of circumstances convinced many liberals that the killer must have benefitted from nationalist, state-connected networks in the execution of his crime and some subsequently pointed at the notorious "Deep State" (*derin devlet*) as the culprit.

The idea of the Deep State had captured the broader public imagination in Turkey in the aftermath of the November 1996 "Susurluk incident." On November 3, a car crashed into a truck in Susurluk, a northwestern Turkish town halfway between Istanbul and Izmir. When the emergency crews arrived on the scene of the accident, they were shocked to pull out of the wrecked car a prominent police chief, a notorious mafia leader with connections to the Grey Wolves (a far-right MHP militia that made a name for itself hunting leftists in the 1970s), a Kurdish deputy with connections to state-sponsored Kurdish village guards (infamous for their human-rights abuses against pro-PKK Kurds), and a beauty queen. This served as a sign that Turkey had a nefarious underworld, a "Deep State," in which security officials, criminals, and hard nationalists rubbed shoulders.

Following the 1997 "soft coup," the Islamists heartily embraced the Deep State idea that a malign, invisible hand ultimately ran Turkey. As they saw it, the Deep State orchestrated Turkish politics behind the scenes, including the 1997 coup, in which "the deep state did not want to share deep power with moderate Islamists."[4] Since the earliest days of the republic, Islamist journalists argued, the Deep State had been the secret weapon of those who sought to undermine the people's will.[5]

The roots of the Deep State theory can be traced to the Turkish War of Independence (1919–22) and the preceding collapse of the Ottoman Empire.[6] In 1912, a union of Balkan states defeated the empire, seizing all Turkish territory in Europe, with the exception of Istanbul and nearby Thrace, the southeasternmost corner of the continent. And in 1918–19, following the empire's defeat at the hands of the Allied forces during World War I, the Allies, along with Greece, occupied Thrace, Anatolia, and Istanbul (all part of modern Turkey). A furtive group of mostly military officers from the ruling Young Turkish CUP stepped in to organize a resistance movement against the occupation, coalescing around the Black Hand Society (Karakol Cemiyeti). The Young Turks mostly hailed from the Balkans, the intellectual and economic heart of the Ottoman Empire prior to its collapse. Many of them, as Black Hand Society members, had fought against Balkan nationalists while among the ranks of the Ottoman army to preserve the fraying empire. These Balkan nationalists had secret outfits of their own that were aimed at sedition against the Ottoman Empire (and also the Habsburg Empire in the case of the Serbs). One of the most famous of these secret societies was the Serbian Black Hand (Crna Ruka). The Young

Turk Black Hand Society that helped organize the Turkish military campaign against the Allied occupation of the empire was, ironically, inspired by Serbia—a nemesis of the Ottoman Empire.

The Turkish Islamists of the late 1990s, and the AKP in the early years of the new century, believed that the Black Hand Society had never died and had in fact survived as the Deep State. The liberals thought that Turkey had to embrace successfully its Islamist movement, the AKP, in order to become a true democracy. Some leftists and liberals, mainly those who had been brutalized by the military in the aftermath of the 1980 coup, sided with the Islamists too. Neither the Islamist nor the leftist–liberal proponents of the Deep State theory, however, clearly articulated who precisely was part of this clandestine organization. Dink's murder only served to awaken fears of the lurking and brutal invisible hand that hovered over Turkey, one that no elected politician could truly control.

Although the police apprehended Dink's killer within a few weeks, chummy photographs of policemen posing with the assassin while the latter held up a Turkish flag leaked to the public. This further fueled liberal outrage and seemed to confirm the Deep State theory.[7] More than 100,000 mostly liberal protestors carried signs at his funeral that read: "We are all Hrant Dink; we are all Armenian."[8]

At a time when the AKP had been working to present a human rights-focused, EU-ready Turkey to the outside world, Dink's murder revealed the dissonance between the image the party cultivated abroad and the reality at home. The trial provided an opportunity for the AKP to prove that it had reformed the judiciary in order to guarantee human rights, but instead the party proved to Turkey's liberals that it would only use legal institutions to pursue its *own* political agenda, and the clouds over Dink's murder never cleared.[9] Dink's killer's life sentence was commuted to just over twenty years, since the assailant was a juvenile. What is more, allegations over officials' complicity in the murder were never properly investigated. In an open letter published six years after Dink's death, his family directly criticized the AKP government for its indifference to their plight:

> [The AKP] boasted, "No murder has remained unresolved
> during our term," ignoring the slaying of the only Armenian
> in republican history who had waged a vocal struggle for
> human rights. We are no longer part of this show. We have
> no expectation from anything in which the state is either in
> front of or behind the curtain.[10]

The AKP's moderation had its limits, and while Erdogan's democratizing reforms were intended to strengthen pious Muslims' religious
freedoms, such as lifting the ban on the hijab, they often stopped
short of protecting the rights of Turkey's political and ethnic minorities. The fully articulated Deep State theory undoubtedly rests to a
degree on exaggerations and generous leaps of faith—but if we take
the more modest version of an unspoken cooperative network of like-
minded soldiers, bureaucrats, businessmen, and politicians intent
on maintaining shared ideology and interests over time, something
like it has certainly been a consistent feature of Turkey's republican
history. If there was a Deep State, the AKP's plan was not to take it
down, but to take control of it.

The 2007 "e-coup"

In April 2007, the AKP nominated Abdullah Gul to be president.
The secularists were outraged and found it alarming that a man
whose wife wore a hijab and argued against the headscarf ban could
become head of state. The nomination prompted the most significant
political crisis in Turkey since the 1997 "soft coup." On April 27, 2007,
the TAF responded to Gul's nomination by issuing an online press
release, which would come to be known as the "e-memorandum." In
it, the military reiterated its role as the guardian of secularism and
threatened "certain groups" who were working to undercut Turkey's
secular principles.[11] In past showdowns between the government
and the TAF, such as the 1971 coup by memorandum, the former
had bowed down to the latter's threats; disputes between Islamists

and the TAF had historically ended similarly, such as when Erbakan abdicated in 1997. In 2007, armed with much wider and deeper popular support than Erbakan, and being a more skilled political player, Erdogan refused to follow his predecessor and called the TAF's bluff to stand behind Gul's presidential run. In what was later dubbed the "e-coup," the military failed to take any further action in blocking Erdogan or Gul's nomination, and Erdogan was able to present the armed forces, traditionally considered the most powerful institution in the country, as a paper tiger. This was the beginning of the end of the TAF's dominance in Turkey.[12]

In the July general election that followed this pseudo-confrontation, the AKP won 47 percent of the vote, followed by the CHP at only 21 percent. Erdogan owed this electoral victory in large part to Turkey's economic growth, as well as to the continued absence of any center-right alternatives. But anti-coup sentiment, too, helped Erdogan. At the same time, the AKP's strong standing in this election and victory against the military, a first for any Turkish Islamist or any other civilian movement, convinced Erdogan that he had built enough popular support to attack the checks and balances in the Turkish political system with the help of a key ally: the Gulen movement.

Enter the Gulen movement

Built around the charismatic and messianic figure of Fethullah Gulen, the Gulen movement is a tight-knit Islamic brotherhood with political ambitions and endowed with a strong, near devotional, attachment to its founder. Although it has many members who publicly declare their association, the Gulen movement also has a non-transparent core known only to a few, at the center of which is Gulen himself. Gulen was born in 1941 (his birthdate is disputed) in the conservative northeastern Turkish city of Erzurum, near the country's border with the southern Caucasus. The son of a small-town imam, Gulen obtained his preacher's license in 1959, and seven years later moved to the liberal Aegean port city of Izmir, where he began to cultivate his network of supporters.[13] Following a 1999 secular government crackdown on Turkey's Islamist leaders and in the aftermath of the 1997 "soft coup," Gulen fled to the United States (although the movement officially claims he moved following his doctor's recommendation to seek treatment). In 2001, he obtained an immigrant visa in the United States as a "religious worker," and spent the following seven years in legal battles with the US government over obtaining permanent residency. He submitted letters from former Turkish and US officials in order to prove his "extraordinary abilities" en route to obtaining permanent residency as an "educator" under a special program.[14] In July 2008, a federal district court judge ruled in Gulen's favor, and he became a permanent resident of the United States. Educational institutions form the core of Gulen's global network, which calls itself "Service" (Hizmet). These institutions are located in more than 180 countries worldwide, primarily in Turkey, Central Asia (where the group has its oldest and strongest networks outside Turkey), and the United States.[15] The movement also holds strong networks in sub-Saharan Africa and the Balkans, where the highest-quality schools are often Gulenist and educate the children of the political elite.[16]

The first chain of Gulen-inspired US charter schools opened in Cleveland, Ohio, in 1999, and there are now around 160 Gulen-affiliated schools in at least 20 US states. These schools share distinguishing features: they are opened by Turks; they emphasize math, science, and technology; their teachers set an example of pious Islamic living (as per Gulen's teachings); and they offer Turkish language or culture classes. Hizmet also has extensive political influence in the United States through organizations such as the Rumi Forum in Washington DC, the Pacifica Institute in California, and the Niagara Foundation in Chicago. Their members attend government dinners and donate tens of thousands of dollars to political campaigns.[17]

Tracing connections across these political organizations, as well as tying them back to Gulen, proves challenging. Organizations are rarely transparent—federal records often do not name contributors, and the hierarchy and sources of funds are unclear. US charter schools deny ties to Gulen and the network, yet share the same structure and mission statement. Emre Celik, the president of the Rumi Forum in 2016, de-emphasized connections to the network:

> All institutions have a board, and the boards are legally responsible for what they do and don't do [...] Gulen doesn't hold any official office or any official position. And his day-to-day duties, beyond writing and speaking, do not involve the running of any single institution in any country.[18]

Despite these attempts at disaffiliation, US officials have raised concerns. In May 2006, the US consul general in Turkey, Deborah K. Jones, reported: "[Gulen supporters] are almost uniformly evasive about their purpose of travel and their relationships to Gulen."[19]

Following the AKP's electoral victory in 2002, the movement threw its support behind Erdogan via its media arms, including the daily *Zaman* and its English-language, and more liberal, counterpart, *Today's Zaman*. In addition to media and educational institutions, Gulen's network has focused its efforts on the police and the judiciary—and now, in the wake of the July 2016 coup attempt, on the military. With the help of the AKP, Gulen's supporters infiltrated at least the ranks of Turkey's police force and its judicial system. As a result, when Erdogan wanted to take on the TAF, he could rely on Gulen's extensive network to aid him in his efforts to purge secular opponents through court cases.

Conspiracies and show trials

Having successfully pushed back against the military, when Turkey's Constitutional Court launched a case in March 2008 to shut down the AKP, Erdogan knew he did not have much time to act against the secularist court and its most important ally, the TAF, in order to avoid the same fate that befell Erbakan. To this end, with more help from the Gulen movement he launched the infamous "Ergenekon" case, using the murder of Dink to go after the "Deep State." The case involved a set of trials, the first of which was aimed at prosecuting members of "Ergenekon," an alleged enigmatic ultra-nationalist organization (named after the Turks' place of origin in Central Asia according to Turkic mythology) connected to the Deep State and plotting to overthrow the government through murders such as the assassination of Dink. New show trials were added to Ergenekon, such as "Sledgehammer," between 2008 and 2011, which with each addition became less convincing.

Ergenekon began in early 2008 when 31 retired military officials (some of whom were indeed connected to Turkey's criminal under-world) were detained by the government. Following the assassination of Dink and the discovery of weapon caches held by coup plotters, these arrests seemed justified and were welcomed by a public concerned with safety and stability. In the beginning, there was at least partial evidence that the military had likely discussed a contingency coup against the government, and therefore many Turks lined up behind the case. The government detained prominent generals Aytac Yalman and Sener Eruygur in July 2008, together with a number of other military officials, alleging that they had discussed a coup during a 2004 war game.[20] It appeared that such a war game had indeed taken place, but suspicious irregularities emerged in 2010 during the "Sledgehammer" phase of Ergenekon, throwing the case into doubt. While prosecutors presented a seemingly incriminating document said to prove the organization of a coup attempt, software analysis later determined that the document had not been created until 2006 and thus was a forgery.[21] Soon, the arrests and indefinite detentions of key military officers became even more difficult to rationalize as the government launched even less convincing cases. Altogether, more than 300 military officers, including active duty admirals and generals, were arrested and sentenced, although the prosecutors did not provide a full and convincing account of the alleged plot. Various indictments produced by prosecutors argued that a coup plot existed but was so well hidden that it could not be proven.

The Gulenists and leftist–liberals build their own jail

Subsequent waves of arrests were similarly based less on evidence and more on paranoia about the Deep State and a simple desire to remove opponents such as secularist leaders and the TAF. Some of the more flagrant and high-profile actions taken during the Ergenekon era involved renowned physician Turkan Saylan, NATO general Ergin Saygun, and journalists Ahmet Sik and Nedim Sener. Saylan, a 73-year-old, terminally ill cancer patient who had founded one of Turkey's most prominent NGOs promoting girls' education, had been at the forefront of anti-Islamist and NGO-led rallies during the 1997 "soft coup"—and now it was time for the Islamists to extract a pound of flesh from her. In an early-morning raid in April 2008, the police seized Saylan from her deathbed and illegally searched her home for evidence of her alleged involvement in a coup plot. Nothing was found in the house and no charges were pressed against her. She died a month later.

General Saygun was one of the most popular Turkish officers in Washington and one of the most respected at the Pentagon. Through his service in NATO, he had developed a working relationship with practically all US generals and gained a positive reputation in Washington DC as one of the finest officers in the alliance. Thus, when he was arrested for supposedly taking part in the Ergenekon conspiracy—a plot that, according to the prosecutor's indictment, attempted to carry out "Islamist and Marxist attacks to overthrow the government"—Washington and the Pentagon were shocked and skeptical about the ruling.

The arrests of journalists Ahmet Sik and Nedim Sener, known for their criticism of the Gulen movement and the Ergenekon case, in March 2011, were just two acts of many that took place in a troubling anti-media atmosphere that would endure for the following years. *Zaman* (along with police and prosecutors loyal to Gulen) promoted the Ergenekon trials and the ensuing witch-hunt in which anti-AKP and often secularist journalists, academics, and scholars were labeled as "coup plotters" and threatened with jail. The newspaper illegally accessed victims' phone and email conversations through Gulen-aligned police and prosecutors and leaked their contents to the public. In this regard, *Zaman* found a helping hand from another daily, *Taraf*. Launched in 2007 at the onset of the Ergenekon trials, *Taraf* would become a major pro-AKP voice regarding the hearings. Begrudging allies, many leftist–liberals united with Islamists in their hatred for the military, and these formed the backbone of *Taraf*. The spunky paper took an unabashedly anti-military line, often depicting not just the TAF, but any intellectuals or journalists opposing the AKP, as coup plotters. When Sik and Sener were arrested, *Taraf* came out with the headline: "They were not arrested because of their journalism."[22] Driven by the leftist–liberals' hatred for the Deep State bogeyman and the military, *Taraf* joined *Zaman* to become one of the building blocks of the environment of fear that the Ergenekon case would create: opposing Erdogan became synonymous with plotting a coup. In a twist of bad karma, following the failed coup of 2016, writers from both *Taraf* and *Zaman* would be arrested for allegedly plotting against Erdogan.

The amount of evidence compiled against accused Ergenekon sympathizers is impressive: state prosecutors eventually submitted a record-breaking indictment of more than 8,000 pages to the court.[23] The way in which this mountain of evidence was compiled, however, is perhaps even more noteworthy. Reminiscent of the McCarthy investigations of the 1950s in the United States, Erdogan's government and his police (a body under the government's direct control in Turkey and heavily infiltrated by Gulenists at the time) carried out hundreds of legally dubious house raids like the one used against Saylan. Detentions, wiretaps, and knowingly falsified documents were used as evidence against suspects in court. Pro-AKP news outlets, such as the aforementioned *Zaman* and *Taraf*, proliferated, emboldening the conclusions derived from these questionable practices while attacking AKP opponents.[24]

In the years following the first Ergenekon arrests, individuals accused of involvement in the plot were incarcerated by the hundreds and put on trial in proceedings tellingly called the "Sledgehammer" (Balyoz) case. Academics, police officers, journalists, secularists, and any perceived opponents of Erdogan and the AKP were among those arrested, but TAF personnel bore the brunt of these detentions. By 2011, around half of all Turkish admirals—the navy, considered the backbone of the 1997 "soft coup," suffered especially severely, demonstrating the vindictive nature of the trials—were jailed, and the pro-AKP media accurately reported that more of the top brass would soon be forced to resign.

Gulenists attacked the military with as much ferocity as the AKP or sometimes more, removing secularist officers and, it now appears, replacing them with Gulenist sympathizers. Following the failed coup of July 2016, prominent Turkish journalist Sedat Ergin pointed out that there was likely a long-term motivation for this purge. While a full account of the 2016 coup is yet to be produced, as this book goes to print it appears that it was carried out by an unusually high number of these alleged Gulenist appointees, many of whom were able to secure their positions in the military thanks to purges of secularist officers during the Ergenekon trials.[25] If this is indeed true, the Gulenists appear to have used allegations of a plot in 2008–11 to pave the way for their own alleged coup attempt in 2016.

The conflict between the AKP and its allies and the TAF came to a head in July 2011 when the commanders of the Turkish ground, naval, and air forces resigned. Pro-AKP, Gulenist, and leftist–liberal journalists deemed the resignations an act of protest from a military whose popularity and power were waning. Indeed, the shift in power was palpable. In the words of Yusuf Kanli, a Turkish journalist: "It seems that, in the past, when the military expressed dissatisfaction with the government, the government would leave. Nowadays, when the government expresses displeasure to the top generals, the top generals are leaving. There is a change of roles."[26]

Another journalist, Asli Aydintasbas, called the resignations "the symbolic moment where the first Turkish republic ends and the second republic begins."[27]

"Republic of fear" rising

If a second republic had begun, it would be the "republic of fear": an environment of intimidation in which the leader and his AKP could openly harass dissidents. The Ergenekon trials had sent a message to anyone opposing Erdogan that they could easily be jailed; their private phone conversations or emails could be leaked to the public; and they could be linked to coup plotters by the pro-Erdogan media. The Ergenekon case made it infinitely more difficult for Turks of all stripes to oppose Erdogan.

While all verdicts from the Ergenekon case were overturned in April 2016 (once he broke the military's back, Erdogan, ever the skillful tactician, moved to co-opt the generals as allies against the Gulen movement and the PKK), the AKP leader had successfully made a strong statement to the TAF, secularists, and the world at large: the traditional guardians of secular Turkey were no longer the grand arbiters of politics. The resignation of the military's top brass, Erdogan's most feared adversaries, served as a de facto white flag signaling that Erdogan and his government were no longer forced to adhere to a center-right platform to assuage the concerns of the TAF's allies about the AKP's Islamist pedigree. Without the military the courts, the media, business communities, and the secularist NGOs were weak. Erdogan had just broken the strongest link in the 1997 "soft coup" chain, and the rest would fall under his power like ripe fruit picked from a tree.

Not surprisingly, after the indispensable role played by liberals in the defanging of the military, Erdogan and his party began interpreting its popular mandate as carte blanche to ignore democratic checks and balances and the liberal intelligentsia (and even, in time, the conservative Gulenists). Erdogan's crackdown on the liberals and freedoms ensued in due course.[28] Standing against Erdogan was now the most dangerous political position in Turkey; the Turkish leader was free to shape the country in his own image. A new "Ataturk," obsessed not with Westernization but Islamization, was about to be born.

Canary in the coal mine: Turkey's slide on freedoms and gender equality under the AKP after 2007

In September 2010, just as the Ergenekon case was coming to an end, Turkey held a referendum to decide whether or not to carry out 26 proposed amendments to the military-drafted constitution instituted in the aftermath of the 1980 coup. According to Erdogan and the AKP, the main purpose of the amendments was to create a constitution that more closely matched the style of those of EU member states, thus potentially facilitating Turkey's accession. Supporters pointed to specific amendments that would seemingly address gender inequities, improve citizens' rights to privacy, and, they claimed, break up the guild-like nature of the judiciary by giving elected officials more influence over judicial appointments. Opponents (rival political parties and secularists among them) maintained that any purportedly progressive amendments were unlikely to be executed. They also highlighted the dangers of judicial reforms that would give the ruling government far-reaching powers over the courts. At least some voters found the amendments confusing, and the referendum consisted of a single "yes or no" vote on all 26 amendments, rather than 26 separate votes. Thus, the referendum came to be seen primarily as a vote of confidence in the Erdogan government rather than a substantive assessment of the value of the amendments. Not surprisingly, proponents of the Erdogan-led initiative (leftist–liberals and Gulenists among them once again) proved victorious, winning the referendum by 58 percent to 42 percent.

While the referendum passed, the significant number of Turks who opposed many of the amendments had evidence to support their concerns. Their worry that Erdogan and the AKP would fail to implement liberal policies involving gender and privacy rights, for example, was not unsubstantiated. In Turkey today, women hold between a third and half of jobs in the medical, legal, academic, and engineering fields, thanks to Ataturk's reforms in the 1930s; yet the AKP has failed to appoint a woman to any of the 35 executive posts in the ministries of energy, justice, transportation, public works, or health. Whereas one amendment claimed to defend personal privacy by giving citizens more control over their personal information, the government that proposed it oversaw a documented twofold increase in wiretapped phone calls.[29]

Erdogan's record on human rights and liberties at that time should have acted as a warning to those who supported the amendments as a way to give the leader a mandate to liberalize Turkey. Whereas the country made great improvements to press freedom and legal institutions between 2002 and 2007, it plateaued on those same indices after Erdogan's election win in 2007 and victory against the military in the Ergenekon case. Between 2007 and 2011, Turkey's score changed from 0.577 to 0.595, a negligible 0.018, on the World Economic Forum's "Gender Gap Index" (where 0 is inequality and 1 is equality).[30] Soon, such indicators would begin to fall (see Figure 1), demonstrating the broader erosion of democracy that the AKP and Erdogan would effect.[31]

Court power

Did the Turks who rejected the referendum recognize the potentially destructive impact that some of these amendments would have in the hands of Erdogan, a man of growing authoritarian tendencies? Indeed, having stripped the military, the most powerful of his adversaries, of its influence, Erdogan was now ready to turn his attention to the other building blocks of the 1997 "soft coup" alliance: the high courts, which had shut down the RP and FP and recently threatened to shut down even the AKP, and the secular media and the business

FIGURE 1   LIBERAL DEMOCRACY IN TURKEY 1950–2014

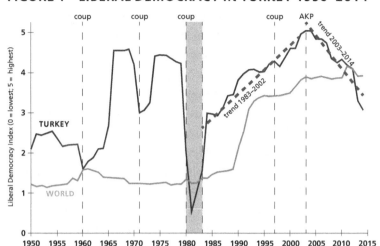

Source: Varieties of Democracy, V-Dem Data Version 6.2,
https://www.v-dem.net/en/data/data-version-6-2/
(Y-axis label added for clarity)

community, which had thrown their support behind the ban and the military during the "soft coup." While many of the amendments had the ability to undermine democracy, the impending changes to the judicial system were the most troublesome.

One amendment increased the number of judges in the Constitutional Court, the highest in Turkey, from 11 to 17. President Gul was tasked with choosing two of the new members to this court (without the need for a legislative confirmation process), where a number of AKP supporters already sat. This change effectively handed control of the most powerful court in the country to Erdogan.[32] Another amendment would see the High Council of Judges and Prosecutors (HSYK) raise its membership from 12 members to 34.[33] This committee, which provides peer oversight to judges and prosecutors, had four new members chosen by President Gul, and it continued to be led by the AKP justice minister. These changes provided Erdogan and the AKP, already in control of the executive and legislative branches, authority over the third and final branch of government, effectively extinguishing the possibility of any genuine separation of powers or checks and balances in Turkey.

Perhaps the HSYK and the high courts had never truly proved to be the effective checks and balances required of a liberal-democratic system. Jurists with a dim view of egalitarian democracy have historically staffed both institutions. With the exception of certain relatively bright periods, such as parts of the 1960s, the late 1980s, and early 1990s, Turkey has functioned as an *illiberal* democracy. Nevertheless, the complete folding of the judiciary under an illiberal ruler, as Erdogan's autocratic side became dominant, meant that soon even the past illiberal years of Turkish democracy would be missed dearly. At the time of the referendum, however, the zeitgeist in Turkey centered on a shift in direction from the country's illiberal past. The irony is that many didn't see that such a shift could not be achieved by a movement that itself was deeply illiberal.

Erdogan exploited the Turkish aversion toward this past, particularly in regard to the history of undemocratic military coups. As the bitter referendum campaign raged on, he charged individuals against the mandate "of being 'in favour of army coups' and went as far as to warn that they would be 'eliminated.'"[34]

Taming the media...

Once Erdogan had effectively established a grip over the three branches of government and sapped the power of the military, he felt it necessary to subdue the media and the business community, the two other key building blocks of the "soft coup" alliance that once dueled with his fellow Islamists. Large independent or anti-government newspapers such as *Sabah*, *Aksam*, *Star*, *Milliyet*, and *Vatan*, and their popular sister television networks, were subsequently seized by pro-government watchdogs who afterward installed Erdogan-approved management and ownership. Historical problems in the media facilitated the unchallenged nature of these takeovers and allowed Erdogan to move forward with his agenda.

When Erdogan came to power, most of the Turkish media was owned by large businesses that would often pressure their media companies to editorialize in order to appease the government. With some exceptions, major newspapers and television networks could change their tone toward government depending on the relationship between their owners and political elites. Thus, although the Turkish media was technically free, it was not completely independent. Erdogan was intent on placing the bulk of the media into the hands of owners friendly to his agenda, simultaneously preventing any media support for his opposition. To this end, the AKP exploited legal loopholes and passed new restrictive media laws. The transfer of "Sabah-ATV," a shorthand for Turkey's second-largest media conglomerate, to pro-AKP businessmen happened in the following way. The government first charged the owners of "Sabah-ATV" with improper business practices and then passed control of the company to a national regulator. The regulator then sold the media group at an auction that had only one bidder: an AKP supporter who then received a loan from a state-owned bank to finalize his purchase. This would prove to be a common occurrence: just after the AKP rose to power in 2002, pro-government businesses owned less than a quarter of the Turkish media; by 2011, pro-AKP businesses owned around 50 percent. Today, the vast majority of the Turkish media is in the hands of pro-Erdogan businesses.

Before the government confiscated it, *Sabah* was known as the *New York Times* of Turkey due to its liberal content; now it is one of Erdogan's key allies. What is more, the Turkish media today cannot criticize, satirize, or discuss corruption allegations about Erdogan in the way they once did in relation to Demirel, Ecevit, Ozal, Yilmaz, or Ciller. Corruption charges discussed in the press targeting Ciller and Yilmaz brought their governments down, and Demirel, Ecevit, and Ozal were once upon a time the butt of jokes in the Turkish media. But they lived with and tolerated such satire. Indeed, Ozal, who was often depicted as various animals, and at one time also as an unflattering and overweight Marilyn Monroe, trying to hold his skirt in place while standing on a subway grate, exhibited such cartoons in his office.[35] Under Erdogan's leadership, when a Turkish caricaturist sketched Erdogan as a cat, he responded by suing the artist and the publication for 10,000 lira, equivalent to almost $7,000 at the time.[36] The death of political satire in Turkey, a genre going back to the days of the late Ottoman sultans, is itself indicative of the AKP's ahistorically tight grip over free speech and the media.

...and the business community

The intimidation of the business community moved in tandem with Erdogan's rearrangement of the media. In 2009, the media firm Dogan Yayin, a conglomerate owned by Turkish billionaire and TUSIAD member Aydin Dogan, was fined almost $2.5 billion for tax evasion; this fine nearly exceeded the company's total net worth.[37] The penalty is largely thought to have been politically motivated: Dogan Yayin owned around 50 percent of the Turkish media at the time and had long supported secular, liberal, and nationalist views, which often criticized the AKP and the Islamists. For instance, during the 1997 "soft coup," the Dogan-owned media had stood with the military against Erbakan, and columnists in Dogan-owned publications had been at the forefront of criticism of Islamists. Dogan-held companies were then subjected to an excruciating and politically motivated tax audit, during which Erdogan publicly called for a boycott of the Dogan-owned media, including *Hurriyet*, Turkey's most prominent and most widely circulated daily newspaper. In the end, Aydin Dogan buckled under the pressure and agreed to sell some of his media companies, including the influential liberal *Milliyet* newspaper, to pro-AKP businesses.

Erdogan's successful subjugation of the Dogan family proved to have an effective and chilling effect on the broader media and business community. At the same time that the tax fines and selective audits were being leveled against Dogan, the companies of the Koc family were also being targeted. This family, the wealthiest in Turkey and a supporter of secular and liberal causes through their philanthropic organizations, came under a similarly intensive audit. The business community gradually surrendered to Erdogan. The alliance between the military, courts, media, secular NGOs, and business that had brought down Erbakan in 1997 was no longer an obstacle.

Erdogan's second report card

When did Erdogan abandon his moderate, center-right platform? An early warning sign should have been the ejection of center-right-origin politicians from the AKP. In 2001, the AKP was established with many center-right politicians on board. The first AKP cabinet, formed under Gul in 2002 and then chaired by Erdogan in 2003, too, included key center-right figures. However, starting in 2007, and each time Erdogan won an election subsequently, fewer of these politicians made it into his government. And at each AKP convention, fewer center-right figures ended up assuming positions of power in the party. Between 2002 and 2011, the AKP went from being a broad right-wing movement embracing the center-right brand of Turkish politics to an Islamist party run by Islamists. (In 2014, and following the departure of prominent AKP founder Gul and other former RP figures, the AKP would evolve further, becoming a politburo-like structure dominated by Erdogan loyalists.[38])

While Erdogan had distaste for the powerful, wealthy, and secular from his early life, it began to manifest itself more overtly in his politics as the years and his power progressed, especially during his second term in government. Whether during the Ergenekon trials or the suspiciously motivated referendum of 2010, Erdogan built momentum for a presidency that he would seize and transform into a new, personal position that could advance his rule in time and scope. His supporters would prove vehemently passionate, but so too would his long-term opponents, who were not finished fighting. Erdogan's illiberal policies strengthened once he was able to eliminate three key checks and balances: one undemocratic (the TAF), and two democratic (the high courts and the media). His successful intimidation of the business community and civil society also neutralized a potential force of opposition, and Erdogan became brazen in his disregard for democratic institutions.

9

The Revolution Devours Its Children

2011 election victory: Erdogan's illiberal side

The AKP began June 2011 heavily favored to win its third consecutive general election since the party's inception ten years earlier and, sure enough, Erdogan achieved a whopping 49.8 percent of the vote. But Erdogan achieved such popularity only by fueling societal polarization. He had always had a penchant for demonizing and cracking down on demographic groups that were not likely to vote for him, starting with the secularists, and this became a key part of his strategy in the aftermath of the 2011 election as he went on to demonize others, including liberals, leftists, Kurds, and Alevis. Accordingly, his right-wing conservative base, a plurality and, at times, a majority of the Turkish electorate, rallied around him. In addition, there is a large segment of the population that supports Erdogan regardless of his indiscretions, as a result of the significant improvements to infrastructure and living standards brought about by his party's policies. With Erdogan and his party in charge of the executive, legislative, and judicial branches, a comprehensive and thorough crackdown on opposition media taking place, a significant part of the public aligned behind him, and, perhaps most importantly, the TAF in a severely weakened state, Erdogan's illiberal alter ego encountered even fewer constraints after 2011.

This "illiberalization" took many forms. Internationally, Erdogan apparently intended to sour Turkey's historic relations with Israel, the only non-Muslim-majority country in the Middle East. The AKP hardly missed an opportunity to criticize Israel on the international stage, condemning its policies as "genocidal." And AKP officials did more than just talk. They seem to have actively stoked a crisis in bilateral relations. In 2010, Israeli commandos raided a flotilla, led by the Turkish ferryboat *Mavi Marmara*, that was carrying Turkish activists attempting to break the Israeli blockade of Hamas-held Gaza. In the ensuing confrontation in international waters—now referred to as the "*Mavi Marmara* incident"—nine activists were killed; a tenth died four years later after being in a coma. The slaying of these Turks—including one Turkish American dual citizen—sent Ankara's relations with Israel into a tailspin. But this crisis was seemingly partly of Ankara's own making. There were reports that the mission had been supported in Turkey by "top levels of the governing party," in the words of the *New York Times*. Erdogan and the AKP surely knew the stunt would prove inflammatory, confirmed by the fact that party members' planned presence on the boats was canceled when they were "warned off at the last minute by senior Foreign Ministry officials concerned that their presence might escalate tensions too much."[1]

Erdogan called Israel's actions a "bloody massacre," publicly asked why the UN would not impose more sanctions on Israel, and only accepted Israel's apology after first refusing it and then referring to Zionism as racism.[2] In the end, Erdogan banished the Israeli ambassador from Turkey and reduced military cooperation with Israel.[3] One European diplomat said of the reactions to the event: "Erdogan is making a big play to become the leader of the Islamic street [...] We need to watch this dynamic very closely."[4] While the international community largely condemned the actions of Israel, Erdogan and the AKP clearly promoted the actions of the flotilla, and were not shy in exploiting the situation for their benefit to the fullest possible extent.

Islam and everyday life

Domestically, Erdogan has increasingly introduced religion into everyday public life, including by constructing 9,000 mosques over a ten-year stretch of AKP rule, from 2005 to 2015.[5] Among these is the grand "Erdogan Mosque" on Istanbul's Camlica Hill, which includes a 105-meter (344-feet) minaret, rivaling even that of the Prophet's Mosque in the Muslim holy city Medina. The similarities between this and the legendary Ottoman Blue Mosque created suspicion regarding the motives behind its construction: "Erdogan is trying to compete with the sultans," claimed Oguz Oztuzcu, former president of an Istanbul architecture firm. For many it is evident that this mosque is meant not merely to host worshipers but to add to the religious legacy of Erdogan and his party; the Istanbul minister of environment and urban planning even asserted that the mosque was an attempt to "represent the era of the AKP."[6]

Beyond such tangible signs of piety, Erdogan has taken overt steps toward the Islamization of Turkish society, most notably through education policy. For example, in 2014, the Council of National Education, a government advisory body, issued a policy recommendation suggesting that mandatory courses on Islam be taught to all students as young as six in public schools.[7] As a result of Erdogan's changes, kindergarten-age children of other faiths or no faith, or from non-practicing families, will be forced to take courses in Sunni Islam in publicly funded schools. In 2012, the parliament passed an education bill, based largely on Erdogan's stated goal of "raising a devout generation," which sped up the movement to transform publicly funded secular high schools into government-funded Imam Hatip religious schools.[8] Religiously focused programs replaced extracurricular activities involving arts and athletics across publicly funded secular schools. This education bill also enabled the instantaneous replacement of school administrators by Erdogan-approved pawns picked from a conservative trade union closely aligned with the AKP.[9] Erdogan frequently emphasized the importance of a pious society during this time, and was not shy about lambasting opponents who promoted a more secular education system. He went so far as to accuse rival political leader and CHP chair Kemal Kilicdaroglu of encouraging "an atheist generation," a baseless accusation.[10]

129

Gezi Park rallies: Erdogan bloodies the liberals

When Erdogan had moderated his Islamist platform to create a more inclusive, democratizing policy agenda, liberals had been some of his most important allies. Wishing to support freedom of expression and religion, they had protested alongside hijab-wearing women for their right to wear headscarves at universities. However, when Erdogan began to push Islamization, particularly in the social realm (with public morality campaigns, alcohol-sale regulations and bans, and calls for women to have at least three children), liberals were the first key allies to part ways with the AKP leader.[11] Since then, these liberals, many of whom are young and urban, have formed a small, yet tenacious, opposition to Erdogan's autocratic agenda.

In May and June 2013, the Gezi Park protests signaled the birth of a new type of anti-AKP grassroots politics in Turkey as "environmentalists, feminists, radical leftists, ultra-nationalists, LGBT activists, trade unions, some of them observant Muslims, others not" set aside their differences and rallied together against the government.[12] The protests began when environmentalist groups organized a sit-in to protest against government plans to cut down trees in Gezi Park in the heart of Istanbul to make way for a shopping mall, the design of which was to memorialize Ottoman military barracks that had occupied the site a century earlier. Even more poignantly, the barracks that Erdogan wanted to resuscitate had been the staging ground for the 1909 Islamist-led counter-revolution against the secularist Young Turkish CUP government in the late Ottoman Empire. At that time, Ataturk, as a 28-year-old officer, had marched into the city as the staff officer in the pro-CUP military, to crush the counter-revolution at the Taksim barracks.

The young activists who descended on Taksim, this time in 2013, had over the past decade watched the AKP raze many of the city's precious green spaces to make way for lucrative, and sometimes garish, construction projects, many owned by Erdogan's political allies. When images of police brutality against this small group of protestors surfaced on social media, attendance at the sit-in, later dubbed the "tree revolution," grew quickly into the thousands. When police cracked down even more harshly, the size of the demonstration exploded to transcend the initial scope of the environmental protest, as demonstrators poured into Istanbul's streets in the middle of the night to defend their right—and, perhaps more importantly, the right of people of different ideological stripes—to protest. Though radical-leftist groups eventually began to dominate the square and rallies, this was nevertheless a turning point.

Protestors occupied Istanbul's central Taksim Square for weeks, and the demonstrations spread to more than 70 cities of varying sizes across the country. The wrath of civil society forced the government's hand. On June 2, Erdogan recanted the shopping-mall proposal that had ignited the protests (though he would not stick to this pledge after the protests subsided). After Erdogan left for a trip to Morocco, deputy prime minister Bulent Arinc apologized to the sit-in demonstrators for police violence, and also offered to meet with them.

Certainly, the Gezi movement did not force a fundamental shift in AKP policies. When Erdogan returned from Morocco, he lambasted Arinc and eventually ordered a violent and brutal crackdown that initially led to five deaths, including four protestors and one police officer.[13] Still, the fact that the AKP felt the need to assuage the situation demonstrated the power that grassroots movements held. At the same time, the fact that voices within the AKP were censored signaled Erdogan's strong control over the party. His reaction to the Gezi Park rallies suggested that, by 2013, the AKP was morphing from a broadly center-right movement led by Islamists and supported by liberals, to a narrowly Islamist party led by a single dominant ruler.

Erdogan has a nemesis...

The Gezi Park rallies point to the birth of a new form of grassroots politics in Turkey, which can be accounted for by two main factors. The first is social media, which single-handedly helped turn an environmentalist sit-in into a massive anti-government rally and sustained it for days. During the midnight police crackdown, a social-media campaign brought nearly a million demonstrators onto Istanbul's streets at two in the morning to defy the authorities and Erdogan's rule. Somewhat ironically for Erdogan, his opponents are able to organize with the help of expensive smartphones that they can only afford thanks to the economic prosperity achieved under his tenure. By the same token, the success of Erdogan's social policies, including his campaign to increase public services, has made Turkey nearly universally literate. Accordingly, the Turks are better connected to the world—and each other—than they were before. A 2013 study by New York University, for example, found that while only 35 percent of tweets about the Tahrir Square protests during Egypt's 2011 revolt against Hosni Mubarak's regime came from Egypt, 90 percent of tweets during the Gezi Park protests came from Turkey, and 80 percent were in Turkish.[14]

The second factor was Turkey's new middle class. The twenty-first century has seen the country evolve into a majority middle-class society. The middle class that the AKP has created is committed to individual freedoms and ready to protest against the party's style of governance and political domination should they impinge on these freedoms. Profoundly irksome for Erdogan is the reality that middle-class Turks, effective organizers on their smartphones, are committed to middle-class demands, including freedoms of expression, association, media, and assembly. College students, mostly middle class and thought to be apolitical, emerged as a hugely influential organizing force of the Gezi movement. They set up makeshift clinics, established hotlines for medical help for the injured, and provided legal counsel for demonstrators who were arrested.

...but it is a divided one

The participation of these students offered a glimpse into Erdogan's future challenge. They—along with the environmentalists, hard-leftists, women's-rights activists, ultra-nationalists, LGBT activists, members of the Alevi community, Kurdish separatists, and secular liberals—want their voices to be heard. There is, however, a long way for them to go.

Turkey's liberal Muslim community of Alevis, traditionally marginalized in the country's politics, played an especially visible role in the Gezi Park rallies—tellingly, all civilian casualties during the demonstrations were Alevis. The Alevis, who constitute 10–20 percent of the Turkish population, profess a spiritual understanding of Islam. Their take on religion and staunch pro-secularist views differ from the AKP's emphasis on rigid Islam.[15] Under the AKP's rule since 2002, the Alevis have been excluded from participation in Turkish politics to an even greater extent than has historically been the case. There are no Alevis in the governing party's leadership or among the 27 cabinet ministers. More significantly, Alevis constitute less than one percent of the 27 undersecretaries, 27 deputy ministers, 81 provincial governors, or 81 provincial police chiefs—all key bureaucratic positions filled by central-government appointment.

When the Gezi Park rallies rapidly expanded, the Alevis were at the forefront of the protests. And they sustained these rallies in Alevi-majority neighborhoods of Ankara and other cities for days after Erdogan crushed them elsewhere. In the future, as a secularism-embracing constituency, Turkey's Alevis will be part of any anti-AKP bloc in the country. But this effort will require parts of the majority Sunni society that reach beyond the AKP's base to abandon their prejudices. As a heterodox group of Muslims, the Alevis have long suffered from discrimination, and sometimes outright hostility from many Sunnis in Turkey. Along the same lines, the Alevis have to learn to trust Sunni Turks politically. The Alevi–Sunni divide in the country, which haunts the anti-AKP bloc, encapsulates the problems for Erdogan's opposition that lie ahead: sometimes the gap between various groups in the Turkish opposition can be wider than the gaps between Erdogan and his opponents.

Emblematic of the Gezi movement's diverse and eclectic nature, the rallies also included a number of AKP voters—this was their way of saying to the AKP, "We may vote for you, but that does not mean we will support all your policies." Even Erdogan's allies and supporters, including the Gulen movement, threw some support behind the demonstrations and published a number of editorials in the media criticizing the ruling party. For example, *Zaman* complained that "even those who love Erdogan [were] having a hard time defending his actions."[16]

Even though they ultimately failed to change Erdogan's course on liberal freedoms, the Gezi Park protests exposed the depth of the rift between the democratic vision of large swaths of society and the AKP. The movement was a public battle between Erdogan and his simple interpretation of democracy as majoritarianism (the rigid belief that the will of the majority must be respected without regard for the protection of political minorities) against what was essentially a coalition of minorities flexing their muscles. When combined, these minority groups make up nearly half the Turkish population. Erdogan's own democratizing policies in the economic sphere, which helped usher in his successive electoral victories, also fostered the confidence of the liberals and grassroots movements to hold him accountable in the social sphere and to become key challengers of his policies.

However, Erdogan's opposition has some way to go. Turkey's grassroots movements lack a party and a charismatic leader to carry them to power. What is more, they are spread across the political spectrum between Turkish and Kurdish nationalists, Alevis and Sunnis, leftists and center-right conservatives, among others. If the grassroots movements have not coalesced and found a leader by the time the next Gezi-type movement springs up, Erdogan will not find it difficult to crush it again.

Erdogan splits with the Gulenists

Following the crackdown on the liberals, Erdogan next set his sights on the Gulenists. Their symbiotic relationship first began to show signs of strain after Erdogan's 2011 victory and the mass resignation of the secularist military's top brass. Having then received nearly half the popular vote and broken the back of the military, Erdogan arguably decided that he did not need the Gulenists—whom he had used as a means to help eliminate checks and balances, lock up generals, and intimidate opponents—as much as he had in the past. Their helpfulness in carrying out sophisticated operations, their reach into the police and judiciary, and their ability to wiretap nearly anyone in the country also made them a threat: if they could bring down the mighty Turkish military through their invisible networks, they could surely go after Erdogan himself one day. The Gulenists, too, were questioning the relationship. Having success-fully defanged the TAF, and then secured the appointment of many of their members into the officer corps, and having infiltrated the police and the judiciary, the movement was arguably asking itself whether it really needed Erdogan.

By 2011, the relationship had run its course. Erdogan had provided the Gulen movement with something it did not have: a political party with which to defeat its adversaries. Likewise, the movement had provided Erdogan with assets he lacked: an intelligentsia, media outlets, and a bureaucratic apparatus, including the police, with which to crush his opponents. Now, though, Erdogan and Gulen each felt that Turkey was his to grasp, and neither was willing to settle for a condominium arrangement. What ensued was a raw power struggle.

In the aftermath of the AKP's success in the 2011 election, Gulen-aligned businesses, once some of the main beneficiaries of government-awarded contracts, were suddenly cut out of deals, and the movement's followers were denied new promotions and jobs in government, including the role of head of the National Intelligence Organization (MIT), Turkey's spy agency, something they dearly wanted. The crisis went public when the Turkish government pro-ceeded with peace talks with the PKK in the face of protests from the Gulen movement, which has always had strong Turkish-nationalist tendencies and strongly objected to such overtures. In 2012, Hakan Fidan, the head of MIT and key negotiator of the talks, was nearly arrested by state prosecutors for holding secret talks with the PKK while Erdogan was recovering from surgery. It is widely believed that the Gulenists, attempting to impede the ongoing peace talks, encouraged this attempted arrest.[17] The Gulenists are also suspected of having leaked recordings of the 2008 and 2009 Oslo peace talks between the Turkish government and the PKK, sabotaging the meetings.[18] At that time, Erdogan was still keenly interested in obtaining the Kurds as key allies, and the Gulenists' interference left a bad taste in his mouth.

The tensions came to a head when, in November 2013, Erdogan moved to close Gulen-sponsored preparatory "cram schools" (*dershanes*).[19] In Turkey's education system, high-school students' performance on a single centralized test alone determines which universities they can enter, and the *dershanes* played a key role in readying them for this. Simply put, a high-school senior who did not attend a *dershane* could not hope to enter a good university and, often, he or she would not be able to enter a university at all. Over decades, this set-up turned the *dershanes* into a billion-dollar business, and the Gulenists, known for their commitment to good education, owned a large slice of this pie. What is more, the *dershanes* also provided the Gulenists with a medium for recruiting poor but smart students into the movement at a young age, by providing them with full scholarships, effectively securing them spots in Turkey's "Ivy League" universities. Some of these scholarship grantees would eventually join the movement and form its brain trust, dubbed the "Golden Generation."

Erdogan's ban on *dershanes*, of course, had an official justification. He stated that the institutions had turned students into "racehorses" (and he was right, for the *dershane* was a nightmarish experience for Turkish high-school seniors, who had constantly to memorize and practice tests with little time left for anything else).[20] But in practical terms, by shutting down the *dershanes* Erdogan was threatening to destroy a main fundraising mechanism for the Gulen movement, as well as their ability to spot the country's smartest young people and recruit them into their organization.

The Gulenists did not wait long before retaliating, and a major government corruption scandal broke in December 2013, involving the arrest of 52 people connected to the AKP, including family members of cabinet ministers, who were charged with "bribery, corruption, fraud, money laundering, and gold smuggling."[21] Embarrassing tapes of what appeared to be conversations between Erdogan and his son about managing millions of dollars of cash were leaked to the public in pro-Gulen dailies such as *Zaman*.[22]

Erdogan used the *dershane* ban to provoke the Gulen movement into a fight. Although he had accepted Gulenist aid over the years, he was cautious about allowing them to accumulate too much power, and had discussed "potential measures against the group in the [Turkish] National Security Council" as early as 2004.[23] He knew that shutting the *dershanes*, lifeline of the Gulenists, would force them to attack him openly. Once exposed, Erdogan could cut them down. Subsequently, in 2013 and 2014, following corruption allegations against him and his family members, Erdogan demoted and fired many of the police chiefs, judges, and prosecutors involved in the corruption charges.

Though it was damaging, Erdogan and the AKP survived the 2013 corruption scandal. In the aftermath, the government declared the Gulen movement a terrorist organization, and Gulenists became Erdogan's staunchest opponents. The Gulenist dailies *Zaman* and *Today's Zaman*, once his biggest allies, turned into his biggest critics. And, in 2014, Erdogan gained his revenge when he had more than two dozen major journalists and media executives arrested and implemented a boycott against Gulen-affiliated media outlets.[24] From this point on, Erdogan and the Gulen movement waged all-out war, with the fight reaching its crescendo in the failed plot of July 15, 2016, in which Gulen-aligned military officers allegedly formed the backbone of a *coup d'état* against Erdogan.

Rise and fall of the Erdogan–Kurdish alliance

Just as he did with the liberals and the Gulenists, Erdogan took a utilitarian view of his alliance with another group, the Turkish Kurds, a constituency he would befriend and use only to discard when he no longer needed its assistance. As a minority that rejects Turkish nationalism and is overwhelmingly devout, the Kurds were, like Erdogan, at odds with the military and pro-Kemalist nationalist and secularist Turks. Erdogan recognized an opportunity to align with the Kurds against these mutual enemies and adopted progressive policies aimed at reconciliation. The Turkish Kurds voted for Erdogan in large numbers in 2002, 2007, and 2011.

Beginning in 2009, Erdogan laid the groundwork for what would later be termed the "Solution Process": peace talks aimed at ending the military conflict between the leftist and hard-line Kurdish-nationalist PKK (designated a terrorist entity by Turkey, the United States, and NATO) and the TAF, ongoing since 1984. In January 2009, the government began a publicly funded 24-hour Kurdish-language television channel. Erdogan even inaugurated the station's opening by extending his best wishes in Kurdish, a poignant act given that merely speaking the language, much less supporting Kurdish causes, had previously been banned in Turkey.[25] In addition, the government facilitated the creation of Kurdish language departments in universities and allowed Kurdish to be taught as an elective course in middle and high schools in June 2012.[26] That same year, Erdogan announced that Fidan, the spy chief, had participated in the aforementioned secret peace talks with the PKK in Oslo.[27] This public announcement signaled his willingness to court the Kurds openly in an alliance, a fact that explained nationalist Kurds' absence from the Gezi Park rallies after the initial days of the protest.

The period between late 2012 and 2015 was the height of a—relatively—peaceful era in Turkey's political struggle with the nationalist Kurds and the PKK. In 2013, the PKK announced that it would withdraw all its forces from Turkey, and the government promised to move forward with legal and constitutional changes. However, the Syrian civil war and Erdogan's political calculations halted any further steps toward peace. The conflict in Syria spilled into Turkey; nationalist tensions increased around the Kurdish issue, including territorial gains by the PKK's Syria-based franchise, the Democratic Union Party (PYD). In August 2014, Erdogan abandoned his position as prime minister due to an AKP statute which sets term limits for elected officials. The same month he won the election to become president and therefore head of state, but was also forced to give up his position as head of government and chief executive as per the country's constitution, which stipulated that the president be a non-partisan figure. At this point, Erdogan set his eyes on winning a referendum to change the country's constitution in order to become an executive-style president, so he could simultaneously assume the offices of head of state and head of government, as well as returning as the head of the AKP. This is when Erdogan realized that a liberal and amenable stance on the PKK would not win him enough Kurdish-nationalist votes to offset the many Turkish-nationalist votes he would lose. Perhaps most importantly, the pro-Kurdish Peoples' Democratic Party (HDP), which entered parliament in June 2015 as the third-largest legislative bloc, ran on a platform of blocking Erdogan's presidential ambitions (HDP co-chair Selahattin Demirtas competed for the presidency under the hashtag #wewillnotmakeyoupresident), posing a direct threat to Erdogan's consolidation of political power. This was the final nail in the coffin of Erdogan's alliance with the Kurds.

Erdogan's success has been to divide the groups that oppose him, by extending an olive branch to one while persecuting or prosecuting the other. The fault of Erdogan's detractors is that they were never unified: when Erdogan cracked down on the secularists, the liberals and the Gulenists helped him. When he beat up the liberals, the Gulenists and the Kurds stood away. When he went after the Gulenists, the Kurds looked the other way, and the secularists basked in *Schadenfreude*. Once Erdogan came down on the Kurds, allies were either on the run themselves or too cowed to speak up.

Ataturk's seat: the siren call of Turkish politics

The nationalist Kurds and Demirtas could not have found a better way to enrage Erdogan. Standing between him and his ultimate ambition of an executive-style presidency was unforgivable in Erdogan's eyes. Turkey is a parliamentary democracy with the prime minister as the chief executive, while the president, though he or she is head of state, has traditionally held limited executive powers in comparison. In spite of this, the presidency is the most coveted position in the Turkish system. Just as sailors in Greek mythology were lured to their doom by siren song, in Turkish politics leaders are enticed to their political ends by the call of the Turkish presidency. The reverence for this institution can be traced to Ataturk, who was also Turkey's first president, between 1923 and 1938. As Turkey's simultaneous liberator, reformer, and founder, Ataturk has an inescapable pull over the Turkish citizenry, and even over his detractors.

Every Turkish politician dreams of having the prestige of Ataturk one day.

The 1982 Turkish constitution stipulates that the presidency is a non-partisan post. Two previous powerful Turkish prime ministers, Ozal and Demirel, resigned from their posts and their parties to become president, in 1990 and 1993, respectively, only to see their political careers ended. After losing their charismatic leaders, Ozal's ANAP and Demirel's DYP fragmented, undermining Ozal's and Demirel's political legacies.

In 2007, the AKP led a constitutional referendum that included amendments to the presidency. It passed, mandating that future presidents be elected by direct, popular vote rather than by parliament, that his or her term would be five years instead of seven, and that he or she could be re-elected for a second term.[28] At the time of this referendum, Erdogan's ally Gul had already been elected as president; the changes in the referendum would thus not take effect until Gul's seven-year term expired in summer 2014. In the early months of 2014, some thought that Gul could be re-elected as president. While the Constitutional Court ruled that Gul was eligible to run for a five-year term, he followed his well-established reflex, stepping aside for Erdogan.[29] Erdogan's opting for the presidency also allowed him to bypass the aforementioned AKP statute—having won three elections as prime minister, Erdogan was facing a term limit in 2015.

But there was another reason for Erdogan's presidential run: he, like so many before him, dreamed of sitting where the "Father of the Turks" had sat. In this regard, the 2007 referendum was a stroke of prescience. Erdogan was at the height of his popularity during this time, and took advantage of this, winning the presidential election of 2014 with more than 50 percent of the vote in the first ballot, meaning the contest did not go to a second round, as had been expected. The result also showed that his split with the Gulen movement had cost him virtually nothing in the polls. Of course, Erdogan was only too happy to occupy the position once held by Ataturk. But unlike Demirel or Ozal, and as an "anti-Ataturk Ataturk," Erdogan would also refuse to move into the Cankaya Palace built for Ataturk, and occupied by every Turkish president since. Erdogan moved instead to a recently reconstructed 1,100-room palace in Ankara dubbed "Ak Saray," a play on the AKP's name and its claim to be *ak*, or white, in the abstract sense—pure and clean. Perhaps coincidentally, the name also evokes Washington's White House. Erdogan's $615 million presidential residence also signaled the blending of ruling party and state.[30]

Erdogan's victory was not without controversy. The Turkish leader's increasingly generous delivery of state resources to the ruling party, discussed by *Time* magazine in an article entitled "Turkey's first presidential elections were no democracy," is a case in point. The article pointed to a report by the Organization for Security and Co-operation in Europe (OSCE) that highlighted Erdogan's enormous advantage in the media, including the state-funded broadcaster TRT. According to the report:

> TRT1 devoted 51 per cent of coverage to Mr. Erdoğan, while covering Mr. İhsanoğlu and Mr. Demirtas [two opposition candidates] with 32 per cent and 18 per cent, respectively. In addition, 25 per cent of Mr. İhsanoğlu's coverage was negative in tone, while Mr. Erdogan's coverage was almost all positive.[31]

Charges of journalist intimidation also arose when the OSCE accused "the highest authorities in Turkey" of attacking well-known Turkish journalist Amberin Zaman.[32]

By 2014, then, Erdogan had successfully outmaneuvered opponents to become the undisputed Ataturk of modern Turkey. Most of the nationalist, Islamist, and conservative half of Turkey was coalescing around him while the country's liberal, secular, and leftist forces were receiving the brutal end of his oppressive policies. Of course, not everything was rosy for Erdogan. The Turkish president knew very well that to avoid the outcome suffered by Ozal and Demirel, who watched power slip from their hands after leaving their positions as head of government and the ruling party, he would need to make himself a partisan president and chief executive. This is why, after 2014, all Turkish politics has boiled down to one goal for Erdogan: changing the constitution so he can become an executive-style president, assuming the titles of head of state, head of government, and head of the ruling party all at the same time. As far as Erdogan was concerned, a clear path emerged for him to realize his contorted vision for the presidency: winning over more Turkish-nationalist voters by declaring full-scale war against the nationalist Kurds.

10

The Future of the Turkish Kurds: Peace or Fire?

E rdogan's success or otherwise in dealing with the Kurdish issue will determine how long he stays in power. Turkey's Kurdish and PKK policy has implications for the country's democracy and security, relations with its neighbors, and alliance with the United States, which has relied on the Syrian Kurds, linked to the PKK, to combat ISIS. More than 20 million Kurds live in the Middle East, although they are spread across four countries—Iraq, Iran, Syria, and Turkey—and are divided by three mutually unintelligible dialects (Kurmanji, Sorani, and Zaza), among others, two alphabets (Arabic and Latin), and nearly a dozen antagonistic ideological movements, ranging from socialist to jihadist. As a result, the Kurds often find themselves among the most disenchanted groups in the Middle East. The Kurds in Turkey face a similar conundrum: they are trapped between Erdogan and the PKK.

Turkey's Kurdish movement is at its most important turning point since the Ankara government captured Abdullah Ocalan, the founder of the PKK, in February 1999.[1] At that time, Turkey had just managed to defeat a full-blown Kurdish insurgency supported by at least two of its neighbors, Iran and Syria. The following decade promised a period of calm for Turkey regarding its Kurdish issue, given that Ocalan was in jail and the PKK had declared a ceasefire. Even after the PKK broke its ceasefire in June 2004, Ankara held the upper hand, particularly when the United States began providing intelligence assistance in 2007. The PKK declared another ceasefire in March 2013 after entering into secret peace talks with the Turkish government in December 2012: it appeared that Turkey's Kurdish issue was heading toward a peaceful resolution.[2]

Kurdish fire

But the Syrian conflict cut the peace process short, and Erdogan's plan to become an omnipotent president led him to harden his position. A hawkish stance on the PKK allows Erdogan to siphon off votes from the hard-line Turkish-nationalist faction (the MHP). The PKK, too, was eager to fight. In 2015, it mobilized against Ankara, emboldened by the ability of its Syrian franchise—the PYD—to capture large swaths of Syrian territory, notably the self-declared autonomous region of Rojava. The PKK was hoping to recreate the "Rojava model" inside Turkey by taking control of cities and then declaring them autonomous.

All this put Turkey on a dangerous trajectory beset with worsening clashes with the PKK in the country's southeast and terror attacks conducted by the PKK's urban franchise, the Kurdistan Freedom Falcons (TAK), across the country. As the Turkish police and military gradually reduced the PKK presence in the urban centers of the country's Kurdish-majority southeast in 2016, the group increasingly focused on urban centers in the west. Two strikes that the TAK carried out in Ankara in 2016 killed at least 65 people.[3] And, on December 10, the TAK targeted downtown Istanbul in twin suicide-bomb attacks, killing 48 people. This upsurge in violence came on the heels of a new PKK-led insurgency in the country's southeast, which has further exacerbated tensions with the PYD. Turkey began shelling PYD positions in Syria in 2016, and, in August, Turkish forces led an incursion into northern Syria to take territory from ISIS, which also allowed them to block territorial advances by the PYD. Fueled by developments in Syria, the Kurdish issue in Turkey could lead to a crisis with Washington, which relies on the PYD, more specifically the PYD's People Protection Units (YPG) militia, to push back against ISIS.

Can Turkey prevent a reversion to full-blown war like that between Ankara and the PKK of the 1990s, in which around 35,000 people are said to have died? The answer rests on an understanding of the historic Turkish–Kurdish relationship and the newly emerging dynamics between Turkish Kurds and other Kurdish groups in the Middle East, especially in Syria.

A brief history of the Kurds in Turkey

Turkey is a multi-ethnic, although almost entirely Muslim, nation. The Kurds are one part of this diversity, in some ways standing out from other Muslim groups.[4] Most surveys suggest that around 15 percent of the country's population of 80 million could be ethnically Kurdish.[5] The presence of this rather substantial non-Turkish group is not so surprising, as the country's population also includes a large number of other non-Turkish Muslim ethnic communities. For instance, approximately 1 million Muslim Circassians migrated to Turkey in the middle of the nineteenth century after the Russian Empire expelled them from the northern Caucasus. At that time, the Muslim population of Turkey stood at nine million.[6] Today, Circassians likely constitute around 10 percent of the country's population. Yet, despite their relative size, the Circassians, and millions of other non-Turkish Ottoman Muslims, from Bosnians to Greek Muslims, have integrated into the mainstream. Some Kurdish groups, most notably the Alevi Kurds (who have mostly adopted a secular Turkish identity that they share with Turkish Alevis) and many Kurds living in western Turkey, have also integrated into the country's overall population by intermarrying with Turks.[7] But many others have not, leaving the Kurds in a unique position among other non-Turkish Muslim groups in the country.

A number of factors help explain the Kurds' distinctive status.[8] The first is historical. Turkish nationalism became a potent force in the late Ottoman Empire as the fabric of the multi-ethnic and multi-religious empire was disintegrating. In order to achieve a homogeneous identity, Turkish nationalism substituted the patriotism of "Ottoman Muslim-ness" with that of "Turkishness," thereby establishing a new standard of citizenship in which Bosnians, Circassians, Kurds, and other Ottoman Muslims had to identify themselves as Turkish in order to become participating citizens in the new country. Unsurprisingly, this late Ottoman–Kemalist stance presented few challenges for the Balkan Muslims, such as Bosnians, or for other immigrant non-Turkish Muslims, such as the Circassians. Like the Turks, these groups lived in the core Ottoman territories in the southern and central Balkans and western and central Anatolia, and could easily make the switch from Ottoman to Turkish. The Kurds, however, lived beyond the core Ottoman territories in southeastern Anatolia and the Middle East and were not exposed to Ottomanizing influences to the same extent. Kurdish areas were largely autonomous from Istanbul, and local leaders (beys) ruled over these lands, which the Ottomans called Kurdistan.[9] In the Ottoman era, a Kurd in what is now southeastern Turkey most likely did not see himself as "Ottoman" in the way that a Bosnian Muslim in the Balkans would have. This is why passing from "Ottoman-ness" into "Turkishness" has been harder for Kurds in Turkey than for all other non-Turkish Muslim groups.[10]

Furthermore, expelled from their homes by Russia and the newly independent southeastern European states, such as Greece and Bulgaria, the Ottoman Muslims from the Balkans and the Caucasus had nowhere to go but Turkey, and therefore no choice but to accept the Turkish nationalism that awaited them there. This was not the case for the relatively sovereign Kurds, who are autochthonous to southeastern Anatolia and thus were not subject to the same survival imperative that led others to embrace Turkish national identity.

Relative poverty has also hindered Kurdish integration into the Turkish republic. Eastern Turkey has always been poorer than the rest of the country—indeed, the region never fully recovered from the multiple infrastructure collapses during and after World War I. Armenian, Ottoman, and Russian armies burned cities in the area and crippled the local economy in a matter of six years. The region's remoteness (it is distant from navigable seas) and rugged terrain (the average altitude in eastern Turkey is 6,500 feet or nearly 2,000 meters) did not allow it to develop in the 1980s when the rest of the country took off economically under Ozal. Turks too live in this area, where they form the majority of the population in the rugged and remote northeast—a region that saw even more destruction during and after World War I than did southeastern Turkey. But while these Turks in the northeast are as poor as the Kurds in the southeast, their resentment has naturally not become an ethnic one. In contrast, although they are not a monolithic unit and certainly not wholly supportive of the PKK, the Kurds' relative deprivation compared to the rest of the country has led to ethnicity-based discontent among them, following the rise of leftist Kurdish nationalism in the late twentieth century.

Enter the PKK

Diyarbakir in southeastern Turkey is a laboratory for observing the dominant leftist brand of Kurdish nationalism governed by the PKK. The centripetal forces that have kept Diyarbakir's Kurds away from the heart of the Turkish nation were compounded in the late twentieth century by fighting between the Turkish government and the PKK. This Kurdish left-wing group has been waging a war against the Turkish state since its foundation by Ocalan in 1978. Although Turkey has been able to keep the PKK in check since the organization launched a military campaign against Ankara, the fighting has left an indelible scar on the public consciousness as well as caused tens of thousands of deaths.[11]

In the 1980s, Turkey responded to the PKK's Kurdish-nationalist message by reinforcing its ban on the Kurdish language in the courts, municipal government, and the media; even Kurdish songs were banned. This move proved to be counterproductive, and, coupled with the PKK's strategy of violence to intimidate the rural Kurdish population, the ban in fact helped the PKK build a popular base among the Kurds in the 1980s and the 1990s.[12]

In recognition of its failure to stifle Kurdish nationalism, Ankara switched tactics and adopted progressive policies regarding the Kurdish issue in the first years after the AKP came to power in 2002. The government removed restrictions on public Kurdish-language use and began the aforementioned publicly funded 24-hour Kurdish-language television channel.[13] Moreover, Ankara now facilitates Kurdish-language departments in universities, and, since June 2012, has allowed Kurdish to be taught as an elective course in middle and high schools.[14] These reforms began during the 2009 "Kurdish Opening" and continued during the so-called "Solution Process" that followed, at which time Erdogan initiated negotiations with the jailed PKK leader Ocalan in an apparently sincere attempt to foster peace. The situation has since deteriorated, however, and since July 2015 the fighting between Turkey and the PKK has been as ferocious as it has ever been. Moreover, the renewed violence has nullified the progress of the past decade; any future negotiations will have to be rebuilt from the ground up.

Kurdish politics in southeastern Turkey: a two-party system

Turkey's national political arena is contested among four parties, namely, the AKP, the CHP, the HDP, and the MHP. In contrast, politics in southeastern Turkey is a two-way rivalry between the HDP and the AKP: combined, the two received more than 93 percent of the vote in the 12 southeastern Kurdish-majority or -plurality provinces during the most recent general election in November 2015.[15] While the ruling AKP appeals to more conservative, pious Kurds in the region, the HDP's left-wing platform draws in ethno-nationalist Kurds.

The HDP took a historic step when it decided to enter the June and November 2015 general elections as a party—previously it only fielded independent candidates—and managed to cross the

10 percent electoral threshold for the first time, enabling it to enter parliament.[16] In the June election, the party received more than 13 percent of the vote, gaining 80 out of 550 seats, while in November its popularity slipped somewhat: it garnered 10.8 percent of the vote, winning 59 seats. Nevertheless, the HDP's entry into parliament in both elections, passing the country's rather high 10 percent electoral threshold, was a huge success. Historically, pro-Kurdish parties have received about 5 to 6 percent of votes, meaning that the Kurdish political movement could only be represented by independent members of parliament, which gave them a much smaller bloc of deputies (20–30) compared to the HDP's current delegation.

The HDP's overall gains in the June 2015 election and limited success in the November 2015 election have been attributed to several internal and external factors. The party rode the wave of rising Kurdish nationalism thanks to recent regional developments. The PKK's Syrian offshoot, the PYD, made territorial gains in northern Syria after 2013 to establish self-rule, and fought a 112-day resistance in the Syrian city of Kobani in 2014 to defend the town against ISIS. Ankara's refusal to provide support to the Syrian Kurdish forces during the initial attack in September 2014 left many Turkish Kurds disgruntled with the AKP and Erdogan. As the Kurdish regions in northern Iraq and northern Syria received international recognition and support in their successful fight against ISIS and their nascent political autonomy, Turkey's Kurds began to develop broader expectations for their own areas. The HDP, led by their charismatic co-chairman Selahattin Demirtas, capitalized on this regional Kurdish moment to consolidate the Kurdish vote.[17]

But three-way competition: AKP vs. HDP vs. PKK

Viewing itself as the champion of civil rights for the Kurds, the AKP government felt betrayed by the HDP's success, and chose to resort to old-school military tactics to defeat the new Kurdish insurgency.[18] Another reason for Turkey's hard-line shift towards the Kurds is

Erdogan's previously mentioned desire to become an executive-style president.[19] In the most recent general election, in November 2015, the Turkish leader's party received 49.5 percent of the vote. Erdogan needs to build further support, and to this end he will continue his attempts at peeling off right-wing votes nationally from the MHP, a strongly Turkish-nationalist faction that bitterly opposes the PKK and the HDP. For this reason, Erdogan will maintain a tough line on the Kurdish movement, and continue fighting to boost his image as a strongman until he wins a referendum to become an executive-style president. In addition to these overtly political considerations, Erdogan increasingly sensed that PKK field forces were utilizing the period of non-belligerence during the "Solution Process" to deepen their capabilities and pose an even sharper threat to the security of the country. His hard-line policies are supported by the Turkish security forces, including the TAF, which is concerned about the PKK's so-called underground-state infrastructure, including arms caches, courts, and tax offices, which developed in southeastern Turkey during the "Solution Process."[20] Accordingly, when the PKK broke the ceasefire with Ankara in July 2015, the entire security establishment was happy to move militarily against the group.[21]

For its own part, the PKK, too, has eagerly embraced the renewed fighting with the government, since it undermines the rise of the HDP and Demirtas. In the aftermath of the June 2015 election, having more than doubled the HDP's votes, Demirtas had become a household name across Turkey, a first for a Kurdish-nationalist politician in the country. By returning to violence, the PKK, a group that believes in using violence as a political tool, has blocked Demirtas' rise and, subsequently, prevented a peaceful solution to the Kurdish problem in Turkey. The PKK, therefore, came out as winners in the Kurdish conflict, ironically along with President Erdogan, whom the group opposes diametrically on the Kurdish chessboard. The government's policies against the Kurdish insurgency have thus far not fully defeated Kurdish nationalism. Curfews lasting for weeks, heavy bombardments, and urban warfare in HDP strongholds appear to be pushing Turkey's Kurdish population away from the state.

Increasing polarization and violence in the southeast between the Kurds and the government is a challenge, especially with rising concerns over Erdogan's autocratic style of government. The question is what sort of political rights to grant to the Kurds. The HDP often pushes for an extensive set of group rights, including acknowledgment of the Kurds as a national community, as well as recognition of Kurdish as an official language in the country's constitution and, most importantly, broad autonomy for the Kurdish provinces. But Erdogan seems more interested in changing Turkey's parliamentary system to an executive presidential system with himself at the helm than solving the Kurdish issue once and for all. He knows that a liberal stance on the Kurdish issue would not win him enough Kurdish-nationalist votes to offset the many Turkish-nationalist votes he would lose. Turkish nationalists oppose any political reconfiguration of Turkey into a binational state of Turks and Kurds—in other words, a federal structure of self-autonomous regions, the stated goal of Turkey's Kurdish nationalists. This Turkish-nationalist constituency is the one that Erdogan most hopes to court in a 2017 referendum to change the constitution and allow him to become an omnipotent president.

Nevertheless, the Turkish government would do well to re-examine its role in the current escalation with the PKK, if not for political reasons then for the long-term stability of the country as a whole. Turkey's Kurdish issue will not simply disappear on its own. And due to shifting regional dynamics following the Arab uprisings, Turkey is now more pressed than ever to develop a permanent response to its Kurdish issue. The Syrian civil war, instability in Iraq, and the rise of ISIS have caused Turkey's doorstep to crumble into chaos. In fact, five of the deadliest terror attacks in Turkish history have taken place in the period between 2013 and 2016, and they are all connected to the fallout from the Syrian war. Together, these attacks have killed over 500 people and injured over a thousand others.[22] Furthermore, three key ISIS attacks in the country, namely, the June 2015 attack in Diyarbakir, the July 2015 bombing in Suruc, and the October 2015 bombing in Ankara, all intentionally targeted pro-PKK and pro-HDP groups, demonstrating the broader, regional aspect of Turkey's Kurdish issue, as well as showing how dangerously and easily the war between ISIS and the Syrian PYD can be imported into Turkey as an ISIS–Kurd battle.[23]

Solutions in the Middle East: better ties with Iraqi and Syrian Kurds

To solve its Kurdish issue at home, Turkey first must overcome its fear of Kurds abroad, especially in Iraq and Syria, where weak states have made the Kurds important political actors. Whereas Turkey's ties with the Iraqi Kurds have improved in recent years, Ankara's relations with the Syrian Kurds have become rather bitter. This is because, unlike in Iraq's Kurdistan Regional Government (KRG), where Iraqi Kurdish groups hold more sway than the PKK, Ocalan and the PKK are very popular among the Syrian Kurds. Bashar al-Assad's father provided Ocalan with refuge, as well as allowing the PKK to grow inside Syria in order to use it as a proxy against Turkey, and this bond between the two has remained. Syria's disintegration as a result of the war has opened a door of opportunity for that country's Kurds: somewhere between 10 and 20 percent of the Syrian population is Kurdish—a fact that has created a strong case for a greater Kurdish zone of control and eventual autonomy.

However, the cross-border dynamics of the Syrian civil war and imminent security threats from multiple actors against Turkey present an important case for the conquering by Ankara of its deeply rooted fear of Kurds in Syria. Turkey might actually be better served by supporting strong buffer entities such as Syrian Kurdish Rojava (as it already does with the KRG) instead of attempting to maintain the far less defined ground realities of today. If Ankara were to make peace with the Syrian Kurds, it would benefit from having a friendly force that guards more than 400 miles of Syria's 510-mile-long Turkish border against ISIS and other threats. Furthermore, as has been the case with Iraqi Kurdistan, Turkish infrastructure companies have been among the prime beneficiaries of the region's investment boom, winning major contracts for road and airport construction. Turkey is the necessary outlet for Kurdistan's energy resources and a necessary trade partner for any landlocked entity emerging in the post-Syrian environment. Turkey's possession of a strong and vibrant free-market economy would also prove beneficial to an autonomous Syrian Kurdish region in Syria, as it has with the KRG. In this regard, Syrian Kurds could learn from the remarkable shift in relations between Turkey and the Iraqi KRG. Ankara's policy with the Iraqi Kurds has evolved from open hostility in 2003 at the beginning of the Iraq War to open friendship today. When Iraqi Kurds showed goodwill to Ankara, Ankara reciprocated, building good ties with the KRG in Erbil, where today Turkey has a diplomatic mission. Turkish Airlines, the country's national flag carrier, flies directly from Erbil to both Istanbul and Antalya, Turkey's fifth-largest city, facilitating Iraqi Kurdish tourism in the Turkish Riviera. And trade between Turkey and the Iraqi Kurds has boomed to such an extent that Turkey is the KRG's largest trading partner.[24]

Solution at home: broader liberties for all citizens (Kurds included)...

To develop better ties with Iraqi and Syrian Kurds, Ankara also needs to address Kurds' grievances at home. However, simply implementing the models provided by Turkey's neighbors with sizable Kurdish populations—Syria, Iraq, and Iran—is not necessarily the best way to go about it. The overwhelming majority of these countries' Kurds live within the boundaries of their traditional homeland, or Kurdistan, making territorially based autonomy a realistic outcome. In Turkey, by contrast, nearly half of Kurds have migrated out of their homeland in the country's southeast, and Istanbul is the most populous Kurdish city in the world. Thus, a potential autonomous Kurdish region inside the country would have to exclude nearly half the country's Kurds, who live in western Turkey. Furthermore, a majority of the Turkish population would object to such a step. Given Turkish political and demographic dynamics, territorial Kurdish autonomy looks unlikely.

The solution to the Kurdish issue in Turkey is, therefore, not necessarily narrow political autonomy but broader liberties for all citizens. Turkey needs to provide its population with the widest individual freedoms imaginable if it is to satisfy its Kurdish citizens regarding their rights, including those of Kurds in western Turkey. The Kurdish population is not only diffused geographically in Turkey but also quickly integrating. One out of every six Kurds is married to a Turk.[25] Accordingly, addressing Kurdish demands in Turkey means granting comprehensive cultural rights to all the country's citizens, Kurd or not, irrespective of location. Reforms would include access to both education and public services not only in Kurdish but in other minority languages as well.

Kurds and Turks alike would almost certainly embrace a framework based on strengthening individual rights. In the short term, the government could take a number of specific and feasible steps. For instance, removing the legal uncertainties that surround the use of indigenous names for villages and landmarks would be a welcome symbolic gesture to Kurdish and other linguistic minorities. Many buildings, towns, and streets with Kurdish names—as well as Armenian, Bulgarian, Georgian, Greek, or Syriac—were reassigned Turkish names in the twentieth century. A reversal of this forced renaming would serve as an acknowledgment of Turkey's linguistic and ethnic diversity.

...and the "Spanish model"

Turkey is a large country in need of decentralization. Many nationalist Kurds want self-government in the southeast, but an overwhelming majority of Turks oppose outright federalization. In this regard, Turkey might look to Spain's administrative reforms beginning in the 1980s as a model. In Spain's asymmetrical political system, areas such as the Basque region have stronger administrative autonomy than others, even though all areas remain under central-government control. By providing the Basques with local political power, Spain ultimately negotiated a non-federalized government that deflated the violent wing of the Basque movement.

Turkey could follow a similar path of decentralization, allowing for stronger administrative autonomy in Kurdish provinces and other non-Kurdish outlying areas, while maintaining constitutional unity. By simultaneously granting broad individual freedoms and greater administrative autonomy to the Kurds, Ankara could win their support while also satisfying the country's greater populace. Many Turks are uncomfortable with the country's current military-written constitution, which reads like a list of "don'ts" rather than a document outlining the country's political system. Not only the Kurds but Turks of all stripes would welcome a fresh constitution that lists their freedoms and those alone. This would be the best way to help Turkey consolidate as a liberal democracy. But as explained in the following chapter, Erdogan's current political trajectory mostly excludes this scenario.

Can Turkey capture its Kurdish moment?

It will be hard for Turkey to maintain leverage over the Syrian and Iraqi Kurds when Turkish Kurds are locked in a violent struggle against Ankara. To secure influence and stability in Syria and Iraq, Ankara has to make peace with its Kurdish community. And the Kurds, too, have an interest in peace with Turkey. Kurdish nationalists and some others believe that this is the Kurds' moment in history. The Kurds may indeed turn the Middle East's post-World War I alignment and their division by four countries on its head, but they cannot do this without Turkey.

This could indeed be Turkey's Kurdish and Middle East moment. But it all depends on Erdogan's political agenda. If the Turkish leader continues to fight the PKK to maintain his strongman image in the

hopes of transforming Turkey into a presidential system of govern-
ment with himself at the helm, Ankara could miss the proverbial
Kurdish train, not only in Syria, but also inside the country. The
PKK could launch all-out war, expanding violence further to cities
in western Turkey. Even if Turkey successfully prevents a contiguous
Kurdish corridor in northern Syria through interposition of Sunni
Arab-controlled, Turkish-supported areas, it will face a quantita-
tively and qualitatively deeper military threat from the PKK and the
PYD for years. Turkey could survive these challenges, but only at
a huge humanitarian and material cost as well as by damaging its
human-rights record and potentially its relationship with the United
States, should Washington continue to rely on the PYD to defeat
ISIS. It is Turkey's Kurdish moment to seize; if Ankara plays its hand
right, it could become long-term friends with the Kurds.[26] But the
Kurds, too, must play their hand correctly: continued PKK terror
attacks, such as the bombing that killed 48 people in Istanbul on
December 10, 2016, will make it impossible for any Turkish leader
to extend an olive branch to the Kurds.

11

Foreign-Policy Gambit

ogether with the Kurds, foreign policy will be one of Erdogan's biggest challenges in the future. If he can keep transnational threats at bay, he can maintain his position at Turkey's helm. Ankara needs to rethink large parts of its ambitious foreign-policy agenda in the last decade, during which time Erdogan tried to make Turkey a stand-alone Middle East power. This agenda has left Ankara badly entangled in the Syrian civil war, isolated in the Middle East, and exposed to many enemies. If left to smolder on their own, these factors will add to the country's domestic tensions, as well as exacerbating its crisis.

Good intentions

From 2005 to 2007, between the end of his first term and the beginning of his second as prime minister, Erdogan gradually rolled out a new foreign-policy agenda for Turkey, departing from the twin pillars of Ankara's traditional approach: neutrality in Middle East politics and a focus on ties with Europe and the United States. In the beginning, this shift seemed to be entirely non-ideological. Ankara wanted to focus a little less on Europe and the United States, and use its energy instead to build ties with countries in the Middle East, Latin America, Africa, and Asia in order to expand markets and gain international influence. Accordingly, following the AKP's rise to power, Turkey established dozens of new diplomatic missions in Africa, compared to just three new missions in EU countries. And

Ankara reaped the benefits of this policy when it secured a seat at the UN Security Council in 2009–10, its first entry to the UN's top body since 1961.

Slanted vision

However, a subterranean motive soon emerged for this new foreign-policy drive: Turkey was pivoting to Islamist causes. Signaling this shift in 2006, the AKP invited Khaled Mashal, the Damascus-based leader of Hamas' military wing, to Ankara for meetings with top-level officials. Previously, Turkey had positive ties with the Palestinian Authority and Israel, but now it was reaching out to an armed Islamist organization in the Palestinian theater. This reaching out to Hamas, which is aligned with the Islamist Muslim Brotherhood (MB), should have been an early warning sign to all Turkey watchers. The Turkish Foreign Ministry, a bastion of secular-minded and liberal bureaucrats in the country, didn't want to touch Mashal: its spokes-person announced that the AKP, and not the Foreign Ministry, had invited the Hamas leader to Ankara. Nevertheless, Mashal showed up in the capital in February 2006, and met Erdogan and his advisor Ahmet Davutoglu, as well as obliging Foreign Ministry officials.

Bad neighbors

Erdogan's shift toward Hamas and other Islamist parties in the region aimed to make Turkey an autarchic power in the Middle East through the use of such new proxies and allies. In envisioning this eventually doomed foreign policy, Erdogan had a helping hand from Davutoglu, whose core political philosophy is that Turkey can become a regional power by developing better ties with its Muslim neighbors, some-times at the expense of its relationships with the United States and other traditional Western allies. Davutoglu wished Turkey to have "zero problems with its neighbors," which he believed would allow it to become a decision-maker country with broad regional influence.[1] Of course, this grand ambition did not quite work out. The problem with the Davutoglu foreign-policy school is that Turkey's neighbors are not Luxembourg, Belgium, and the Netherlands, but rather ISIS, Iran, Iraq, Syria, and, across the Black Sea, Russia. In fact, after a decade of AKP rule, Turkey is anything but a country with influence over the Muslim powers of the Middle East, whether it is the Assad regime in Syria, which Ankara has been trying in vain to oust, the Islamic Republic of Iran, which has undermined Turkish policies in Syria and Iraq, or the Sisi government in Egypt, which despises Ankara—not to mention the ISIS threat. And the AKP has made for itself a feared adversary in Moscow, a relationship it has since struggled to repair. Worse, Turkey's ties with Washington are now riddled with problems.

Signaling recognition of this failure, in May 2016 Erdogan fired Davutoglu—whose rise to household-name status clashed with Erdogan's strategy of holding a monopoly on power—hoping to use his ouster to shift away from some of the foreign-policy moves of the last decade. Still, it will be a long time before Ankara achieves game-changing influence in the Middle East. Russia and Iran will continue to undermine Turkish policies in the region, and the relationship with Washington will be fraught with tension for the foreseeable future under the AKP.

Obama's appeal to Turkey and the Muslim world

It didn't have to end like this for Turkey. In April 2009, less than three months after his inauguration, US president Barack Obama made a historic visit to Turkey. Aside from his visit to Canada and stops in Europe for international summits, this was the president's first overseas bilateral visit, highlighting the importance he put on Turkey and his ties with Erdogan. In the aftermath of a rocky period in relations with the United States under George W. Bush, this move was welcomed in Ankara. As the new president, Obama conveyed his ardent intention to establish Turkey as a key ally of his administration and as a model for its dealings with the Middle East and Muslim-majority countries. A senior advisor to Obama remarked that the US president believed that Erdogan "was going to show that you could be democratic and Islamist at the same time."[2] During his visit, Obama addressed the Turkish parliament, and voiced support for the country's entry into the EU, continually stressing the sentiment that "the United States is not and will never be at war with Islam." He was, as one BBC correspondent described, "on a mission to charm."[3] Indeed, it was a forthright effort to bring about a new chapter in US–Turkish relations—a chapter dedicated to recognizing and advancing mutual interests important enough to overlook disagreements.

Turkey, too, saw this time as a potentially prosperous one, with Erdogan heralding the rise of "*Bizim* [our] *Huseyin*" (evoking the US president's Muslim middle name in Turkish), as he and his inner circle privately nicknamed President Obama. Turkey's booming economy had remained relatively stable after the 2008 global crisis, and it had initially begun to reap the benefits of its more cordial regional foreign policy. Its economic and cultural power in the Middle East was growing and Erdogan's future prospects looked bright. Erdogan cherished being America's window onto the Muslim world at a time when Turkey itself was pivoting toward that world as a soft-power nation.

Turkish soft power

During the middle of the first decade of the twenty-first century, the conventional wisdom in Ankara was that Turkey should stop looking to Europe, which had continually snubbed it, and instead focus on the Middle East and other areas in order to regain the regional leadership role it had lost with the dissolution of the Ottoman Empire at the end of World War I. That, the AKP maintained, would best be accomplished not through displays of military force but rather by building up soft power, a concept that was deeply rooted in Gul's brand of international politics inside the AKP.

The growth of Turkish soft power in Muslim countries—that is, its increasing commercial, economic, and cultural might in foreign policy in the last decade—can be largely attributed to its burgeoning economy under Erdogan. As proof of this success, Turkey became a majority middle-class society for the first time in its history, a fact the CIA recognized in September 2013 by listing the country as a developed economy. Individual Turkish businesses exemplify the country's broader economic success. For example, Turkish Airlines flew from Istanbul to about 75 destinations in 2002, many of them domestic routes. Today it services nearly 300, many of them in the Middle East, Eurasia, and Africa. In Iraq alone, the carrier now has six scheduled destinations, compared to zero in 2002.

In the last decade, Turkey has emerged as a strong Middle Eastern economy due to better connectivity. Much of the country's growth has come from a strong export sector. Turkish products—from trucks to canned tomatoes—have found happy consumers across the Middle East, bringing Turkey clout in the same way that cars did for Japan in the 1970s and 1980s (to borrow a comparison from Washington Institute scholar Ambassador James Jeffrey). Turkish soap operas, once obscure dramas produced solely for local audiences, are now beamed into living rooms from Alexandria to Beirut. To name just one example, *Noor*, a classic rags-to-riches story, has enthralled more than 85 million viewers. In 2012, such soap operas earned Turkey about $130 million from abroad, mostly from the Arab world.[4] For a time, Turkey's quest for influence, and its apparent success as an affluent, high-functioning Muslim-majority society, seemed to be having the effect desired by Ankara. In a 2011 Brookings Institution poll of the citizens of five Arab countries, Turkey was ranked first among countries believed to have played a "constructive role" in the Arab Spring. In the same survey, Erdogan's popularity towered above that of other world leaders.[5]

Building upon its soft power, Ankara attempted to facilitate stronger diplomatic ties with its Muslim neighbors, as Turkish officials routinely made high-level visits to Baghdad, Damascus, Tehran, and other regional capitals. Between November 2002 and April 2009, the Turkish foreign minister visited Iran and Syria eight times in total. In addition, Turkey opened scores of new embassies and consulates across the Arab world, giving the country a visibility in the region that it had lacked since the Ottoman era, after which the Arabs had fallen principally under British and French rule.

And hubris

Turkey's achievements in this period propelled Davutoglu and Erdogan's belief that Ankara could become a stand-alone power in the Middle East in this way. Turkey flaunted its perceived influence in the region by bandying the idea of a "Shamgen zone," a play on the EU's Schengen free-travel area and "Sham," the traditional name in Arabic for Syria, covering the Levant. The idea was that Turkey, Syria, Jordan, and Lebanon would come together, excluding Israel, under a customs and political union. With Erdogan brimming with confidence from the attention bestowed on him by Obama, Turkish foreign-policy elites followed in turn, and soon a strong current of opinion in Ankara held that Turkey had played second fiddle to Washington for too long in the Middle East. Turkey could become a regional power only by going its own way, even when this meant sometimes breaking with Washington.

Turkish resistance to US policy in the aftermath of the 2003 Iraq War conferred legitimacy on the new regime in the eyes of the region's peoples. Similarly, Turkish aims to exert regional soft power were behind its 2010 effort to enlist Brazil to help forge a nuclear deal with Iran. Here, Turkey saw an opportunity to use its supposed magic touch on an issue that Europe and the United States had failed to resolve. The initiative was actually launched by Obama directly with Brazilian president Luiz Inácio Lula da Silva and Erdogan, but by joining with Brazil, Turkey signaled that as new, emerging powers, they could solve problems that the older and more established powers could not. But the approach back-fired for the Turks, and in no small part because Washington had cheered Ankara and Brasilia, but did not take Turkey's initiative very seriously. At first, Washington encouraged Turkey and Brazil to negotiate a nuclear deal between Tehran and Washington. The United States, which had originally been focused on passing Security Council sanctions against Iran, then rejected the deal, dubbed the "Tehran Agreement." In turn, despite a phone call from Obama asking Erdogan to abstain, Turkey voted against sanctions at the UN Security Council, where Ankara had secured, by dint of its soft power, a non-permanent seat for the first time since 1961.[6] All told, this series of events demonstrated both Turkish hubris and Washington's unwillingness to embrace Turkey's newly enhanced self-image. The vote prompted disapproval from both US defense secretary Robert Gates and US secretary of state Hillary Clinton, and a debate emerged in Washington over whether the Americans were "losing" Turkey.[7]

Disagreement nearby

At first, Turkey's bid for warmer ties with other countries in the region, such as Syria, seemed to work. The new tone gave Turkey ample influence over its smaller southern neighbor, which it hoped to peel away from Iran. But when, in 2011, open rebellion broke out against the Assad regime in Syria, and as the region's hard-power political interactions surfaced, Ankara was confronted with the limits of its soft power.

Turkey's policies in the Arab Spring, and more specifically in the Syrian war, have exposed the mismatch between the AKP's approach to the Middle East, its soft-power ambitions, and regional realpolitik. To build soft-power influence, Erdogan went out of his way to court the Assad regime. For instance, in 2008, the Erdogan and Assad families vacationed together on Erdogan's private yacht along the Turkish Riviera.[8] Moreover, Ankara lifted visa restrictions for Syrians traveling into the country, boosted trade with Damascus, and even organized joint sessions for the two countries' cabinets. Therefore, when the Arab uprising arrived in Syria, Turkey thought that it could use its influence over the Assad regime to stop it from brutalizing protestors. Initially, Ankara encouraged Assad to enact reforms, expecting him to heed its words. In August 2011, Davutoglu spent hours pleading with the Syrian leader to stop killing civilians and to form a government with Syrian MB members in it, hoping that Turkey's good ties with the regime would be enough to propel a change in its behavior. Assad not only disregarded Davutoglu, but within hours of the Turkish official's departure from Damascus sent tanks into Hama, a center of the rebellion. Assad's snub suggested that Turkish soft power was not a Middle Eastern currency. Ankara later severed all diplomatic ties with Assad. What is more, Turkey's consequent anti-Assad policy put Ankara and Tehran at opposite ends of the regional and political spectrum. Traditionally democratic Turkey's support of the revolution and protestors clashed with authoritarian Iran's continued support for the Assad regime and its brutal crackdown on civilians.[9]

Up with the United States

The reignited conflict with Tehran, Turkey's historical regional competitor, has led Ankara gradually to turn back toward the United States. President Obama initiated the turnaround when he had a heart-to-heart conversation with Erdogan at the G20 summit in Toronto in July 2011, explaining to him his concerns over the Iran nuclear deal and the *Mavi Marmara* incident. The Obama overture worked: the two leaders started to speak often again and exchange empathetic views. During the Arab Spring, Obama phoned him more than any other foreign leader except the British prime minister, who traditionally gets the most calls from the White House.[10] Collaboration appeared especially deep on the issue of Syria. Turkey had emerged as the region's key opponent of Assad, which was just fine for Obama, who was focusing on domestic issues ahead of the 2012 US presidential election. Washington and Ankara both hoped for a "soft landing" in Syria—not to mention an end to Assad's rule without the country descending into chaos. Obama appreciated that Ankara was willing to bear the burden of policy toward Syria, from imposing sanctions against Assad to supporting the opposition, following a strategy originally designed by Davutoglu.[11]

Ankara's statements on the Arab uprisings led to a warming of Obama's relations with Turkey—a NATO member that uniquely fit Obama's quest to find powerful Muslim-majority allies happy to work with the United States. After Ankara concluded that dictators such as Libya's Muammar Gaddafi would fall sooner or later, once they were challenged by the masses, the two countries began coordinating their policies on the Arab Spring.[12] Turkish cooperation with Washington in Libya—implemented after Ankara's initial reluctance to join military action against a Muslim leader—reinforced the United States' positive view of Turkey.[13]

Down with the United States

The improvement in ties with the United States proved to be short-lived, however. Turkey once again jumped the gun and started punching above its weight in the Syrian civil war, hoping that it could induce Obama to follow. Ankara went directly for an ambitious policy of regime change in Damascus in 2012 and tried to persuade Washington to join its efforts and significantly support the opposition. At the time, the United States was not willing to put its full weight behind the rebels. Turkey's sense of abandonment was heightened further in the aftermath of the chemical-weapons deal US and Russian officials brokered in September of 2013, which, in Turkish minds, provided a lifeline for the Assad regime.[14] Turkey began to signal its disappointment with the Obama administration's Syria policy—or what it saw as the lack thereof.

In the following year, Ankara turned to China to purchase air-defense systems, complaining about US constraints on technology transfer during arms sales and chafing at what it perceived as a lack of US support in Syria, among other things. Ankara thought that by turning to the Chinese it could induce US companies to offer a better deal, including transfer of sensitive weapons technology to Turkey. This strategy led to a major backlash from Washington: the United States simply told Turkey that such a system would not be plugged into the NATO network.[15] The mood between Ankara and Washington soured further.

Turkey pursued other policies that upset Washington. In an attempt to depose Assad, Ankara turned a blind eye to the jihadists who were entering Syria through Turkey to fight the Damascus regime. Turkey did not intend to support the jihadists; rather, Ankara believed that "Assad will fall, and good guys will take over, and then these good guys will clean up the bad guys."[16] Of course, that has not happened. In the interim, at least some of the fighters who crossed into Syria morphed into ISIS.[17] Ankara's inability to predict and pre-empt the jihadist backlash added to Washington's concerns over Turkey. Accordingly, some in Washington, especially at the Pentagon, started to view Turkey as a country that worked with America's adversaries in Syria. Ankara, on the other hand, saw the radicalization process in Syria differently, and blamed the lack of US support for the moderate rebels in the early phases of the rebellion as the primary cause for the rise of jihadists later in the conflict. The Syrian civil war has remained the crux of the differences between the two countries.

Bad investments

Turkey's Middle East focus failed to deliver Ankara regional power or keep its alliance with the United States strong, but it did achieve another goal, namely, bringing Ankara close to MB-style parties. Unfortunately, eventually this strategy, too, would fail to deliver regional greatness as the MB's power across the Middle East has plummeted.

Once shunned by Westerners as a hard-line Islamist party, the AKP saw itself as a model in whose image the MB-affiliated parties might evolve during the Arab uprisings. Parties linked to the Arab Islamist MB movement, such as those in Egypt, Tunisia, Libya, and Syria, according to the AKP's logic, could moderate and come to power through democratic elections. For Turkey, such an outcome would have the added benefit of creating natural regional allies. Indeed, with the MB's initial rise to power in Egypt, Turkey's vision seemed to be coming to fruition. Likewise, in Syria, Ankara began supporting the MB to help it emerge as the leader of the country's opposition. Similar strategies were pursued in Tunisia and Libya.

On the Palestinian scene, too, in an attempt to position itself as a mediator in a decades-old conflict, Turkey threw its support behind MB-linked Hamas, hoping to use its newfound regional influence to convince the radical Palestinian group to moderate. In this regard, Ankara hoped Hamas would recognize Israel and renounce violence. Hamas, however, did not heed Turkey's counsel, and even after losing its Syrian bases during the fighting, and appearing more isolated than ever, did not fall under Turkish influence. Furthermore, while Turkey's Hamas policy has yet to deliver results, it also poses a challenge to the traditionally good relationship between Ankara and the Palestinian Authority, and will consequently place stress on Turkish–Israeli ties. Turkey's glory proved to be short-lived also in Tunisia and Egypt, where Ankara-backed and MB-aligned actors were soon sidelined from power by 2014. And in Syria, more radical and violent Islamist groups have overshadowed MB-aligned factions.

Egyptian troubles

Other events have further upended Ankara's vision of gaining power in the Middle East through a pro-MB policy. Following the MB's ouster in Egypt through anti-government protests led by the military, Turkish ties with the country came undone when Egypt fell under the new leadership of General Abdel Fattah al-Sisi. Taking issue with Ankara's strongly pro-MB stance, Sisi pulled his ambassador from Ankara, and put in place sanctions against Turkish economic interests. Turkish businesses have suffered in Egypt as a result, undermining Turkey's cherished soft-power goals. Turkish–Egyptian relations will remain anemic until either Erdogan or Sisi exits politics. This is due to the fact that the two leaders are diametrical nemeses—Erdogan is the Islamist leader who survived anti-government protests, such as the Gezi Park rallies, while Sisi is the secularist dictator who took over when such anti-government protests toppled the MB-led Islamist government in Cairo.

Sisi continues with his efforts to undermine Erdogan's influence in the region by, for instance, carrying out joint military exercises with Russia and Greek Cypriots.[18] For its part, Turkey hosts Sisi's opposition, including key figures in the Egyptian MB, as well as allowing the anti-Sisi and pro-MB Egyptian media to beam its messages from Istanbul to Cairo. In the bigger picture, regardless of who is in power in Ankara or Cairo, ties between Turkey and Egypt, the two largest Sunni Muslim powers in the Eastern Mediterranean, will always be competitive given the two countries' sense of grandeur.

More importantly, Turkey's pro-MB policy in Egypt soured Obama's views of Erdogan. As noted earlier, Obama reached out to Erdogan early in his presidency, valuing a relationship with a Muslim leader, and the two spoke often between 2009 and 2012, despite occasional spats. Erdogan enjoyed a state visit to Washington in May 2013, although ties between the leaders were strained following the Erdogan government's violent suppression of protests in Gezi Park soon afterward. However, Obama's view of Erdogan took an irreversible negative turn that summer. In May, Erdogan publicly chastised the West for its complicity in the coup in Egypt. Later that summer, Erdogan claimed to have proof that Israel was behind the coup, and the White House publicly condemned his statement.[19] At this point, Obama's view of Erdogan turned sour, a state of mind he would maintain until the end of his presidency in January 2017. For instance, when Erdogan visited the United States in the spring of 2016, he hoped President Obama would join him for the opening of a large mosque and social-services complex in Lanham, Maryland, supported by the Turkish government. The White House refused. It looked as if Erdogan was ready to walk away, too. But then Russia returned to threaten Turkey, and this changed everything, at least for a time.

Enter the Russian menace

For Turkish security analysts, no country is dreaded more for its military power and expansionist tendencies than Russia. Between 1568, when the Ottomans and Russians first clashed, and the end of the Russian Empire in 1917, the Turks and Russians fought over a dozen large-scale wars. In each encounter, Russia was the instigator, and in most cases the overall victor. In these defeats, the Ottomans lost vast, and solidly Turkish and Muslim, territories spanning from Crimea to Circassia. These lands' inhabitants, such as the Crimean Tatars or the Circassians, were killed or forced to flee deeper into the interior of the Ottoman lands, where they and their descendants became living reminders of the Russian threat. To this day, the joke in Turkey is that if you scratch a Turk, you get a Circassian. Many Turks are woefully aware of Russia's role as their country's historical nemesis.

Following the collapse of the Ottoman Empire, Ataturk cultivated pragmatic ties with the Soviet Union and Turkey stayed out of World War II. But soon, the terrifying prospect of Russian aggression arose once again when Moscow demanded territory from Turkey. Fearing the worst, Ankara rushed into the open arms of the West. After sacrificing precious blood and treasure to the war effort in Korea, Turkey attained NATO membership in 1952.

Taking this history into account, the most jarring event ever to push Turkish foreign policy back toward the United States came in November 2015, when a Turkish F-16 shot down a Russian plane that had briefly violated Turkish airspace from Syria. In what appeared to be a rash decision made in seconds, an irate Vladimir Putin fumed that the incident would "have serious consequences for Russian–Turkish relations" and referred to Turks as "accomplices of terrorists" before immediately threatening sanctions against Ankara.[20] Turkish officials claimed that the plane was inside Turkish airspace and that it was not the first time that Russia had violated its borders. In the aftermath of the incident, Russia declared that it would shoot down any Turkish planes or troops that made their way into Syria, placing in jeopardy Turkey's clandestine program to support the anti-Assad rebels. Putin also imposed economic sanctions on Turkey, and deployed additional troops to Armenia, thus encircling Turkey on three sides: with a military presence in Crimea to the north, Syria to the south, and Armenia to the east.

The Russians soon started harassing Turkey more directly in the cyber, military, and intelligence realms. For instance, rolling power blackouts through Istanbul and many other large cities in March 2016 elicited suspicions of Russian involvement. Moscow escalated tensions further: on May 13, the PKK released a video of one of its fighters downing a Turkish military helicopter. Notably, the weapon in the video appeared to be a variant made for Russian domestic use, not a stripped-down export model sold to the Syrian regime, whose stockpiles of anti-aircraft missiles have been raided repeatedly during the Syrian civil war.

Fearing that Russia could be providing weapons to the PKK and its Syrian franchise the PYD, Erdogan reacted. The logic here was simple: if Russia was arming the PKK–PYD, then Erdogan could not hope to defeat the Kurdish groups. And if Erdogan could not defeat them, he could not win a referendum with support from Turkish-nationalist groups to make himself an executive-style president. Accordingly, Erdogan moved to normalize ties with Putin in order to delink his Kurdish opponents and Moscow. He reached out to his Russian counterpart in June 2016, sending him a letter in which he expressed regret for the 2015 plane incident. Following this gesture, that same month, Erdogan and Putin spoke by telephone to calm festering bilateral tensions.

Ankara's growing perception of being abandoned by its Western allies after the failed coup of July 15, 2016—it took Washington four days to issue a statement to condemn the military's actions—provided Putin with a reason to act speedily following Erdogan's apology. The Russian leader called Erdogan the day after the coup plot to wish him well. Putin was also aware that sustained sanctions against Ankara were punishing Russia more than they were Turkey. The Turks have many customers for their inexpensive yet high-quality wares, and the Russians, already suffering under European and US sanctions and from collapsing oil prices, ultimately need access to the deals available in Turkish markets.

Accordingly, the two leaders met in August 2016, Erdogan compromising by traveling to St. Petersburg to meet his counterpart. At this meeting, they decided to normalize relations between their countries. Putin also declared that sanctions would end. They also nailed down a foreign-policy deal at their meeting: Russia would allow Turkey to go into Syria again without fear of Moscow's retaliation. In return, Ankara would adopt a compliant attitude toward Russia in Black Sea and Ukrainian affairs. As a result, for instance, Erdogan has voiced support for Turkish Stream, a joint Turkish–Russian pipeline put on hold after the F-16 incident. Revitalization of this project, which would allow Russia to export gas while bypassing Ukraine, was central to rejuvenating Turkish–Russian ties.

In the same month, relieved of the Russian threat, Turkey sent troops into northern Syria, taking Jarablus, a major border crossing used by ISIS to smuggle foreign fighters and weapons. The move into Jarablus also allowed Erdogan to block the advance of the PKK-allied PYD in Syria with Turkish forces positioning themselves between the PYD's Kobani and Afrin enclaves. For Erdogan, it was a masterstroke: linking his agenda of an executive presidency to the broader Turkish national goal of defeating the PKK, and then connecting these two objectives to the transatlantic goal of pushing back against ISIS.

Isolated Turkey

Erdogan's tactical victories notwithstanding, lacking in military hardware and powerful proxies, Ankara will struggle to maintain the political gains it has achieved when faced with Middle Eastern realpolitik. Developments—including the Syrian civil war as well as Russia's and Iran's hegemonic designs—have humbled Ankara's regional ambitions. In particular, Turkey's backing for the rebels in the Syrian conflict pitted Ankara against the pro-Assad Iranians in a proxy war—the first time Turkey and Iran had been in such an adversarial position since 1639, when the Ottomans and Persians concluded a 166-year war for regional influence.

Beyond the country's immediate neighbors, Turkish relations with Egypt, Saudi Arabia, the United Arab Emirates, and other Arab regimes were damaged when Ankara chose to support the MB-type political parties during the Arab uprisings, upsetting the Gulf monarchies, many of which have a deep aversion toward the MB. As a result, Turkey was left with few friends in the Middle East, with the exception of Qatar, non-state Iraqi Kurds, and to some extent Saudi Arabia. (Turkish–Saudi ties improved somewhat after Saudi Arabia's vehemently anti-MB King Abdullah died in January 2015.)

In 2010, no one could have predicted that the MB-related parties would be sidelined so fast and so precipitously. Instead of having "zero problems with neighbors," Turkey has ended up having nearly zero neighbors without problems. One issue is not that Erdogan and Davutoglu lacked foresight in supporting the MB, but rather that they limited Turkey's options by putting almost all their capital behind it. In other words, it was as if they put Turkey's money on just one horse in a multi-horse race. Had the MB won, Turkey too would have won, and won big, but because it lost, Ankara ended up losing everything. In hindsight, as crafty foreign-policy practitioners, Erdogan and Davutoglu should have supported the MB as they wished, but also kept lines of communication open with all the key actors in the countries experiencing the Arab uprisings.

Bearing the painful brunt of regional isolation, in June 2016 Turkey agreed to normalize ties with Israel. Going forward, however, relations between the two countries will remain less than harmonious. True, Turkey and Israel will continue to trade: Israel considers Turkey the best conduit for potential natural-gas sales to Europe, while Ankara wants to buy Israeli gas to decrease its own energy dependence on Russia. But bilateral ties are unlikely to return to their 1990s heyday, when policy makers in both countries perceived similar threats to their safety and had an empathetic view of each other. More specifically, Turkey's continued ties with Hamas will remain a particularly tough sticking point for Israel.

Ties with Russia, too, will not completely return to what they were during the 1990s and early years of the new century. Following the rupture in 2015, Russia showed its hostile side, reminding Erdogan why his forebears, Ottoman and Kemalists alike, had good reason to fear Moscow. Turkish–Russian ties went through an unusually warm period from the end of the Cold War until 2015. Booming trade, construction (Turkish companies building Russian infrastructure), tourism links (Russians visiting Turkey), and Ankara's purchase of large quantities of Russian natural gas to feed its growing economy helped build the relationship during these years. This was also a period of warm political relations, something that was boosted by an empathetic relationship between Erdogan and Putin. However, the F-16 incident in 2015 represented the end of this era of close political ties. Moscow's hostile behavior after November 2015 reminded Erdogan what a menacing neighbor Russia had been in the past. Moving forward, although Turkey and Russia will make up economically, Erdogan will be hard-pressed to see a regional friend in Putin as he once did.[21]

Furthermore, even though rising global authoritarian populism should band Erdogan and Putin together as allies, Putin's long-term goal will be to wish and work for Erdogan's downfall. Russia's Muslim community, which constituted at least 10 percent of that country's citizenry in 2010 and is growing at a faster rate than the rest of the Russian population, is almost completely Sunni, and Putin sees the rise of (Sunni) political Islam as a domestic threat.[22] The Russian leader considers his Turkish counterpart the chief patron of Sunni political Islam to Russia's south. His worry is that the success of Erdogan's revolution in Turkey will resonate strongly among Russian Muslims, who share either close historical affinities (as in the case of the Chechens and other northern Caucasus Muslims, many of whom the tsars banished to the Ottoman Empire) or intimate ethnic ties (as in the case of Tatars or other Turkic Muslims, who constitute a majority of Russia's Muslim community) with that country. Moscow fears that the success of Sunni political Islam in Turkey could lead to radicalization (as in the case of Tatars), or further radicalization (as in the case of Chechens), among Russian Muslims. In other words, Erdogan's political success is Putin's nightmare. Putin will be less than forgiving of Erdogan's mistakes and will use opportunities to boost covertly the anti-Erdogan opposition, including the PKK, with which Russia has historic ties going back to that organization's founding with Soviet support in the 1970s. Putin will also eye PKK-allied Rojava and the PYD in Syria as long-term pawns against Erdogan.

The Assad regime will be more of an open foe of Erdogan. The Syrian president will not forgive Erdogan for his policy of trying to oust him in his country's civil war. As far as Assad is concerned, Erdogan has tried to kill him, and he needs to pay for this. The Assad regime, which is already connected to at least one terror attack in Turkey, namely the 2013 Reyhanli bombing that killed 51 people, will use its historic connections to radical far-left groups in Turkey to undermine Erdogan by sponsoring terrorism and creating instability. It will also use Kurdish Rojava as a pawn against Ankara.

Turkey's ties with Iran, too, will be less than warm. Feeling the pressure of two powerful adversaries in Syria, Ankara decided to extend an olive branch to Iran in 2016. This took the form of deeper economic ties, which have helped Iranians find relief from international sanctions. Tehran has reciprocated by bringing Turkish businesses into the Islamic Republic. Yet even with booming commercial ties, competition for dominance in Syria and Iraq will undermine Turkish–Iranian relations. Turkey already has thousands of troops in Syria and Iraq. Whichever way the Syrian war ends, Iran will be uncomfortable with Turkish territorial gains in Syria at the expense of its ally, the Assad regime, and will work with Damascus to undermine Erdogan's troops. Tehran will also continue to back its other regional ally, the Baghdad government, regarding Turkish military presence in northern Iraq.

Accordingly, Turkey's ties with Iraq will suffer further. In that country, Ankara's opposition to former prime minister Nouri al-Maliki and its rapprochement with the Iraqi Kurds, a step that Baghdad considers an affront to its sovereignty, soured Iraq's perceptions of Turkey from 2010. Ankara, for its part, considered Maliki an Iranian pawn and supported the Iraqi opposition to undermine him. In return, Maliki lambasted Ankara's Syria policy and blocked Turkey from using Iraq as a trade route in an attempt to cut it off from the region at large, a development which forced Turkey to develop a shipping route into the Middle East using the Israeli port of Haifa, and to seek better ties with Israel overall.

Turkish–Iraqi relations haven't improved under Maliki's successor, Haider al-Abadi. Today, the widespread perception in Baghdad is that Turkey's and Iraq's Sunnis, including the Kurds, are facing off against Iran, Iraq's Shi'as, and the Iraqi central government. In 2014 and 2015, Turkey deployed troops deep inside Iraq, setting up a forward base, Bashiqa, near Mosul. Ankara said that this base was needed to train Sunni Arabs and Kurds to fight ISIS. To Abadi, this was yet another sign of Turkish interference in Iraq's internal affairs, and Ankara's siding with the country's Sunnis against Abadi's Shi'a-majority government. Together with Iran, Baghdad will challenge the Turkish military presence in northern Iraq, as well as Ankara's proxies, including the militia of the Iraqi Turkmens (who are ethnically related to the Turks), the Peshmerga forces of the Ankara-friendly Kurdistan Democratic Party (KDP), and Ankara-allied Sunni Arab tribes in Mosul. Erdogan's biggest foreign-policy risk in the coming years will be body bags coming from Syria and Iraq.

Erdogan's foreign-policy report card

In a way, Turkey's struggles in the Middle East mirror those of Japan in East Asia. Even today, Japan—the consummate soft-power nation—relies on US hard power for its security in the region. Japan needs US bases, the nuclear umbrella, and treaties to guard itself against China and nuclear-capable North Korea. Similarly, Turkey needs the United States and access to its Patriot missile systems to use against Assad and the Russian threat from Syria, as well as NATO guarantees to protect it against the challenges posed by the Syrian war, ISIS, Iran, and Russia. As long as Turkey fears Russia and competes against Iran, it will rely on America.

Ironically, therefore, despite Erdogan's efforts to shift foreign policy away from that of his secular predecessors, the Turkish position looks now much as it did under Demirel's presidency in 1995: Ankara has bad relations with Russia, Iran, Iraq, and Syria, while the United States and thus NATO are its only reliable allies; ties with Israel have recently improved; and the relationship with the EU is a case of one step forward, one step back.[23] In fact, today good relations with the United States and NATO are even more important for Turkey, given the growing chaos in the Middle East and the menacing posture of Russia.

Washington could take at least part of the blame for Turkey's foreign-policy misfortunes. During the presidency of George W. Bush and in the aftermath of the September 11 attacks, the United States overemphasized Turkey's Muslim identity at the expense of the country's Western vocation. And later on, under President Obama, Washington failed to appreciate on time the hubris emerging in Ankara. In fact, at times the United States contributed to this, such as at the beginning of the Syrian uprising when it encouraged Ankara to play a more active role against the Assad regime.[24] Presidents Bush and Obama often showered Erdogan with praise even as he was cracking down on the media and the courts, undermining democracy. Erdogan has been a Rorschach test for successive US presidents: Bush saw in him a faithful Muslim democrat, and

Obama a multilateralist Muslim democrat. Each was mistaken in his perception. In reality, Erdogan is an illiberal Islamist who thrives on challenging the US-led international order. Now, the US–Turkish relationship faces new challenges under the Trump administration, including rising anti-Muslim sentiment in the United States.

Overall, the AKP's foreign policy under Erdogan has left the country with few allies. Those that do possess military power, such as the United States, have become more hesitant about the idea of working in an unstable region with an illiberal Turkey. Each side, however, needs the other. Washington needs Turkey—which borders Iran, Iraq, and Syria, and is a maritime neighbor to Russia—in order to implement its policies regarding these countries successfully. More importantly, Washington needs Turkey, and access to vital Turkish bases, especially Incirlik, in order to defeat ISIS and jihadists in Iraq and Syria. For his own part, Erdogan needs Washington because he is facing a crisis at home: he cannot afford to be left alone against Russia, Iran, the PKK, the PYD, Baghdad, and the Assad regime.

A NATO radar facility in the Turkish town of Kurecik in the east-central Anatolian Malatya Province, activated in 2012, is perhaps the best example of the symbiotic security cooperation between Ankara and the United States and NATO. The facility is part of NATO's Ballistic Missile Defense shield, serving to protect alliance members against Russia and Iran. Its opening has angered Russia and Iran equally, but most recently the shield was used to guard Turkey against potential threats from the Assad regime in Syria. Erdogan ultimately proved flexible enough to recalibrate relations with Israel and Russia under the pressure of regional events, so it is not inconceivable that he could do so in significant ways with the strained US relationship. Washington will need to do its part, too.

12

Ending Turkey's Crisis

When did Erdogan transform from a democratic leader to an autocratic one, catapulting his country into a crisis? If you ask this question in Turkey, you will hear remarkably different dates. Secularists will single out the 2008 Ergenekon trials; liberals will point to the summer 2013 crackdown on the Gezi Park rallies; Gulenists will draw attention to December 2013, when Erdogan launched a retaliatory campaign against them in response to the corruption accusations leveled against his government; nationalist Kurds will harp on the breakdown of Ankara's ceasefire with the PKK in summer 2015; and former prime minister Davutoglu will likely identify the turning point as May 2016, when Erdogan ousted him from power.

In fact, Erdogan was never fully committed to liberal democracy. Some Turks, such as the leftist–liberals, who hoped that the Islamists could turn into true democrats, assisted him with his campaign against the military during the Ergenekon trials. Other groups, such as the Gulenists, willingly cooperated with Erdogan, believing they could use him to rise to power—but Erdogan outsmarted them and jettisoned them once they had helped him consolidate power. Outside observers hoped that Erdogan would be committed to liberal democracy as per his pre-2002 promise, believing that this would provide evidence that Islam and democracy are compatible. However, developments since 2002 have shown that the Turkish leader's agenda was built not on Islam, but Islamism, an ideology that distorts both democracy and religion. Turkey's experience as a multi-party democracy since 1950 and of living under what is an increasingly autocratic regime since 2002 demonstrates that while Islam and democracy are compatible, Islamism and democracy are probably not, at least not in the Turkish case. Furthermore, developments have shown that Erdogan's agenda was to build power in order to crown himself the country's omnipotent leader. This has been his true interest, not the promotion of liberal values or the maintenance of Turkey's place in the West.

In his early years as a politician, one of Erdogan's biggest successes was broadening the traditionally exclusive Islamist RP platform and persuading different groups of voters and international observers to become invested in his AKP's success as a center-right movement. However, once he secured electoral victories by delivering economic growth, Erdogan's illiberalism and Islamist roots strengthened—due in part to Turkey's 10 percent electoral threshold, which always awarded him lopsided and unrepresentative majorities in the legislature. Beginning with his showdown with the secularists in the Ergenekon trials and the accompanying court cases of 2008–11, Erdogan has gradually alienated large swaths of Turkish society and eventually narrowed his platform to push ultra-conservative and non-egalitarian Islamist social and political values onto the rest of the country. He has made a habit of forming alliances with various groups and actors before promptly abandoning and persecuting them once he no longer requires their services, creating a large, resentful demographic bloc that will aim to undermine him in the future. Erdogan has become the most powerful leader in the country, and he wants to shape it in his image. But while roughly half the country embraces this agenda, the other half bitterly opposes it, and herein lies the crisis of modern Turkey, with the gravest implications for its stability. And in foreign policy, Erdogan has advocated solidarity with Islamists and launched grandiose regional designs, exposing the country to risks, again with severe repercussions for Turkey's security, as well as the security interests of its European and American allies, since sustained instability in Turkey will inevitably render Ankara an ineffective ally for Brussels and Washington.

Erdogan's Kurdish wall

Democracy is the most effective system of checks and balances. As a result of Erdogan's increasing disregard for other groups' political demands, the AKP lost its legislative majority for the first time in the June 2015 general election, securing only 258 of the 550 seats in the Turkish legislature after winning 40.9 percent of the overall vote. Another historic result in this election was the parliamentary entrance of the HDP, a pro-Kurdish–liberal alliance: no other Kurdish party in Turkish history had been able to cross the 10 percent electoral threshold. In addition to having a pro-Kurdish platform, the HDP created an inclusive roster of parliamentary candidates representing Turkey's ethnic and political minorities. More tellingly, nearly half the candidates fielded by the HDP were women. In western, metropolitan Turkey, the HDP increased its popularity through an appeal to liberal Turks. And in the country's Kurdish southeast, it made an appeal to pro-AKP Kurds by adding conservative candidates, including imams, to its lists. With this platform, the HDP banded liberal Turks and conservative Kurds around its core constituency of nationalist Kurds. Thanks to this electoral triad, the party increased its share of the vote from 6.5 percent in the 2011 election, when it had contested seats under the banner of the narrowly Kurdish-nationalist Peace and Democracy Party (BDP), to more than 13 percent in June 2015. Amassing 80 seats in the legislature, the HDP tied for the third-largest bloc in parliament. Suddenly, the Kurdish movement was a potential kingmaker: it did not matter if many Turks did not like the HDP's Kurdish-nationalist demands—such demands could no longer be ignored. Following the election the HDP's co-chair Selahattin Demirtas kept to his campaign promise to block Erdogan from achieving an executive-style presidency. And so Erdogan proceeded to crush the HDP.

The 2015 summer of hell

In the aftermath of the election, the Turkish-nationalist MHP said it would not enter a coalition government with the HDP because of the latter's identification with the Kurdish-nationalist cause and failure to denounce the PKK. Erdogan openly advised the AKP not to join other parties in forming a coalition government, knowing a power-sharing government would sound the death knell for his plan to become an executive-style president. Massive instability during the summer of 2015, in the aftermath of the election—the result of increased PKK and ISIS violence—coupled with frustration about the parties' inability to form a coalition, led the opposition parties to lose votes and the AKP to regain its legislative majority in the snap election that followed in November. The HDP failed to condemn rising PKK attacks, losing its influential liberal Turkish base and support among intellectuals. The breakdown of the government's ceasefire with the PKK in July hurt the HDP, but also helped the AKP. Once fighting with the PKK resumed in earnest, some nationalist Turkish voters changed their votes from the MHP to the AKP in support of Erdogan's strongman tactics against the PKK. At the same time, conservative Kurds (who lacked the PKK protection granted to their nationalist Kurdish counterparts) were afraid that the return of PKK violence to the country's southeast would hurt them most. Ominous in this regard was Prime Minister Davutoglu's October warning that if the AKP did not win repeat elections, "white Tauruses would come back," referring to the unmarked sedans that Turkey's security forces are believed to have used to "disappear" Kurdish activists in the 1990s.[1] Davutoglu's chilling words worked, pulling many conservative Kurdish voters away from the HDP and back to the AKP.

The PKK and ISIS repeatedly targeted Turkey in a string of terror attacks following the June 2015 election, killing more than 40 people.[2] In October 2015, ISIS carried out the most destructive terror attack in Turkey to date, killing 103 anti-AKP demonstrators at a peace rally in front of the central railway station in Ankara. With the parties in parliament unable to form a coalition government, Turkey had descended into chaos just weeks before the November election. This convinced enough Turks to opt for single-party rule again, hoping for a way out, and the AKP returned to power with 49.5 percent of the vote and 317 seats out of 550. Erdogan was safe again, at least for the time being.

Despite the AKP's comeback, the results of the two 2015 elections exposed how tenuous Erdogan's grip on power had become: over the course of a few months, the AKP wavered between losing control of parliament and regaining the majority. It was forced to rely on widespread fear stoked by terror attacks across the country for support for its platform of *istikrar*—stability.

A second war of independence: the failed coup of 2016

These fissures in Turkish society finally erupted on July 15, 2016, when a group of generals, largely concentrated in the Turkish Air Force and at least partially affiliated with the Gulen movement, staged a coup to overthrow Erdogan. The president's most visceral nightmare, that the military might again oust an Islamist government, materialized late that night. As the plane that Erdogan had been sneaked onto hung in the air, his life's work hung in the balance. Abject fear must have permeated his mind, not only for his own life, but also for the fate of the dreams he had long cherished. He had worked tirelessly to become Turkey's most powerful leader, and now his erstwhile allies might kill him.

Turkey has a history of successful coups, but they have tended to be mostly bloodless and to have originated within the hierarchy of the secularist military. Few analysts predicted this coup because it broke some fundamental rules: it was organized by a faction within the military; its backbone comprised not secularists, but rather, apparently, officers aligned with the conservative Gulen movement; and, last but not least, it resulted in massive bloodshed. Ultimately, however, July 15 was ill-conceived and poorly organized, and failed miserably. Contributing to the putsch's failure was its timing: rather than executing the coup in the middle of the night—typically around 3 a.m., when most people are asleep—the conspiring generals, having been forced to bring their plan forward due to the domestic intelligence agency getting wind of the plot, attempted the coup at 10 p.m. on a Friday. This was inauspicious indeed: to generalize, at the time the pro-AKP half of Turkey was out praying (the day's final prayers for Muslims are at around 10:30 p.m. in the summer), and the anti-AKP half was out drinking and dining. Crowds soon mobilized to defeat the plotters.

The coup, therefore, failed within a matter of hours. The putsch-ists only secured one television channel—the government-run TRT, which does not rank among the top-watched networks in the country. In a victory of the internet over traditional media and digital over analog, Erdogan—who had been vacationing on the Turkish Riviera—appeared on FaceTime, calling on his supporters to flood the streets to protect Turkey's democracy. Religious calls were issued from minarets for hours, extolling Erdogan's supporters to come out in his defense, a strategy that worked marvelously. According to official numbers, a total of 161 civilians and 104 coup supporters were killed in the ensuing clashes, but the protestors succeeded in overpowering the military's ill-coordinated forces on the streets.[3]

Although not all the details have been revealed, it appears that the coup forces raided Erdogan's hotel compound in an attempt on his life, only to find that he had been alerted to the plot and had left for Istanbul an hour earlier.[4] Within the first hours of the coup, the commander of the First Army in Istanbul, the largest and most respected of Turkey's four armies, came out against it, signaling to the rest of the TAF the nature of the factional uprising. In a vindication of Turkey's democratic future, TUSIAD, NGOs, major media outlets, liberal pundits, and the leaders of the CHP and the HDP (all persecuted or demonized by Erdogan) came out against the putsch and, indirectly, in favor of Erdogan. A few months later, in a speech addressed to parliament, Erdogan reflected on the attempted coup—and the attempt on his life—by declaring: "Realize this: July 15 was a Second War of Independence for the Turkish nation."[5] If so, it was a brief one. The putsch unraveled in less than 24 hours.

Coup attempt sours relations with the West

Since the coup failed, some international observers brushed it off as a mildly alarming blip in Turkish politics. It took the United States days to condemn it, for example. Furthermore, adding insult to injury, Washington's condemnation came *after* condemnation by Russia. This delay embittered Ankara's view of Washington. The trauma felt in the country after the coup was deep, and in the following weeks the mood was nervous, angry, and dark. It took the authorities almost three months to apprehend all of the assassination squad that descended on Erdogan's resort hotel.[6] Fearing for his safety, Erdogan did not return to Ankara until days after the plot had failed. The bombing, including the targeting of the parliament building, deeply shocked residents of the city, which had not experienced a direct military attack in more than 600 years. Istanbul, too, felt the reverberations of the coup attempt: F-16 planes, operated by plotters who intended to terrorize residents, flew at low altitudes and high speeds over the city, creating supersonic booms that created the illusion that the city was being bombed. Even majestic Istanbul, crown jewel of the Romans, the Byzantines, and the Ottomans, could not avoid being shaken. As the Turks saw it, this was their 9/11.

The abiding trauma was so uniformly deep that it finally provided Erdogan with the unified audience every leader craves. Following the attempted putsch, he focused on two key retributive measures: asking the United States to extradite Fethullah Gulen, whom he fully blamed for orchestrating the violence, and reinstating capital punishment. Speaking a week after July 15, Erdogan vowed to approve the latter measure if the AKP-controlled parliament voted to pass it.

These policies would hurt Turkey's relations abroad, notably those with Washington and Brussels.

Another blow to US–Turkish ties was the belief still held by many in the pro-government camp that Gulen's status as a US resident implicated Washington in the coup. Prominent columnists in pro-AKP newspapers boldly aired these allegations, and at least one other cabinet member, Suleyman Soylu, the labor minister, publicly blamed the United States for being behind the coup. The Islamists' illiberal and shallow understanding of how democratic governance operates has exacerbated the frustrations of the Turkish government. Erdogan views other countries through the lens of his own autocratic ways. For instance, in April 2009, in the aftermath of the Danish cartoon crisis, Turkey objected to then Danish prime minister Anders Fogh Rasmussen's appointment as NATO's secretary general on the basis that he had "allowed" representations of the Prophet Muhammad to be published in the Danish media, among other reasons.[7] Similarly, rather than understanding the deep-seated institutions of the free press or judiciary, Erdogan and his supporters view Gulen's continued residence in the United States, as well as his ability to publish op-eds in American newspapers after the coup attempt, as proof of US indifference and even complicity in one of the most traumatic events in Turkish history.

In the aftermath of the failed coup, as discussed in Chapter 11, Russia quickly took advantage of the mood in Ankara, normalizing ties with Turkey and giving Erdogan the green light for the August 2016 Turkish incursion into northern Syria. This incursion showed that Ankara was finally reshuffling its priorities in Syria. For nearly five years, Turkey had obsessed over the goal of ousting Assad. But now, seeing the writing on the wall—the survival of its enemy, the Assad regime, and even a potential US–Russian settlement on Syria—Turkey decided to prioritize two other objectives: driving ISIS away from its border and blocking Kurdish advances. The incursion into Jarablus allowed Turkey to do both simultaneously.

Why Turkey matters

The 2016 Jarablus operation provided Turkey with a bridgehead in Syria that has increased Ankara's value to the United States as a partner in fighting ISIS. But Erdogan has also cast Turkey into the Syrian war in a dangerous attempt to aid the Islamist groups vying for power. Furthermore, for some time now the United States and the EU have had to revisit their faith in Erdogan. Turkey was once regarded as the model of a Muslim-majority democracy: many Western analysts hoped that Arab Spring countries could adopt the AKP model. But since then, Erdogan's democratic credentials have come under serious scrutiny. He has reneged on his early commitments to political liberalism and democratic reforms, and outside observers have lost faith in the AKP as an exemplar.

Now, US and European policy makers are watching Ankara's Syria policy come under pressure as Turkey faces increased domestic instability. At the same time, though, events and geography, such as the Syrian refugee crisis, have enhanced Ankara's role on the global stage, which is why the EU made efforts to meet Turkish demands for the March 2016 deal on refugees and why in April of the same year Germany acquiesced to Erdogan's demands to bring a legal case over a satirical video ridiculing him in Germany.[8] However, the accusations that Turkey leveled against the United States after the coup have angered many US policy makers, and EU leaders are uncertain about which sources of information coming out of Turkey can be trusted anymore. After a decade of increasingly arbitrary foreign policy and domestic political attitudes, Erdogan's Turkey will be willing to commit to, at best, a transactional relationship with the United States and Europe. This is a dire conclusion for those who have watched the AKP in the past decade, hoping that Erdogan would successfully blend Islam, Turkey's Western vocation, and democracy. Unlike previous Turkish leaders, such as Ozal, who saw himself as a conservative Muslim and a Westerner, Erdogan views himself as a conservative Muslim but not a Westerner. Accordingly, he no longer regards NATO as central, seeing it not as a club of nations with shared values, but rather as an outlet where he can purchase security through transactional deals. Whether or not the Turkish leader is the partner that the United States and the EU want, he is the ally they have been dealt at a critical juncture. Of course, the extent to which Turkey takes NATO seriously will also depend on the future of US–Russian relations. If Washington under President Donald Trump moves to reset its relationship with Russia, this could expose Turkish–Russian ties to the vicissitudes of US–Russian relations. In turn, Ankara could move to cut its own bargain with Moscow.

In any case, Erdogan's transactional view of the NATO alliance will limit US ties with Turkey. Erdogan's dim view of the EU and its liberal-democratic values will endow the EU with even less influence in Turkey. At best, Turkey's Western allies can hope that the security they provide to Turkey against ISIS, Russia, and the Assad regime will be enough to keep Erdogan on their side. They can also dream that, in Erdogan's wake, liberals will run Turkey one day, pivoting the country toward its traditional allies in the West—a long-term vision and hope.[9]

Erdogan's final report card—a tortured mix

- **DETERIORATION OF FREEDOMS:** After 15 years of AKP rule, Turkey is worse off when it comes to rights and liberties. According to Freedom House, between 2002 and 2016, Turkey's "press freedom" score worsened from 58 to 71 (on a scale of 0 to 100, 100 being the worst), and its "legal environment" score, despite yearly fluctuations, remained at 26 (on a scale of 0 to 30, 30 being the worst). Furthermore, its "political environment" score worsened from 23 to 30 (on a scale of 0 to 40, 40 being the worst).[10] The NGO Reporters without Borders, which measures freedom of information, determined that Turkey ranked 100th out of 139 countries in 2002, and 151st out of 180 countries in 2016.[11]

- **ERODING WOMEN'S RIGHTS:** Some of the deep changes Erdogan is implementing in Turkish society may be difficult to reverse, at least in the short term. According to *The Global Gender Gap Report 2016* composed by the World Economic Forum, Turkey ranked in 105th place among 115 countries in 2006 (the first year of publication) and 130th place among 144 countries in 2016.[12] Under Erdogan, women's rights have been eroded and repurposed as family rights. This has shifted the focus away from the individual woman and instead toward her traditional role as a mother and a wife. In 2011, the AKP rebranded the Ministry of State for Women's Affairs, changing its name to the "Ministry of Family and Social Policies." Erdogan has also instructed all women to have three children in order to boost Turkey's birth rate. In 2012, despite heavy pushback from the medical profession, the government made it illegal for women to choose to have a caesarean, banning the procedure in the absence of an emergency. Erdogan called the procedure "a secret plot" aimed at slowing Turkey's population growth, on the basis that there is a lower birthrate among women who have had caesareans.[13] Recently, the Ministry of Family and Social Policies has unveiled a 10,000-lira marriage credit (the equivalent of around $3,200 in 2016) for newly wed couples between the ages of 18 and 24.[14]

  In addition to this emphasis on traditional family structures, the AKP has also been encouraging gender segregation. In 2013, Tamer Kirbac, the government-appointed director of education in Trabzon Province, responsible for overseeing schools, teachers, and curricula, made national headlines when he lamented high-school dormitories in which male and female students cohabited in the same buildings (though not in the same rooms, or even on the same floors) and had to "use the same staircases" to get to their sleeping quarters.[15] The following year, Fethiye Atli—the mayor of the district of Keban in central-eastern Elazig Province, and one of Turkey's first mayors to wear the hijab—created a bus system to be used exclusively by women, allowing them to travel without the presence of men.[16] Speaking at the first annual

International Women and Justice Summit in 2014, Erdogan declared that for "women and men to be equal [is] against [their] nature," and that they should be considered not "equals," but "equivalents."[17] In Erdogan's Turkey, displays of religious piety guarantee government contracts, jobs, promotions, and access to power. Having a hijab-wearing wife is the surest way to get a job in the Erdogan administration or to receive a lucrative government contract. This is especially significant in light of the fact that only about half of Turkish women cover their heads. Erdogan has been rolling out policies gradually over the past few years to reverse restrictions on students and public servants donning the veil, culminating in the total overhaul of the ban in February 2017, which finally allowed women in the military to wear the hijab.

- **UNDERMINING SECULAR EDUCATION:** If the emancipation of women is one of Ataturk's two greatest contributions to modern Turkey—contributions that continue to set a precedent for other Muslim-majority countries today—the other is his establishment of a publicly funded, secular, universal education system. This is also of importance to the West: generations of Turks have shied away from radicalization because they were educated in a free secular education system. This could change following the demise of Turkey's secular education system under Erdogan.

  Erdogan and his allies are essentially a group of Imam Hatip graduates-cum-political warriors. A May 2016 study by the Washington Institute for Near East Policy documents that over one-third of Turkey's new AKP cabinet, which took office on May 24, 2016, were graduates of Imam Hatip schools; less than 10 percent of the Turkish population has the same educational pedigree.[18] After Erdogan and the AKP came to power in 2002, they were relieved finally to have the chance to dismantle the secularist educational system, as well as the Kemalist establishment that had marginalized them since the early days of the Turkish republic. It began a bitter contest that continues to this day. The most dramatic change to Turkey's primary-education system came with the 2012 passage of a sweeping education-reform bill, dubbed the "4+4+4" plan because it mandates that students receive four years each of primary, middle, and secondary education. Among many other things, this bill marked the final vindication of the Imam Hatip system, which had been for so long at the mercy of Ankara's mercurial political currents. It called for the return of Imam Hatip education at the middle-school level, and it required that even secular public schools provide elective courses in the Qur'an and the life of the Prophet Muhammad at the middle- and high-school levels.[19]

The AKP government has been busy converting secular high schools into Imam Hatip schools.[20] The number of such institutions has exploded in the last few years. Between 2002 and 2016, the number of Imam Hatip students increased from 60,000 to 1.5 million.[21] Following curriculum- and exam-based changes to the country's education system, a growing number of pupils have been forced to study in these Islamic high schools. No one is spared—not even the grandson of Turkey's chief rabbi, who was placed, along with many Christians, in an Imam Hatip high school in 2014, suggesting that students' placement in such schools in Turkey is no longer a choice, but increasingly an imposition.[22]

Today, Turkey's public education system can no longer be considered completely secular. Critics argue that, with these new reforms, it is now the non-religious who are becoming marginalized, just as the religious once were. They point out that proliferating Imam Hatip schools are becoming the only option for students whose parents are unable to afford expensive private schools, and for those students who do not score high enough in entrance exams to gain entry into the secular public schools, which are diminishing in number as Erdogan converts more and more of them into Imam Hatip-style institutions. For Erdogan, this sweeping restructuring is the culmination of decades of struggle: a victory for democracy—or, at least, democracy as Erdogan understands it. Addressing the youth wing of the AKP shortly after the passage of the "4+4+4" bill, Erdogan boasted: "This law—passed with your efforts and your struggle—is more than just a law about the national education system. This law is further proof, confirmation, of who the real owners of the nation's sovereignty are."[23]

• **A MAJORITARIAN, DOMINANT-PARTY SYSTEM:** AKP rule in Turkey today resembles a dominant-party political system, similar to that of South Africa since 1994 under the African National Congress (ANC) and Mexico from the 1920s to the 1980s under the Institutional Revolutionary Party (PRI). These parties came to power following revolutionary developments, garnering strong popular support. Thereafter, they promoted their vision to transform their respective societies, interpreting their persistent popular mandate as a justification for ruling in a majoritarian but also revolutionary fashion. The ANC and the PRI can be classified as majoritarian dominant parties in post-revolutionary societies. Likewise, since coming to power in 2002, the AKP has carried out its own revolution: it has eliminated the legacy of Kemalism and secularism. In just one reminder of this transformation, as discussed in Chapter 9, Turkey's Council of National Education issued a policy recommendation in December 2014 suggesting that courses on Islam be taught to all public-school students as young as six. Such recommendations reflect the revolutionary instincts of the AKP in the mold of a majoritarian dominant party. The contrasts between the AKP and the ANC/PRI models of dominant-party systems, however, point at a democratic regression in Turkey. The ANC and PRI represented a transition to democracy in South Africa and Mexico, respectively; Turkey, on the other hand, was already a democracy, albeit frequently an illiberal one, and had been for more than 50 years when the AKP came to power.

The Turkish case differs from other dominant-party systems in another crucial respect. The movements in South Africa and Mexico captured at least 60 percent of the vote, and usually much higher. In South Africa, the ANC has regularly won 60 to 70 percent of the vote since 1994, while in Mexico the PRI consistently took between 70 and 98 percent between 1929 and 1982—albeit in elections that were not always free and fair.[24] Such overwhelming dominance is not evident in Turkey. In the past four parliamentary elections—in 2007, 2011, and twice in 2015—the AKP has garnered, respectively, 46.6, 49.8, 40.9 and 49.5 percent of the vote. In the brightest assessment for the AKP, therefore, the Turkish electorate is split between pro- and anti-AKP constituents.

Given its limited electoral dominance compared to the ANC or PRI, Turkey's AKP might better be seen as resembling another set of dominant parties in split societies, including the Swedish Social Democratic Party (SAP) and Japan's Liberal Democratic Party (LDP). As the dominant party in Sweden from 1932 to 1973, the SAP received 30 to 50 percent of the general vote, peaking at 53.8 percent in 1940. Similarly, the LDP maintained between around 36 to 50 percent of the Japanese vote from 1958 to 1993, reaching its apex of 56 percent in 1963.[25] The SAP and LDP both ruled through consensus-building. By contrast, the AKP, although operating in a similarly split society, tends to eschew consensus for the majoritarian assertion of power. This trend presents a unique dilemma: Turkish society, split down the middle, has fallen under a dominant-party system run by Erdogan. This is a recipe for long-term political crisis.

• *APRÈS* **ERDOGAN**, *LE DÉLUGE*: Turkey's crisis will not be over even after Erdogan. The longer the center-right constituency of Turkish politics languishes under him, the more difficult it will become for this bloc, which has traditionally championed democratic values and pro-Western foreign policy, to rejuvenate itself after he has gone. So who will govern Turkey after Erdogan? The Turkish leader's powerful personality—at times respected and at times feared—keeps the AKP together. But the same personality has also sidelined politicians with leadership skills, such as

Gul, from the AKP leadership, as well as undermining political alternatives to the AKP from the center-right. After Erdogan, and in the absence of a charismatic leader, the AKP may not remain unified, and the longer the AKP rule, the harder it will be for the center-right to resuscitate itself. These outcomes could leave Turkey potentially rudderless after Erdogan, a development that will usher in a period of deep political uncertainty.

- **CRISIS UNDER ERDOGAN:** In the short term, Erdogan's trajectory has polarized the country socially and politically—the crisis of modern Turkey—and this split will be difficult to mend. Though Turkey was not for extended periods a truly liberal democracy, the AKP era stands out when compared to the country's overall record. For instance, Turkey has an infamous law that allows sitting presidents to sue citizens who have allegedly insulted them. According to figures calculated in January 2016 relating to Turkish presidents' first 18 months in office, Ahmet Necdet Sezer, the tenth president (a secularist Kemalist who was not known for his liberal tendencies), used this law 26 times; Gul, the 11th president and an AKP member, used it 139 times; and Erdogan, the 12th and current president, has used it more than 1,800 times.[26] Following the failed coup, Erdogan pardoned all those convicted of this crime and dropped ongoing prosecutions, though the state of emergency declared after the coup has allowed him to consolidate his power further.

Turkey resilient?

The Turkish political system has successfully weathered many crises in the past, but it could be different this time. During the 1970s, the country's economy collapsed, and the instability led to civil war-like fighting that killed thousands of people. In the 1990s, Turkey was pummeled by triple-digit inflation, multiple economic crises, and a full-blown Kurdish insurgency that killed tens of thousands.

Turkey survived both decades. But though it has proven to be a resilient country, Turkey's chances of continuing to overcome these crises have become more and more uncertain with an increasingly autocratic president at the helm, coupled with a split society, rising violence, terror attacks, external and jihadist threats, and the brewing Kurdish problem.

- **THE KURDISH PREDICAMENT:** Although the historian in me says that Turkey could withstand the coming shock, the analyst in me suggests that it might not. Firstly, the nature of Turkey's Kurdish issue has changed. Although the re-emergence of PKK violence in July 2015 scared some Kurds away from the HDP, the HDP remains the dominant party in Turkey's solidly Kurdish-majority southeastern provinces. Despite the defections in late 2015, the political consolidation of the Turkish Kurds under the pro-PKK HDP means that Turkey's battle with the PKK risks starting a war with nearly a majority of its Kurdish community. The nature of fighting over the past year offers a case in point. In September 2015, the government enforced a week-long curfew, shut down the electricity as well as internet and phone access, and sent in thousands of troops and police to establish a hold on Cizre, a Kurdish-majority town of 130,000 on the Turkish–Syrian–Iraqi border. When the government fought the PKK in the past, it could count on help from the local Kurdish population; that is no longer the case. Ankara's war with the PKK is a retaliatory battle that will only escalate. Every time the government strikes the PKK, the group hits a target in western Turkey, as they did with the most recent bombings in Ankara and Istanbul, as well as in Yuksekova and Diyarbakir in southeastern Turkey—in 2016 alone, Kurdish militants killed over 200 people.[27] Events out of the control of both Erdogan and the PKK, such as Kurdish gains in Syria as a result of the civil war, have had an impact on average Kurds, changing their views of what they want from a peaceful resolution of the Kurdish issue, and what they would accept from Ankara. In other words, average Kurds in the country's southeast may no longer be willing to settle for a personal deal between Erdogan and Ocalan, which would not offer them a significant amount of autonomy. This is the Kurdish crisis that faces not just Erdogan, but also the PKK.

- **THE SULTANATE OF CARICATURE:** Despite the alarming situation, the Kurdish crisis is not the biggest of Turkey's concerns. Turkey is undergoing a fundamental shift to make Erdogan's interpretation of conservative Islam the uncompromising core of public life. Over the years, Erdogan has methodically eliminated Kemalism, introducing conservative and rigid Islam into the country's politics, education system, and, to an extent, foreign policy. While Kemalism required Turkish citizens to treat religion as a private matter and empowered the government to discriminate against overtly religious people, Erdogan considers citizens who are not outwardly conservative to be second-class.[28] Furthermore, as detailed in the following sections, this development has had the unintended consequence of opening the country to jihadist recruitment.

Over the past few years, Erdogan has been replacing Kemalist traditions and symbols in the public sphere with Islamic and Ottoman equivalents. Since 2011, the government has either limited or canceled more than 12 national holidays dedicated to celebrating the secular state and Kemalism. The AKP has instead supported elaborate commemorations of forgotten Ottoman battles, such as the successful siege of British forces at Kut-al-Amara in Iraq in 1916 during World War I, after which captured British soldiers were marched to Aleppo, an ordeal during which many of them died. Overall, Erdogan has been reshaping the public sphere in line with his vision of recapturing Turkey's glorious Ottoman past.[29]

Kemalism no longer offers the social glue with which to bind the country together. Instead, Erdogan wants to rely on Islam and a skewed perception of the Ottoman past. The blame for his "Ottomania" and obsession with flooding Turkey's political system and daily life with religion lies, indirectly, with Ataturk. A general in the Ottoman military before the empire collapsed at the end of World War I, Ataturk was a product of the Ottoman system. He was an ordinary middle-class citizen who received a secular education in Ottoman public schools. As a young man, he lived in an empire that already had a significant body of secular laws, courts, and institutions, and a tendency to see itself as part of the European state system. Thus, Ataturk's uniqueness lies not in the fact that he secularized or Westernized Turkey, but in the fact that he took the Ottoman trajectory to its fullest extent. He enshrined secularism in the Turkish constitution and strongly confirmed Turkey's Western vocation.

Revolutions need to portray the political systems they overthrow as being utterly useless in order to justify themselves, and so, in his revolution, Ataturk cast the Ottomans in an entirely different light. Ataturk and the Kemalist elites depicted the Westernizing Ottomans as religious fanatics who were obsessed with Islam, and who subsequently and consequently failed. They caricatured the Ottomans: the empire, they alleged, was a sort of Salafist state, a pre-modern version of Saudi Arabia. Kemalism, on the other hand, was all about progressive secularism and would enlighten Turkey. Over 80 years, Turkey became one of the most ideologically secularist Muslim-majority states, and such falsified ideas about the Ottomans were taught to generations of pupils and citizens, including Erdogan, who have internalized them.

Counter-revolutions and revisionist movements aim to rewind the political order back to the past, and this is what Erdogan is doing in Turkey. Thus he claims that Kemalism was all darkness and that Turkey would be better off going back to the pre-Ataturk era. His counter-revolution is focused on making Islam the centerpiece of Turkish politics, and he believes that the country's foreign policy should be primarily anti-Western. This, Erdogan thinks, is how he will bring the Ottomans back. The irony is that while claiming to revive the pre-Ataturk empire,

Erdogan is actually reviving the caricature of the Ottomans that he was taught by the Kemalists.

The Ottomans were a sophisticated bunch. To be sure, there were brief lapses to theocracy in the empire's six-century span. Such episodes, though, occurred in the early modern period, such as in the seventeenth century, when the sultans banned alcohol, or curbed the rights of Jews and Christians on religious grounds. And in the modern era, the Ottomans instrumentalized religion: in the nineteenth century, Sultan Abdulhamid II dispatched emissaries to Central Asia and the Indian subcontinent to agitate among Muslims against their nemeses, respectively, the Russian and British empires. The Ottomans were not singularly Islamic, however. From its inception, the empire saw itself as a European power and was so deeply Westernized that by the late nineteenth century, under Abdulhamid II, it provided education for women, ran secular courts, and taught its pupils, including Ataturk, to take religion out of politics. And, in foreign policy, the Ottomans always hoped to be a Muslim and European power, even as their power waned. If Erdogan can grasp the Ottoman legacy beyond the Kemalist caricature that shapes his thinking, Turkey still has a chance to walk away from a ruinous policy of Islamization at home, which ISIS and other jihadist groups will only exploit.

• **FOREIGN ENEMIES:** Erdogan's foreign policy has exposed the country to outside threats, ranging from ISIS to Russia, from Iran to the Assad regime. And despite these mostly Middle East-related risks, the Turkish leader seems unwilling to abandon his preoccupation with casting Turkey as a Middle Eastern nation in a non-Kemalist fashion—the sultanate of caricature in foreign policy.[30] In the fall of 2016, as countries in the Eastern European time zone, which Turkey shared for decades, added an extra hour to end daylight saving time, Erdogan decided to skip the time change in order to align Turkey permanently with its Middle East allies, the Persian Gulf monarchies. Symbolically speaking, Turkey moved from Eastern Europe to the Persian Gulf overnight. Even more symbolically, this change took place on October 29, the anniversary of the foundation of the Turkish republic by Ataturk in 1923. Playing with time-keeping like most revolutionaries, Ataturk himself had instituted the "Calendar Reform" after coming to power, at which time Turkey abandoned the Islamic Hegira calendar and the year 1344, moving to the Western Gregorian calendar and the year 1926.

With his symbolic time change, Erdogan is telling the whole world that, as far as he is concerned, Turkey and its foreign policy remain in the Middle East. Indeed, as of early 2017, Turkey is still mired in the ruinous Syrian civil war, which began in 2011, exposing itself to a variety of external enemies. Hard as it is to believe, Turkey has even supported radical Islamist groups in Syria such as Ahrar al-Sham, which has ties to al-Qaeda, in its effort to bring down the regime of President Assad. Whichever way the Syrian civil war ends, this is concerning for everyone who hoped that Erdogan would successfully blend Islam, moderation, and Turkey's traditionally pro-Western foreign-policy orientation. Of course, the blame for Turkey's drift away from the West also lies with its partners. The EU, for instance, has blocked Turkey's accession, allowing Erdogan to pivot away from Europe. Today, even liberal Turks do not believe that the EU will ever deal them a fair hand, and therefore almost no one in the country takes Europe seriously. The joke in Turkey is that the country will become an EU member during Kosovo's presidential term in the EU—a dim prospect given that Kosovo has yet to be recognized by all EU member states. This is bad news: EU–Turkish relations, one of Turkey's key historical anchors to the West since 1959, are damaged for the foreseeable future.

• **THE JIHADIST THREAT:** Turkey's woeful drift away from the West and the EU is ever more alarming because of rising jihadist elements. During the Muslim holy month of Ramadan in 2016, these groups violently attacked citizens who chose not to fast and targeted establishments that served alcohol. These are both unusual and disturbing developments in Turkey, which hitherto has been known for its liberal interpretation of Islam. Making things worse, the government has neither arrested nor prosecuted these vigilantes.

Not only has the AKP failed to condemn such action, the government has in fact tried to engineer this social change itself—albeit in more subtle ways. For the past decade and a half, the AKP has been working to refashion Turkish social, cultural, and aesthetic practices to align them more closely with Turkey's Islamic Ottoman past (as Erdogan envisions it in caricatured form). But forcing the country to become more Islamic is dangerous—not because of any violence inherent in the religion, but rather because by encouraging Islamization and abandoning secularism at home, Erdogan and the AKP are actively making Turkey receptive to radicalization from abroad, especially from jihadists across the border in Syria and Iraq. This reorientation is sometimes accomplished through not very benign steps: a draft educational curriculum circulated by the Ministry of Education for public review in early 2017 described jihad as a "national and spiritual value."[31]

This dangerous cocktail of events—Islamization at home, the jihadists' use of Turkey as a staging ground for Syria, and the rise of ISIS next door—has encouraged violent radicalization among Turks. The problem with Turkey's Islamization under Erdogan is that *religion in politics is a competition in which the ugliest wins.* There are already worrying signs of radicalization. For instance, Turkish citizens recruited by ISIS in Syria have carried out a number of attacks since summer 2015, killing scores of people. Jihadist propaganda is proliferating on the Turkish Web, and ISIS is accepted in certain circles, including various Istanbul neighborhoods where, as of 2016, people can buy ISIS paraphernalia on the streets. Unlike in the Turkey of yesteryear, jihadists do not stick out like a sore thumb: take for instance the three who killed 45 people at Istanbul's Ataturk Airport on June 28, 2016.

The radicalized men who planned the attack had traveled more than 750 miles from Syria, rented an apartment in Istanbul, and then assembled bombs for a month. They did so without raising the alarm for a simple reason: *Turkey itself is radicalizing, and the jihadists are blending in.*

Torn Turkey

Turkey is theoretically powerful enough to withstand the threats from ISIS (and the PKK) with US backing, especially with crucial US intelligence assistance, weapons, and technology. America's support would also help Turkey resist international pressure to end the fighting in case of an all-out war with the PKK. But it is not clear that the Erdogan administration has the domestic support it needs to withstand such attacks over an extended period of time. Herein lies the crux of my worries: at another time, most Turks would have, however grudgingly, stood behind the government—even at the cost of life and liberty—for the sake of national security. That no longer seems to be the case in today's political climate. And whatever unity Turks of all stripes showed after the coup quickly dissipated as the leader went back to his reliable tactic of demonizing groups that do not support him.

Erdogan's political style has become a dangerous source of polarization in Turkey. To be sure, since 2002 domestic and international structures and currents—from the electoral threshold, which rewarded him with lopsided majorities in the legislature, to the Sisyphean accession path offered by the EU in 2005—have made Erdogan the recipient of various unfortunate gifts, boosting his autocratic side and weakening his commitment to liberal democracy.

Accordingly, he has won successive elections since 2002, but he has also built a cult of personality as a kind of authoritarian underdog, portraying himself as a victim who is forced to crack down harshly on those whose "conspiracies" threaten to undermine him. In this crisis, the country is torn, with the pro- and anti-AKP blocs hating each other more than they fear ISIS or terrorism in general. And as Erdogan moves forward in the mold of a revolutionary leader to shape the country in his Islamist image, only half the country will embrace this agenda, while the other half will do nearly anything to undermine him. Even more worrisome in this time of instability, deep societal polarization between the camps that either love or despise Erdogan trumps what ought to be shared Turkish concern over ISIS and the PKK. In the wake of the July 2015 Suruc ISIS attack, anti-Erdogan protestors blamed the government for failing to stop it. Each new PKK and ISIS attack drives a wedge deeper into Turkish society between these two blocs. When the PKK attacks, the pro-AKP bloc blames the anti-AKP bloc; when ISIS attacks, the opposition blames the government. And, even more worrisome, jihadists in Syria and Turkey are poised to take advantage of these trends.

Two "Ataturks," one dead

Thankfully, there is also good news for Turkey: the AKP, though it controls the country, no longer represents an idealized future. What brought the Islamists to power in Turkey in the last decades was their ability to portray themselves as the agents of change in a poor society, which was cursed with inept elites. Having eliminated the legacy of Ataturk, the Islamists now represent the status quo in Turkey. The AKP has made Turkey a middle-class society, and for this it enjoys broad support. The World Bank reported in 2014 that between 1993 and 2010 "the share of Turkey's middle-class increased from 18 percent to 41 percent of the population."[32] Furthermore, the income of people in the bottom 40 percent has increased at nearly the same rate as that of the overall population, meaning that growing prosperity has been shared across income groups in the country.[33] But the flip side of this story is that Erdogan rules with an iron fist while a growing number of middle-class Turks conflictingly and increasingly want a free society, and the stagnation of incomes following this miraculous economic surge has diminished their patience.[34] Indeed, this stagnation, coupled with brain drain and a decrease in FDI, has left this newly prosperous group feeling unsettled.[35] In the future, Erdogan's biggest challenger will be the amorphous liberal desires of the growing middle-class majority. In fact, Turkey's future could have liberalism written all over it. Just as the Islamists came from the margins in the 1990s after years in the political wilderness under strictly secularist Kemalist rule, since the 2013 Gezi Park rallies a new generation of liberals is emerging as a grassroots movement, using the power of social media to sell their own dream: a truly democratic and egalitarian Turkey.

But the problem for these liberals is that while Erdogan has become an "anti-Ataturk Ataturk," shaping the country in his own conservative and Islamist image—ironically, the legacy of Ataturk continues to influence the strategies of the new "Ataturk"—the secularists, and lately the liberals' Ataturk (that is, the real Ataturk) is of course dead. The secularists and liberals lack a charismatic leader or a party to bring them to power, as the Islamists did before Erdogan and the RP in the 1990s. The CHP, the country's main opposition, is a mix of hard-line secularists, some liberals, and die-hard leftists. It needs to undergo a metamorphosis to become a real liberal force. And although the Kurdish-led HDP has promoted a decidedly liberal message and increased its share of the national vote from 5 to almost 10 percent, it remains a small party, and the continued presence of violent Kurdish nationalists among its ranks will not help it win broader support.

Liberal trajectory?

Turkey's future opposition movement will have to bring together the peaceful wing of the Kurdish-nationalist movement, the liberal wing of secular Turks, anti-Erdogan nationalist Turks, and the center-right wing of conservative Turks under its own "Ataturk," a charismatic leader with a unifying and—at least in principal—liberal *Weltanschauung*. Such a leader has yet to emerge, and when he or she does, he or she will face a tall order: bridging the gap between rightists and leftists, conservatives and secularists, Alevis and Sunnis, Turkish and Kurdish nationalists, and many others in the disparate opposition bloc. Nevertheless, the energy and ideology of liberal Turkey are already there, and such a leader could one day step forward to transform Turkish politics the same way Erdogan revolutionized the country after emerging from the youth branch of his party. A successful liberal movement should also prompt a new Turkish constitution with broad protection of freedoms. Remember, the secularist system that created Erdogan was one that protected freedom *from* religion, but not freedom *of* religion. Erdogan has turned the tables. Moving forward, in order to make sure that the rights of both Turkey's pious and secular halves are respected, the constitution will need to guarantee both forms of religious freedom. These protections will in turn allow adherents of various sects and belief communities in Turkey, including *tariqat* members and Alevis, to practice their traditions freely, or not practice at all, bridging Turkey's sectarian rifts. A new liberal charter would also allow Turkey to solve its Kurdish issue by guaranteeing broad rights for everyone, including the Kurds. If Turkey can make peace with its Kurds, then it can also make peace with the Kurds in northern Syria, a welcome development that would in turn endow Ankara with a cordon sanitaire against instability, jihadism, sectarian conflict, and civil war, all of which are likely to hail from Syria and threaten Turkey for decades.

Erdogan and Turkey's future

Erdogan's personalization of power and domination of political and civil institutions has rendered Turkey politically brittle, in a state of permanent crisis. He has achieved enormous success in elections by demonizing and politically brutalizing various demographic groups that will not vote for him. When combined, these groups make up nearly half the Turkish electorate, and there are still plenty of enemies waiting for him to fall from power. In any case, Erdogan knows that the corruption charges brought against him and members of his family in 2013 have left him with no graceful way to exit the scene. What's more, he does not appear to be interested in listening to other views or reaching a compromise; instead, he treats any sign of dissent as unreasonable and conspiratorial. When Erdogan does leave office—and one day he will—there will be few institutions left standing to keep the country together.

Erdogan will go down in history as the great leader who transformed Turkey economically, but so far it does not appear that his political legacy will be entirely positive. The protagonist in Turkish Nobel laureate Orhan Pamuk's 2015 novel *A Strangeness in My Mind*, Mevlut, in the end fails to make it across the proverbial tracks in Istanbul. At the end of the book he laments: "I will be selling *boza* [a millet-based fermented drink from the Balkans and Anatolia] until the day the world ends," referring to his days and nights spent selling the drink on the streets of Istanbul to make a living.[36] Unlike Mevlut, though, Erdogan has crossed the tracks not just in Istanbul, but also in all of Turkey, becoming the most powerful person in the country. However, like Mevlut he nurtures a grudge against the country's (former) establishment, as well as Western values and all Kemalism-embracing groups.

Can Erdogan stop being like Mevlut, and instead become a president for all Turkish citizens? This requires him to appreciate the political dreams and aspirations of all his citizens. If Erdogan can provide for a new constitution that brings together the country's disparate halves and opens the path for peace with the Kurds, he may leave behind a positive political legacy as well, as Erdogan the Great. Erdogan's path to greatness also requires him to recognize that the time for an Ataturk—involving top-down social engineering in Turkey (or, for that matter, anywhere else)—has passed. The Turkey that Ataturk shaped in his own image in the 1920s was 75 percent peasantry. Barely 11 percent of Turks were literate, and moreover many of these more educated people supported Ataturk's agenda. Contemporary Turkey, which Erdogan hopes to shape in his own image, is 80 percent urban and 97 percent literate. It is unlikely, if not completely impossible, that Erdogan will be able to impose his vision of rigid conservative Islam on the whole of Turkish society, a melange of social, political, ethnic, and religious groups, many of whom oppose Erdogan's agenda. Despite Erdogan's efforts to create a class of crony Islamist capitalists, the bulk of the country's wealth is still aligned with TUSIAD, Turkey's Fortune 500 club, which is wedded to secular, democratic, pro-Western and liberal values. Turkey is simply too diverse demographically, too big economically, and too complicated politically for one person to shape it in his own image against the background of a democratic system and competing political forces.[37] Democratically, Erdogan cannot have his political cake and eat it. In other words, he can continue to shape Turkey from the top down only by ending democracy.

Erdogan ought to be interested in avoiding this scenario for his own sake. The Turkish president wants to make his country a great power. He has made Turkey a middle-income country, and it now has a chance to become an advanced economy if he builds an information society driven by value-added production, including software and information technology. In other words, Erdogan's Turkey can continue to rise if it transforms itself from a country that exports cars (its key export) into one that is a hub for Google. Turkey's capital and creative classes will flee if the government continues on its current path, and international capital and talent will avoid it if its leaders cannot provide unfettered access to the internet and ensure freedoms of expression, media, assembly, and association, and respect for individual rights, environmental concerns, urban spaces, and gender equality—key demands of the Gezi Park protestors and Erdogan's critics on the political left and right. If Turkey remains an open society, it will continue to rise. If it ceases to be democratic, it will not.

Turkey's growth and Erdogan's political fortunes are closely linked. They are also connected to the global economy and the freedoms available to citizens of most developed countries. In fact, the economy is Erdogan's Achilles heel. Although Turkey's economy has grown significantly in size since 2002, it is still small enough to be woefully exposed to potential international shocks. Take note of the global downturn that nearly wiped out South Korea's economy in 1997, at a time when that country's economy was roughly comparable in size to that of Turkey in early 2017. It was an economic collapse that brought Erdogan to power in 2002, and a similar economic collapse could mean the end of his reign.

If Erdogan fails to listen to this advice, he will expose the country to conflict between its pro- and anti-AKP blocs, and ISIS and PKK attacks and foreign enemies will only exacerbate the ensuing crisis. On this unfortunate trajectory, Erdogan will further embrace authoritarian nationalism.[38] This is the "muddle through" scenario whereby Turkey remains in a permanent state of crisis and social conflict. Regrettably, there is a chance that things could get even worse. While Erdogan strives to shape Turkey in his own image, cracking down on that half of the country that opposes him, his opponents will work tirelessly to undermine his agenda: violence will beget violence. Turkey's domestic polarization will expose it to the machinations of its foreign enemies: Moscow, which will work behind the scenes to undermine Erdogan's revolution; Damascus, which will take advantage of its ties with radical Turkish leftists and Kurdish nationalists to hurt Erdogan; and, last but not least, the jihadists, who will ultimately challenge Erdogan's brand of Islamism from the violent far right. Coupled with these external threats, the country's crisis could catapult Turkey into a dangerous civil war. In this scenario, Erdogan would be remembered as the "failed Sultan" who brought about the breakdown of modern Turkey. The choice is Erdogan's to make.

Notes

Introduction: Meet Recep Tayyip Erdogan

1 Soner Cagaptay, "The coup attempt is bad news for Turkey's democracy," *Washington Post* (July 16, 2016).

2 Tim Arango, "Nightclub massacre in Istanbul exposes Turkey's deepening fault lines," *New York Times* (January 1, 2017).

3 "Turkey's charismatic pro-Islamic leader," BBC News [website] (November 4, 2002).

4 "Turkey: GDP per capita (current US$)," World Bank [website] (n.d.). Available at http://data.worldbank.org/indicator/NY.GDP.PCAP.CD?locations=TR.

5 Ibid. For a good and concise analysis explaining the dynamics that drove Turkey's economic growth between 2002 and 2008 and the slowdown of this growth since, see Daron Acemoglu and Murat Üçer, "Why Turkish growth ended: an institutional perspective," Centre for Economic Policy Research [website] (November 18, 2015). Available at http://voxeu.org/article/why-turkish-growth-ended.

6 "Quarterly national accounts: quarterly growth rates of real GDP, change over previous quarter," Organisation for Economic Co-operation and Development [website] (n.d.). Available at https://stats.oecd.org/index.aspx?queryid=350#; "Turkish economy shrinks for first time since 2009," *Hürriyet Daily News* (December 12, 2016).

7 Andrew Mango, *Ataturk: The Biography of the Founder of Modern Turkey* (New York: Overlook Press, 1999), xi.

8 M. Hakan Yavuz, *Islamic Political Identity in Turkey* (New York: Oxford University Press, 2003), 139.

9 Soner Cagaptay, *The Rise of Turkey: The Twenty-First Century's First Muslim Power* (Lincoln, NE: Potomac, 2014).

10 "Turkey: freedom on the net 2016," Freedom House [website] (n.d.). Available at https://freedomhouse.org/sites/default/files/FOTN%202016%20Turkey.pdf.

1 Growing up Poor and Pious in Secular Turkey

1 Orhan Pamuk, *A Strangeness in My Mind* (New York: Vintage International, 2015).

2 *Ustanın Hikayesi* [Beyaz TV documentary, September 3, 2013].

3 Ibid.

4 Ruşen Çakır and Fehmi Çalmuk, *Recep Tayyip Erdoğan: Bir dönüşüm öyküsü* (Istanbul: Metis Yayınları, 2001), 16.

5 "Erdoğan: Babam çok otoriter bir babaydı; yanlış yaptığımızda hesaplaşırdı," T24 [website] (September 3, 2013).

6 Howard Reed, "Turkey's new Imam-Hatip schools," *Die Welt des Islams* 4, no. 2/3 (1955), 150–63.

7   Çakır and Çalmuk, *Recep Tayyip Erdoğan*, 17.
8   Ibid., 22.
9   Can Dündar, *Lider Portreleri: Recep Tayyip Erdoğan* [NTV documentary, 2007].
10 *Ustanın Hikayesi.*

2   Turkey after Ataturk

1   John M. VanderLippe, *The Politics of Turkish Democracy: İsmet İnönü and the Formation of the Multi-Party System 1938–1950* (Albany, NY: SUNY Press, 2005). See also Ceren Belge, "State buildings and the limits of legibility: kinship networks and Kurdish resistance in Turkey," *International Journal of Middle East Studies* 43, no. 1 (2011), 95–114.

2   Howard Reed, "Turkey's new Imam-Hatip schools," *Die Welt des Islams* 4, no. 2/3 (1955), 150–63.

3   M. Hakan Yavuz, *Islamic Political Identity in Turkey* (New York: Oxford University Press, 2003), 53.

4   VanderLippe, *The Politics of Turkish Democracy*, 192; Yavuz, *Islamic Political Identity*, 48.

5   Erik Zurcher, *Turkey: A Modern History* (New York: I.B.Tauris, 2004), 177.

6   Metin Heper, *İsmet İnönü: The Making of a Turkish Statesman* (Leiden: Brill, 1998), 186.

7   Cihat Göktepe, "The Menderes period (1950–1960)," *Journal of Turkish Weekly* [website] (April 13, 2005).

8   For a thorough analysis of the Young Turks, see M. Şükrü Hanioğlu, *The Young Turks in Opposition* (Oxford: Oxford University Press, 1995) and Zurcher, *Turkey: A Modern History*, 93–206.

9   İlber Ortaylı, "Atatürk–İnönü çatışması," *Milliyet* (December 4, 2015).

10 Zurcher, *Turkey: A Modern History*, 221.

11 "Erdoğan, Menderes'in anıt mezarını ziyaret etti," *Cumhuriyet* (September 17, 2010).

12 Arnold Leder, "Party competition in rural Turkey: agent of change or defender of traditional rule?" *Middle Eastern Studies* 15, no. 1 (1979), 85.

13 Banu Eligür, *The Mobilization of Political Islam in Turkey* (New York: Cambridge University Press, 2010), 162.

14 Malik Mufti, *Daring and Caution in Turkish Strategic Culture: Republic at Sea* (New York: Palgrave Macmillan, 2009), 30.

15 "Danıştay kararları yatırımı engelliyor," *Yeni Şafak* (April 6, 2006).

16 VanderLippe, *The Politics of Turkish Democracy*, 50.

17 Göktepe, "The Menderes period."

18 Yavuz, *Islamic Political Identity*, 62.

19 Zurcher, *Turkey: A Modern History*, 230–1.

20 Feroz Ahmad, *The Turkish Experiment in Democracy, 1950–75* (London: Hurst, 1977), 97.

21 For a detailed discussion of Menderes and the DP years, see Zurcher, *Turkey: A Modern History*, 221–40.

22 "Cumhurbaşkanı Erdoğan: Menderes gibi beyaz kefenimizi giyerek yola çıktık," *Sabah* (May 27, 2016).

23 "'Ottoman Hearths' accused in attacks targeting parties, media," *Hürriyet Daily News* (September 12, 2015). For more on the "Ottoman Hearths" (in Turkish), see

Hayrullah Beyazıt, "Hakkımızda," Osmanli Ocaklari [website] (n.d.). Available at http://osmanliocaklari.org.tr/hakkimizda.

24 "Vali ve Jandarma Komutanı meydana birlikte seslendi," *Milliyet* (July 16, 2016).

25 Ruşen Çakır, İrfan Bozan, and Balkan Talu, *İmam Hatip Liseleri: Efsaneler ve Gerçekler* (Istanbul: TESEV Yayınları, 2004), 62.

26 *Ustanın Hikayesi* [Beyaz TV documentary, September 3, 2013].

27 Ruşen Çakır and Fehmi Çalmuk, *Recep Tayyip Erdoğan: Bir dönüşüm öyküsü* (Istanbul: Metis Yayınları, 2001), 24.

28 Ibid.

3   The Foundations of Political Islam in Turkey

1   Feroz Ahmad, *The Turkish Experiment in Democracy, 1950–75* (London: Hurst, 1977), 219.

2   Email conversation with Hasan Bülent Kahraman, December 5, 2016.

3   Ahmad, *The Turkish Experiment in Democracy*, 225–6.

4   *Ustanın Hikayesi* [Beyaz TV documentary, September 3, 2013].

5   Ruşen Çakır, *Ayet ve Slogan: Türkiye'de İslami oluşumlar* (Istanbul: Metis Yayınları, 1990), 229.

6   Emin Yaşar Demirci, "Modernisation, religion and politics in Turkey: the case of the İskenderpaşa community," Ph.D., University of Manchester (1996), 252.

7   Yusuf Ziya Durmuş, "Erbakan commemorated on anniversary of his death," *Daily Sabah* (February 27, 2015).

8   Reşat Nuri Erol, "Erbakanın Adil Düzen söyleminin teorisi," *Milli Gazete* (March 2, 2016).

9   Feroz Ahmad, *The Making of Modern Turkey* (London and New York: Routledge, 1993), 154.

10 Ibid., 161; Çakır, *Ayet ve Slogan*, 232.

11 Demirci, "Modernisation, religion and politics," 255.

12 Çakır, *Ayet ve Slogan*, 232.

13 Ibid., 233.

14 M. Hakan Yavuz, *Islamic Political Identity in Turkey* (New York: Oxford University Press, 2003), 125.

15 Ruşen Çakır, İrfan Bozan, and Balkan Talu, *İmam Hatip Liseleri: Efsaneler ve Gerçekler* (Istanbul: TESEV Yayınları, 2004), 15.

16 For more on Islamist movements in Turkey before the rise of the AKP, see Yavuz, *Islamic Political Identity*.

17 *Özallı Yıllar* [online documentary series, January 13, 2016]. Available at http://32gun.com/video/konu/ozalli-yillar.

18 Ruşen Çakır and Fehmi Çalmuk, *Recep Tayyip Erdoğan: Bir dönüşüm öyküsü* (Istanbul: Metis Yayınları, 2001), 33; Svante Cornell and M. K. Kaya, "The Naqshbandi–Khalidi order and political Islam in Turkey," Hudson Institute [website] (September 3, 2015). Available at http://www.hudson.org/research/11601-the-naqshbandi-khalidi-order-and-political-islam-in-turkey.

19 Raphael Israeli, *Muslim Anti-Semitism in Christian Europe* (New Brunswick, NJ: Transaction, 2009), 108. For a collection of anti-Semitic statements made by Erbakan, see also "Antisemitism and the Turkish Islamist 'Milli Gorus' movement: Zionists/Jews 'bacteria,' 'disease,'" Middle East Media and Research Institute [website] (September 1, 2007). Available at https://www.memri.org/

reports/antisemitism-and-turkish-islamist-milli-gorus-movement-zionistsjews-%E2%80%9Cbacteria%E2%80%9D-%E2%80%9Cdisease%E2%80%9D.

20 Joe Parkinson, "Dismay over Turkish rates," *Wall Street Journal* (January 12, 2012).

21 Gerald MacLean, *Abdullah Gül and the Making of the New Turkey* (London: Oneworld, 2014), 63.

22 "MTTB 49. Genel kurul faaliyet raporu," quoted in Çağatay Okutan, *Tek parti döneminde azınlık politikaları* (Istanbul: İstanbul Bilgi Yayınları, 2004), 189.

23 Can Dündar, *Lider Portreleri: Recep Tayyip Erdoğan* [NTV documentary, 2007].

24 Gareth Jenkins, *Political Islam in Turkey: Running West, Heading East?* (New York: Palgrave Macmillan, 2008), 184.

25 Sabri Sayari and Bruce Hoffman, *Urbanization and Insurgency: The Turkish Case, 1976–1980* (Santa Monica, CA: RAND Corporation, 1991), v. Available at http://www.rand.org/pubs/notes/N3228.html.

26 Çakır and Çalmuk, *Recep Tayyip Erdoğan*, 24.

27 Ibid., 32.

28 Jenkins, *Political Islam in Turkey*, 184; Mustafa Ünlü (dir.), *12 Eylül* [documentary, Cine5, 1998].

29 "Erdoğan: Simit ve su satar, kitap alırdım," NTV [website] (July 23, 2012).

30 "Sevki Yilmaz konusmasi Almanya 1991," YouTube [website] (May 29, 2012). Available at https://www.youtube.com/watch?v=H8Gg0MgpAnY.

4 The Generals Fashion a New Turkey

1 Erik Zurcher, *Turkey: A Modern History* (New York: I.B.Tauris, 2004), 279.

2 M. Hakan Yavuz, *Islamic Political Identity in Turkey* (New York: Oxford University Press, 2003), 89.

3 Feroz Ahmad, *The Making of Modern Turkey* (London and New York: Routledge, 1993), 88.

4 Yavuz, *Islamic Political Identity*, 75.

5 Ibid.

6 For a more detailed discussion of Turkish politics in the 1960s and 1970s, see Zurcher, *Turkey: A Modern History*, 241–77.

7 Can Dündar, *Lider Portreleri: Recep Tayyip Erdoğan* [NTV documentary, 2007].

8 Ibid.

9 İsmail Er and Emre Oktay, "Başbakan Erdoğan Başakşehir Stadı'nı açtı 3 gol birden attı," *Hürriyet* (July 27, 2014).

10 Ruşen Çakır and Fehmi Çalmuk, *Recep Tayyip Erdoğan: Bir dönüşüm öyküsü* (Istanbul: Metis Yayınları, 2001), 47.

11 Yavuz, *Islamic Political Identity*, 83.

12 Banu Eligür, *The Mobilization of Political Islam in Turkey* (New York: Cambridge University Press, 2010), 96.

13 Erkan Akin and Ömer Karasapan, "The Turkish–Islamic synthesis," *Middle East Report* 153, no. 18 (1988).

14 Uğur Akıncı, "The Welfare Party's municipal track record: evaluating Islamist municipal activism in Turkey," *Middle East Journal* 53, no. 1 (1999), 79; Eligür, *The Mobilization of Political Islam*, 154.

15 Ibid.

16 Ibid., 103.

17 *Özallı Yıllar* [online documentary series, January 13, 2016]. Available at http://32gun.com/video/konu/ozalli-yillar.
18 "Kasımpaşa'dan Çankaya'ya, yoksulluktan yolsuzluk suçlamalarına Erdoğan'ın hayatı," T24 [website] (August 10, 2014).
19 Ibid.
20 Ibid.
21 "DYP: Özal İdi Aminleşiyor," *Milliyet* (July 12, 1986).
22 Çakır and Çalmuk, *Recep Tayyip Erdoğan*, 75.
23 Akıncı, "The Welfare Party's municipal track record," 85.
24 Çakır and Çalmuk, *Recep Tayyip Erdoğan*, 60.
25 "Ciller's chance," *The Economist* (June 19, 1997).
26 Jonathan Rugman, "Turkish PM fights off poll threat," *Guardian* (March 29, 1994); Giles Merritt, "Europe should be doing more to bring Turkey into the fold," *International Herald Tribune* (June 28, 1994).
27 Henry Kamm, "Local elections in Turkey may set fate of sagging national cabinet," *New York Times* (March 28, 1994).
28 Jenny B. White, "Islam and democracy: the Turkish experience," *Current History* 94, no. 588 (1995), 8.
29 Hugh Pope, "Turkey's season of discontent: born-again democrats are disappointed with new prime minister Tansu Ciller, corruption and the army's grip on government," *Los Angeles Times* (August 2, 1994).
30 "İstanbul'da gözler Refah'ta," *Milliyet* (October 22, 1992).

5   Erdogan's Meteoric Rise as Istanbul's Mayor

1   Necmettin Erbakan, *Adil ekonomik düzen* (Ankara: Semih Ofset, 1991).
2   Banu Eligür, *The Mobilization of Political Islam in Turkey* (New York: Cambridge University Press, 2010), 160.
3   "Refah'tan yeni sesler," *Milliyet* (September 19, 1993).
4   Sinan Özedincik, "Artık eski Gülay yok," *Sabah* (September 7, 2012).
5   Birol A. Yeşilada, "The Virtue Party," in Barry Rubin and Metin Heper (eds), *Political Parties in Turkey* (London: Frank Cass, 2002), 70; Ruşen Çakır, *Ne şeriat ne demokrasi: Refah Partisini anlamak* (Istanbul: Metis Yayınları, 1994), 56.
6   Christopher Houston, *Islam, Kurds and the Turkish Nation State* (Oxford: Berg, 2001), 1.
7   *Başbakan Prof. Dr. Necmettin Erbakan'ın TBMM Grup Toplantısında Yaptığı Konuşmalar (4 Temmuz 1996–24 Aralık 1996)* (Ankara: Başbakanlık Basımevi, 1997).
8   Çakır, *Ne şeriat ne demokrasi*.
9   Ibid., 56; Yeşilada, "The Virtue Party."
10 Şule Çizmeci, "Tayyip Erdoğan'ın 75 bin kişilik seçim ordusu," *Milliyet* (February 15, 1994).
11 Çakır, *Ne şeriat ne demokrasi*, 29.
12 Eligür, *The Mobilization of Political Islam*, 167.
13 Joost Jongerden, "Crafting space, making people: the spatial design of nation in modern Turkey," *European Journal of Turkish Studies*, no. 10 (2009).
14 Barry Newman, "Turning eastward: Islamic party's gains in Istanbul stir fears of a radical Turkey," *Wall Street Journal* (September 12, 1994).
15 Jenny B. White, "Islam and democracy: the Turkish experience," *Current History* 94, no. 588 (1995), 8.

16 Beyhan Yegen and Bihrat Önoz, "Management of water supply systems of metropoles: Istanbul example," in H. Gonca Coskun, H. Kerem Cigizoglu, and M. Derya Maktav (eds), *Integration of Information for Environmental Security*, NATO Science for Peace and Security Series C: Environmental Security (Dordrecht: Springer, 2008), 473–84.

17 Gül Kireklo, "Yaprak hışırtısını yağmur sanıp cama koşardım," *Habertürk* (August 7, 2007).

18 Aslı Öktener, "Nurdan Erbuğ'un pişmanlığı!" *Milliyet* (February 8, 2001).

19 William Montalbano, "The army's prestige is growing amid political scandal," *Guardian* (November 4, 1994).

20 Öktener, "Nurdan Erbuğ'un pişmanlığı!"

21 "Kasımpaşa'dan Çankaya'ya, yoksulluktan yolsuzluk suçlamalarına Erdoğan'ın hayatı," T24 [website] (August 10, 2014).

22 Eligür, *The Mobilization of Political Islam*, 161.

23 Ibid.

24 Uğur Akıncı, "The Welfare Party's municipal track record: evaluating Islamist municipal activism in Turkey," *Middle East Journal* 53, no. 1 (1999), 77.

25 Ibid., 78; White, "Islam and democracy," 10.

26 Hugh Pope, "Istanbul and Ankara set to fall to Islamists," *Independent* (March 29, 1994).

27 Akıncı, "The Welfare Party's municipal track record," 92.

28 James M. Dorsey, "Judgment day: Islamists in Turkey make deep inroads in mainstream society," *Wall Street Journal* (June 18, 1997).

29 Heather Coleman, Gurdal Kanat, and F. Ilter Aydinol Turkdogan, "Restoration of the Golden Horn Estuary (Halic)," *Water Research* 43, no. 20 (2009).

30 "Farklı zamanlarda Haliç'e çok kafa yormak zorunda kalan üç kişi anlatıyor," *Hürriyet* (November 19, 1997); Henry Kamm, "Cleanup is reviving Istanbul's Golden Horn," *New York Times* (June 1, 1986); Zeynep Gunay and Vedia Dokmeci, "Culture-led regeneration of Istanbul waterfront: Golden Horn Cultural Valley project," *Cities* 29, no. 4 (2012), 215; Coleman, Kanat, and Turkdogan, "Restoration of the Golden Horn Estuary," 5, 11.

31 Eligür, *The Mobilization of Political Islam*, 174.

32 Sefa Kaplan, *Recep Tayyip Erdoğan* (Istanbul: Dogan, 2007), 76.

33 Akıncı, "The Welfare Party's municipal track record," 82.

34 "Eminonu Municipality and the Hizmet Foundation: serving the people of Eminonu?" *Hürriyet Daily News* (December 18, 1996).

6   The Perfect Storm

1   "Kronoloji: 28 Şubat'a giden yol," Al Jazeera Türk [website] (December 27, 2013).

2   "Kaddafi: Türkiye'nin hava sahası neden açık?" *Radikal* (March 9, 2011).

3   "Kronoloji: 28 Şubat'a giden yol."

4   Ibid.

5   Ibid.

6   "Erdoğan: Babam çok otoriter bir babaydı; yanlış yaptığımızda hesaplaşırdı," T24 [website] (September 3, 2013).

7   Ibid.; "Kronoloji: 28 Şubat'a giden yol."

8   Stephen Kinzer, "Pro-Islamic premier steps down in Turkey under army pressure," *New York Times* (June 19, 1997). For a history of Turkey from the Ozal years until

the "soft coup," see Erik Zurcher, *Turkey: A Modern History* (New York: I.B.Tauris, 2004), 278–305.

9 "Albright warns Turkey to guard its democracy," *New York Times* (June 14, 1997).

10 "Declaration by the presidency on behalf of the European Union on the banning of the Refah party in Turkey," European Commission [website] (January 21, 1998). Available at http://europa.eu/rapid/press-release_PESC-98-4_en.htm.

11 "Vural Savaş: AİHM'in kararı doğru," *Hürriyet* (July 31, 2001).

12 "Case of Refah Partisi (the Welfare Party) and others v. Turkey" [judgment of the Grand Chamber of the European Court of Human Rights, February 13, 2003]. Available at http://minorityrights.org/wp-content/uploads/old-site-downloads/download-384-Refah-Partisi-v.-Turkey.pdf; Christian Moe, "Refah Partisi (the Welfare Party) and others v. Turkey," *International Journal of Not-for-Profit Law* 6, no. 1 (2003).

13 Yasmine Ryan, "Uncovering Algeria's civil war," Al Jazeera [website] (December 18, 2016).

14 Koen Brinke, "The Turkish 2000–01 banking crisis," Rabobank [website] (September 4, 2013). Available at https://economics.rabobank.com/publications/2013/september/the-turkish-2000-01-banking-crisis/.

15 "Historic inflation Turkey—CPI inflation," Inflation.eu: Worldwide Inflation Data [website] (n.d.). Available at http://www.inflation.eu/inflation-rates/turkey/historic-inflation/cpi-inflation-turkey.aspx.

16 "Majority of Turks support democratic reforms, but reserved about broadcasts and education in Kurdish," *Hürriyet Daily News* (June 29, 2002).

17 Ünal Ünsal, "Seçim baraji: Anayasa Mahkemesi'nin tarihi sorumluluğu," Diken [website] (December 12, 2014).

18 Ibid.; *Republic of Turkey Parliamentary Elections 3 November 2002* (Warsaw: Organization for Security and Co-operation in Europe/Office for Democratic Institutions and Human Rights, December 4, 2002). Available at http://www.osce.org/odihr/elections/turkey/16346?download=true.

7 Erdogan in Power: The Good Years

1 Mehmet Cetingulec, "Should they stay or should they go? Turkey leaves foreign investors at odds," Al-Monitor [website] (April 1, 2016).

2 Selim Jahan, *Human Development Report 2015* (New York: United Nations Development Programme, 2015). Available at http://hdr.undp.org/sites/default/files/2015_human_development_report.pdf.

3 "Turkey: freedom in the world," Freedom House [website] (2016). Available at https://freedomhouse.org/report/freedom-world/2016/turkey; "Turkey: freedom of the press 2016," Freedom House [website] (2016). Available at https://freedomhouse.org/report/freedom-press/2016/turkey.

4 Roff Smith, "Why Turkey lifted its ban on the Islamic headscarf," *National Geographic* (October 12, 2013).

5 "Türban tartışmaları 60'larda başlamıştı," *Cumhuriyet* (October 5, 2010).

6 "Erdoğan: Türbanda söz hakkı ulemanındır," *Hürriyet* (November 16, 2005).

7 Soner Cagaptay, "Turkey at a crossroads: preserving Ankara's Western orientation," Washington Institute for Near East Policy [website] (October 2005). Available at http://www.washingtoninstitute.org/policy-analysis/view/turkey-at-a-crossroads-preserving-ankaras-western-orientation.

8   Michael M. Gunter, "Abdullah Öcalan: we are fighting Turks everywhere," *Middle East Quarterly* 5, no. 2 (June 1998).
9   Kursat Akyol, "Will Turkey reinstate death penalty?" Al-Monitor [website] (July 29, 2016).
10 Serpil Yılmaz, "Suriye ile yeni bir dönem," *Milliyet* (January 7, 2004).
11 Soner Cagaptay, "Ankara dispatch: eastern heading," *New Republic* (September 8, 2004).
12 Fatma Demirelli, "Turkey not fretting over conservatives," *Hürriyet Daily News* (June 28, 2005).
13 "Policy of zero problems with our neighbors," Republic of Turkey Ministry of Foreign Affairs [website] (n.d.). Available at http://www.mfa.gov.tr/policy-of-zero-problems-with-our-neighbors.en.mfa.
14 Ahmet Davutoğlu, *Stratejik derinlik* (Istanbul: Küre Yayınları, 2001).
15 Soner Cagaptay, "Turkish troubles," *Wall Street Journal* (July 31, 2007).
16 Deniz Zeyrek, "1 Mart mesajının adresi," *Hürriyet* (February 8, 2016).
17 Brian Knowlton, "US warns Iraq on new government," *New York Times* (March 21, 2005).
18 "ABD basını Kurtlar Vadisi'ne giden Emine Erdoğan'ı eleştirdi," Haber Vitrini [website] (February 16, 2006).
19 Yasemin Çelik, *Contemporary Turkish Foreign Policy* (Westport, CT: Praeger, 1999), p. 155.
20 Serkan Demirtaş, "Sezer: the most criticized president ever," *Hürriyet Daily News* (August 29, 2007).
21 Ellen Knickmeyer, "In Turkish vote, ruling party wins by wide margin," *Washington Post* (July 23, 2007).

8   The Silent Revolution

1   Conversation between the author and Hrant Dink, Ann Arbor, MI, 2006.
2   Sabrina Tavernise, "Trial in editor's killing opens, testing rule of law in Turkey," *New York Times* (July 3, 2007).
3   Paul de Bendern and Thomas Grove, "Turkish-Armenian editor shot dead in Istanbul," Reuters [news agency] (January 19, 2007).
4   Abdurrahman Dilipak, "Lanetli süreç: 28 Şubat," *Yeni Akit* (February 27, 2015).
5   Abdurrahman Dilipak, "En derin devlet," *Vakit* (October 16, 2009); "AKP de ittihatçı çıktı," Odatv [website] (June 15, 2014).
6   For a study of the intellectual and political continuities from the Ottoman Empire to the Republic of Turkey, see Fatma Müge Göçek, *The Transformation of Turkey: Redefining State and Society from the Ottoman Empire to the Modern Era* (London: I.B.Tauris, 2011).
7   "Fury after police pictured posing with Dink murder suspect," *Guardian* (February 2, 2007).
8   Benjamin Harvey and Associated Press, "Mass protest at Turkish-Armenian editor Hrant Dink's funeral," *Guardian* (January 24, 2007).
9   "Nedim Şener: Ramazan Akyürek, Dink soruşturmasında kilit isim," BBC Türkçe [website] (February 26, 2015).
10 Yavuz Baydar, "Family boycotts retrial for murder of Turkish-Armenian journalist," Al-Monitor [website] (September 20, 2013).
11 Turkish General Staff, "Press release no. BA-08/07" (April 27, 2007).

12 For the history of civilian and military relations in Turkey, see Steven Cook, *Ruling but Not Governing* (Baltimore, MD: Johns Hopkins University Press, 2007).

13 "Fethullah Gulen: honorary chairman of the Rumi Forum," Rumi Forum [website]. Available at http://rumiforum.org/fethullah-gulen/.

14 Abigail Hauslohner, Karen DeYoung, and Valerie Strauss, "He's 77, frail and lives in Pennsylvania. Turkey says he's a coup mastermind," *Washington Post* (August 3, 2016).

15 Joseph M. Humire, "Charter schools vulnerable to controversial Turkish movement," *The Hill* (March 10, 2016).

16 For more on the Gulen movement, see Jim Zanotti and Clayton Thomas, *Turkey: Background and US Relations* (Washington DC: Congressional Research Service, August 26, 2016). Available at https://fas.org/sgp/crs/mideast/R41368.pdf.

17 Hauslohner, DeYoung, and Strauss, "He's 77, frail and lives in Pennsylvania."

18 Ibid.

19 Ibid.

20 "Sweeping detentions of former top generals exempts Özkök," *Hürriyet Daily News* (February 22, 2010).

21 Dani Rodrik, "The plot against the generals," Dani Rodrik [website] (June 2014). Available at http://drodrik.scholar.harvard.edu/files/dani-rodrik/files/plot-against-the-generals.pdf.

22 Ahmet Altan, "Gazetecilikten tutuklanmadılar," *Taraf* (March 7, 2011).

23 "Ergenekon'da dava sayısı Masonlarla 15 oldu," Haber7 [website] (February 6, 2011).

24 Soner Cagaptay, "What's really behind Turkey's coup arrests?" Washington Institute for Near East Policy [website] (February 25, 2010). Available at http://www.washingtoninstitute.org/policy-analysis/view/whats-really-behind-turkeys-coup-arrests.

25 Sedat Ergin, "O albaylar gitti darbeciler geldi," *Hürriyet* (July 23, 2016).

26 "Turkey's top military leaders quit," Al Jazeera [website] (July 30, 2011).

27 Gul Tuysuz and Sabrina Tavernise, "Top generals quit in group, stunning Turks," *New York Times* (July 29, 2011).

28 Soner Çağaptay, "Ending Turkey's nightmare," *Hürriyet Daily News* (August 3, 2011).

29 Soner Cagaptay, "Turkey after the constitutional referendum," Washington Institute for Near East Policy [website] (September 23, 2010). Available at http://www.washingtoninstitute.org/policy-analysis/view/turkey-after-the-constitutional-referendum-implications-for-washington.

30 "Global gender gap report 2015: Turkey," World Economic Forum [website] (n.d.). Available at http://reports.weforum.org/global-gender-gap-report-2015/economies/#economy=TUR.

31 This chart represents the "Liberal Democracy Index" as calculated by the V-Dem Institute at the University of Gothenburg. See Erik Meyersson, "The reversal of (what little) liberal democracy (there ever was) in Turkey," Erik Meyersson [blog] (October 4, 2016). Available at https://erikmeyersson.com/2016/10/04/the-reversal-of-what-little-liberal-democracy-there-ever-was-in-turkey/.

32 "Anayasa değişikliği 1'inci tur görüşmeleri," *Sabah* (April 28, 2010).

33 "Yeni HSYK üyeleri göreve başlıyor," Anadolu Ajansı [Turkish state-run press agency] (October 26, 2014).

34 "Erdogan pulls it off," *The Economist* (September 13, 2010).

35 Ertuğrul Özkök, "Beni maymun olarak çizseler," *Hürriyet* (March 2, 2009).

36 "Erdoğan'ın karikatüre tazminat davasına ret," *Hürriyet* (November 17, 2006).

37 Joe Parkinson, "Dogan shares jump on sale speculation," *Wall Street Journal* (October 14, 2010).

38   Soner Cagaptay and Cem Yolbulan, "Assessing the new AKP cabinet," Washington Institute for Near East Policy [website] (May 31, 2016). Available at http://www. washingtoninstitute.org/policy-analysis/view/assessing-the-new-akp-cabinet.

9   The Revolution Devours Its Children

1   Dan Bilefsky and Sebnem Arsu, "Sponsor of flotilla tied to elite of Turkey," *New York Times* (July 15, 2010).

2   Semih Idiz, "Islamists in disarray after Israeli apology," *Hürriyet Daily News* (April 11, 2010); Ian Traynor, "Gaza flotilla raid draws furious response from Turkey's prime minister," *Guardian* (June 1, 2010); Ishaan Tharoor, "*Time* meets Turkish prime minister Recep Tayyip Erdogan," *Time* (September 26, 2011).

3   Sebnem Arsu and Alan Cowell, "Turkey expels Israeli envoy in dispute over raid," *New York Times* (September 2, 2011).

4   Traynor, "Gaza flotilla raid draws furious response."

5   "Turkey builds nearly 9,000 mosques in 10 years," *Hürriyet Daily News* (September 16, 2016).

6   Senada Sokollu, "Mosque construction sparks controversy in Istanbul," Deutsche Welle [website] (August 23, 2013).

7   Soner Cagaptay, "Kemal Erdoğan's second Turkish revolution," *Politico* [website] (January 27, 2016).

8   Kadri Gursel, "Erdogan Islamizes education system to raise 'devout youth,'" Al-Monitor [website] (December 9, 2014).

9   Sukru Kucuksahin, "Turkish students up in arms over Islamization of education," Al-Monitor [website] (June 20, 2016).

10   "Debate on religion takes over politics in Ankara," *Hürriyet Daily News* (February 2, 2012).

11   Soner Çağaptay and Cansın Ersöz, "AKP, alcohol, and government-engineered social change in Turkey," *Hürriyet Daily News* (May 10, 2010).

12   "The 2013 Gezi Park protests," Harvard Divinity School [website] (n.d.). Available at http://rlp.hds.harvard.edu/faq/2013-gezi-park-protests.

13   "Gezi Park protest: brutal denial of the right to peaceful assembly in Turkey," Amnesty International [website] (October 2013). Available at https://www.amnesty. org/en/documents/EUR44/022/2013/en/.

14   Güneş Kömürcüler, "Tweet matters between Taksim–Tahrir squares," *Hürriyet Daily News* (June 7, 2013).

15   For more on the Alevis and their relationship with Islamism and the AKP, see Soner Cagaptay, *The Rise of Turkey: The Twenty-First Century's First Muslim Power* (Lincoln, NE: Potomac, 2014), 86–91.

16   A. Turan Alkan, "Başbakan'a mektup," *Zaman* (June 5, 2013).

17   Galip Dalay, "The Kurdish peace process in the shadow of Turkey's power struggle and the upcoming local elections," Al Jazeera Center for Studies [website] (March 24, 2014). Available at http://studies.aljazeera.net/mritems/Documents/2014/3/2 5/2014325104448251734kurds-turkey%20new.pdf.

18   Wladimir van Wilgenburg, "Turkey's Gulen movement could endanger PKK peace process," Rudaw [website] (June 18, 2013).

19   "Turkish corruption probe row deepens," BBC News [website] (January 7, 2014); Daren Butler and Nick Tattersall, "Turkey dismisses corruption case that has dogged PM Erdogan," Reuters [news agency] (May 2, 2014).

20 "Başbakan'dan ilk dershane açıklaması: Kararlıyız," *Sabah* (November 21, 2013).

21 Berivan Orucoglu, "Why Turkey's mother of all corruption scandals refuses to go away," *Foreign Policy* (January 6, 2015).

22 Jack Moore, "Turkey YouTube ban: full transcript of leaked Erdogan corruption call with son," *International Business Times* (March 27, 2014).

23 Daniel Steinvorth, "Scandal and protests threaten Turkey's AKP," Spiegel Online [website] (March 19, 2014).

24 Andrew Finkel, "In Turkey, police arrest journalists and executives," CNN [website] (December 15, 2014); Kadri Gursel, "AKP pursues scorched-earth tactics against Gulenists," Al-Monitor [website] (September 4, 2014).

25 "Turkey's Kurdish TV channel opens to mixed reviews," Reuters [news agency] (January 2, 2009).

26 "Kurdish can be taught in Turkey's schools, Erdogan says," BBC News [website] (June 12, 2012).

27 Sebnem Arsu, "Intelligence chief must testify," *New York Times* (February 10, 2012).

28 "Turkey's first five referendums: a look back," *Hürriyet Daily News* (July 28, 2010).

29 "Turkish president Gül rules out becoming 'Erdoğan's Medvedev,'" *Hürriyet Daily News* (April 18, 2014).

30 Peter Kenyon, "Turkey's president and his 1,100-room 'White Palace,'" NPR [website] (December 24, 2014).

31 *Republic of Turkey Presidential Election 10 August 2014: OSCE/ODIHR Limited Election Observation Mission Final Report* (Warsaw: Organization for Security and Co-operation in Europe/Office for Democratic Institutions and Human Rights, August 10, 2014). Available at http://www.osce.org/odihr/elections/turkey/126851?download=true. The report was quoted in Pinar Tremblay, "Turkey's first presidential elections were no democracy," *Time* (August 17, 2014).

32 "OSCE alarmed over Turkish PM's intimidation of female journalist," *Hürriyet Daily News* (August 10, 2014).

10 The Future of the Turkish Kurds: Peace or Fire?

1 "The capture of a Kurdish rebel," *New York Times* (February 17, 1999).

2 "Turkey Kurds: PKK chief Ocalan calls for ceasefire," BBC News [website] (March 21, 2013).

3 "Ankara'daki patlamada ölenlerin isim listesi," *Habertürk* (February 18, 2016); "PKK's organization game," Anadolu Ajansı [Turkish state-run press agency] (March 18, 2016).

4 For a good discussion of the history of the Kurds in Turkey, see Kemal Kirişci and Gareth Winrow, *The Kurdish Question and Turkey: An Example of a Trans-State Ethnic Conflict* (Portland, OR: Frank Cass, 1997).

5 "The world factbook: Turkey," CIA [website]. Available at https://www.cia.gov/library/publications/the-world-factbook/geos/tu.html.

6 Soner Cagaptay, *The Rise of Turkey: The Twenty-First Century's First Muslim Power* (Lincoln, NE: Potomac, 2014), 98.

7 Ibid., 82.

8 For a different reading of the Kurds' unique position in Turkey, see Henri Barkey and Graham Fuller, *Turkey's Kurdish Question* (Oxford: Rowman & Littlefield, 1998).

9 Soner Cagaptay, *Islam, Secularism, and Nationalism in Modern Turkey: Who Is a Turk?* (London: Routledge, 2006), 19.

10   For a discussion of Ottomanism and Turkish nationalism in the late Ottoman Empire, see Hasan Kayalı, *Arabs and Young Turks: Ottomanism, Arabism, and Islamism in the Ottoman Empire, 1908–1918* (Berkeley, CA: University of California Press, 1997) and M. Şükrü Hanioğlu, *The Young Turks in Opposition* (Oxford: Oxford University Press, 1995).

11   For a good, in-depth discussion of the PKK issue, see H. Akın Ünver, *Turkey's Kurdish Question: Discourse and Politics since 1990* (New York: Routledge, 2015).

12   Aliza Marcus, *Blood and Belief: The PKK and the Kurdish Fight for Independence* (New York and London: New York University Press, 2007), passim.

13   "Turkey's Kurdish TV channel opens to mixed reviews," Reuters [news agency] (January 2, 2009).

14   "Kurdish can be taught in Turkey's schools, Erdogan says," BBC News [website] (June 12, 2012).

15   "Kurdistan," *Encyclopaedia Britannica* [website] (December 9, 2009). Available at https://www.britannica.com/place/Kurdistan; "Turkish general election 2015," *Hürriyet Daily News* (n.d.).

16   Tim Arango, "Kurds have bigger prize in mind after political gains in Turkey," *New York Times* (June 10, 2015).

17   Henri Barkey, "Turkey's turmoil: why Erdogan and the Kurds are both to blame," *National Interest* (September 25, 2015).

18   Emre Peker, "Turkish fight against Kurdish insurgency spreads," *Wall Street Journal* (February 21, 2016).

19   Soner Cagaptay, "Erdogan's next act," *Wall Street Journal* (November 4, 2015).

20   Denise Natali, "Turkey's protracted PKK problem," Al-Monitor [website] (September 1, 2015).

21   "The truce between Turkey and Kurdish militants is over," *The Economist* (July 26, 2015).

22   "Timeline of terrorism in Turkey," Euronews [website] (December 1, 2016).

23   On the Ankara attack, see Tim Lister, "Ankara terrorist attack: what does it mean for Turkey?" CNN [website] (October 11, 2015). On the attack in Suruc, see "Suruc massacre: at least 30 killed in Turkey border blast," BBC News [website] (July 20, 2015).

24   Soner Cagaptay, Christina Bache Fidan, and Ege Cansu Sacikara, "Turkey and the KRG: an undeclared economic commonwealth," Washington Institute for Near East Policy [website] (March 16, 2015). Available at http://www.washingtoninstitute.org/policy-analysis/view/turkey-and-the-krg-an-undeclared-economic-commonwealth.

25   "55 milyon kişi 'etnik olarak' Türk. KONDA," *Milliyet* (March 22, 2007).

26   For a good review of recent dynamics of the Kurdish issue in Turkey, see Ömer Taşpinar and Gönül Tol, "Turkey and the Kurds: from predicament to opportunity," Brookings [website] (January 22, 2014). Available at https://www.brookings.edu/research/turkey-and-the-kurds-from-predicament-to-opportunity/.

11 Foreign-Policy Gambit

1   "Policy of zero problems with our neighbors," Republic of Turkey Ministry of Foreign Affairs [website] (n.d.). Available at http://www.mfa.gov.tr/policy-of-zero-problems-with-our-neighbors.en.mfa.

2   Mark Landler, "Obama's support of Erdogan is a stark reminder of Turkey's value to US," *New York Times* (July 20, 2016).

3   "Obama reaches out to Muslim world," BBC News [website] (April 6, 2009).

4   Yeliz Candemir, "Turkish soap operas: the unstoppable boom," *Wall Street Journal* (April 29, 2013).

5   Shibley Telhami, "The 2011 Arab public opinion poll," Brookings [website] (November 21, 2011). Available at https://www.brookings.edu/research/the-2011-arab-public-opinion-poll/.

6   "Turkish officials hail Turkey's United Nations Security Council seat," *Hürriyet* (October 18, 2008).

7   James Kanter, "Gates criticizes Turkey vote against sanctions," *New York Times* (June 11, 2010).

8   "Hem tatil hem siyaset için Bodrum'da," *Hürriyet* (August 5, 2008).

9   Soner Cagaptay, "Next up: Turkey vs. Iran," *New York Times* (February 14, 2012).

10 Landler, "Obama's support of Erdogan."

11 Soner Cagaptay, "Obama, Erdogan find shared interests," *Washington Post* (November 11, 2011).

12 Ibid.

13 Soner Cagaptay, "How the US military lost its favor for Turkey," Foreign Policy Concepts [website] (September 24, 2015).

14 Soner Cagaptay, "Turkey seeks to lock in long-term security," *Washington Post* (November 8, 2013).

15 Cagaptay, "How the US military lost its favor for Turkey."

16 Ibid.

17 Aaron Stein, "Turkey did nothing about the jihadists in its midst—until it was too late," *Foreign Policy* (July 1, 2016).

18 "Egyptian, Greek military forces start joint exercise in Greece," Ahram Online [website] (December 7, 2015); "Egypt, Russia to hold joint military exercises in mid-October," Reuters [news agency] (October 12, 2016).

19 Mustafa Akyol, "How Morsi matters in Turkish politics," Al-Monitor [website] (May 17, 2015); "Erdoğan'ın sözlerine ABD, İsrail ve Mısır'dan tepki," *Hürriyet* (August 21, 2013).

20 Dion Nissenbaum, Emre Peker, and James Marson, "Turkey shoots down Russian military jet," *Wall Street Journal* (November 24, 2015); Jordan Fabian, "Obama: Turkey has right to defend its airspace," *The Hill* (November 24, 2015).

21 For a review of Turkish–Russian relations in recent years, see Soli Özel, "The crisis in Turkish–Russian relations," Center for American Progress [website] (May 10, 2016). Available at https://www.americanprogress.org/issues/security/reports/2016/05/10/137131/the-crisis-in-turkish-russian-relations/.

22 "The future of world religions: population growth projections, 2010–2050," Pew Research Center [website] (April 2, 2015). Available at http://www.pewforum.org/2015/04/02/religious-projections-2010-2050/.

23 For a discussion of Turkish foreign policy before the AKP, see Lenore Martin and Dimitris Keridis, *The Future of Turkish Foreign Policy* (Cambridge, MA: MIT Press, 2004) and Barry Rubin and Kemal Kirişci (eds), *Turkey in World Politics: An Emerging Multiregional Power* (Boulder, CO: Lynne Rienner, 2001).

24 Brett Daniel Shehadey, "Is Turkey serving up Assad for Thanksgiving?" In Homeland Security [website] (November 23, 2014).

12 Ending Turkey's Crisis

1   "Başbakan Ahmet Davutoğlu'ndan 'beyaz toros' çıkışı," *Hürriyet* (October 20, 2015).
2   Jessica Michek, "Terror attacks in Turkey: what you need to know," Bipartisan Policy Center [website] (March 23, 2016). Available at http://bipartisanpolicy.org/blog/terror-attacks-turkey/.
3   "Death toll rises to 265 in failed Turkey coup: official," Reuters [news agency] (July 16, 2016).
4   Metin Gurcan, "Why Turkey's coup didn't stand a chance," Al-Monitor [website] (July 17, 2016).
5   "'Lozan'da masaya bunlar otursaydı ülkeyi "parsel parsel" satar, "Ne istediler de vermedik" der, sonra da "Kandırıldık" diyerek sıyrılmaya çalışırlardı,'" T24 [website] (September 29, 2016).
6   "11 fugitive soldiers in Erdoğan assassination team captured," *Daily Sabah* (August 1, 2016).
7   Ian Traynor, "Bitter Turkey finally lifts veto on Danish PM as Nato chief," *Guardian* (April 4, 2009).
8   Krishnadev Calamur, "Jokes about Erdogan aren't funny in Germany," *Atlantic* (April 15, 2016).
9   For more on this topic, see Mustafa Akyol, "Whatever happened to the 'Turkish model'?" *New York Times* (May 5, 2016); Kemal Kirişci, "Turkey and the international liberal order: what happened?" Brookings [website] (February 23, 2016).
10 "Turkey: freedom of the press 2016," Freedom House [website] (2016). Available at https://freedomhouse.org/report/freedom-press/2016/turkey.
11 "Reporters without Borders publishes the first worldwide press freedom index," Reporters without Borders [website] (October 2002). Available at https://rsf.org/en/reporters-without-borders-publishes-first-worldwide-press-freedom-index-october-2002; "Data of press freedom ranking 2016: index details," Reporters without Borders [website] (2016). Available at https://rsf.org/en/ranking_table.
12 Ricardo Hausmann, Laura D. Tyson, and Saadia Zahidi, *The Global Gender Gap Report 2006* (Geneva: World Economic Forum, 2006). Available at http://www3.weforum.org/docs/WEF_GenderGap_Report_2006.pdf.
13 Constanze Letsch, "Turkish doctors face fines for elective caesareans," *Guardian* (July 13, 2012).
14 "10 bin TL evlilik kredisi devlet destekli 2016," Habere Davet [website] (December 10, 2015).
15 "Milli Eğitim Müdürü'nden skandal sözler!" *Cumhuriyet* (August 2, 2013).
16 "Kadın belediye başkanının ilk icraatı 'kadın otobüsü,'" *Radikal* (October 4, 2014).
17 "Cumhurbaşkanı Erdoğan Kadın ve Adalet toplantısında konuştu," *Hürriyet* (November 24, 2014).
18 Soner Cagaptay and Cem Yolbulan, "Assessing the new AKP cabinet," Washington Institute for Near East Policy [website] (May 31, 2016). Available at http://www.washingtoninstitute.org/policy-analysis/view/assessing-the-new-akp-cabinet.
19 "İlköğretim ve eğitim kanunu ile bazı kanunlarda değişiklik yapılmasına dair kanun: kanun no: 6287," *Resmi Gazete* [official gazette of the Republic of Turkey] (March 30, 2012). Available at http://www.resmigazete.gov.tr/eskiler/2012/04/20120411-8.htm.
20 Alan Makovsky, *Re-educating Turkey: AKP Efforts to Promote Religious Values in Turkish Schools* (Washington DC: Center for American Progress, 2015). Available

at https://cdn.americanprogress.org/wp-content/uploads/2015/12/09115835/Re-EducatingTurkey.pdf.

21 "Cumhuriyeti asıl yıkacak şey işte bu," Odatv [website] (October 16, 2016).

22 "'Hahambaşı'nın torunu imam hatibe yerleştirildi' iddiasi," T24 [website] (August 30, 2014).

23 "Recep Tayyip Erdoğan address to the AKP youth branch," YouTube [website] (March 31, 2012). Available at https://www.youtube.com/watch?v=RICvSMHJ9q4a.

24 Soner Cagaptay, "Can Erdogan stay at the helm?" Washington Institute for Near East Policy [website] (May 2015). Available at http://www.washingtoninstitute.org/policy-analysis/view/can-erdogan-stay-at-the-helm.

25 Ibid.

26 "Hakaret davası bilançosu," *Hürriyet* (January 31, 2016).

27 "Car bomb kills 18 at a military checkpoint in Turkey," *New York Times* (October 9, 2016).

28 For a discussion on Islamization in Turkey, see Jenny White, *Islamist Mobilization in Turkey: A Study in Vernacular Politics* (Seattle, WA: University of Washington Press, 2002).

29 Şahin Çakmaklı, "İşte tarih tarih AKP'nin milli bayram yasakları," Odatv [website] (October 17, 2016); Elif Batuman, "Ottomania," *New Yorker* (February 17, 2014).

30 For a short but concise review on the instrumentalization of the Ottoman legacy under the AKP, see Nick Danforth, "Turkey's new maps are reclaiming the Ottoman Empire," *Foreign Policy* [website] (October 23, 2016).

31 "Eğitim Reformu Girişimi'nin Milli Eğitim Bakanlığı taslak öğretim programları inceleme ve değerlendirmesi," Eğitim Reformu Girişimi [website] (February 10, 2017). Available at http://www.egitimreformugirisimi.org/tr/node/1807.

32 "New World Bank report looks at Turkey's rise to the threshold of high-income status and the challenges remaining," World Bank [website] (December 10, 2014). Available at http://www.worldbank.org/en/news/press-release/2014/12/10/new-world-bank-report-looks-at-turkey-rise-to-threshold-of-high-income-and-challenges-remaining.

33 "Turkey's transitions: integration, inclusion, institutions," World Bank [website] (December 2014). Available at http://www.worldbank.org/en/country/turkey/publication/turkeys-transitions-integration-inclusion-institutions.

34 "Turkey: GDP per capita (current US$)," World Bank [website] (n.d.). Available at http://data.worldbank.org/indicator/NY.GDP.PCAP.CD?locations=TR.

35 Mehmet Cetingulec, "Where has Turkey's foreign direct investment gone?" Al-Monitor [website] (October 13, 2016).

36 Orhan Pamuk, *A Strangeness in My Mind* (New York: Vintage International, 2015), 584.

37 "Gross domestic product 2015, PPP," World Bank [website] (October 11, 2016). Available at http://databank.worldbank.org/data/download/GDP_PPP.pdf.

38 Halil Karaveli, "Erdogan's Journey," *Foreign Affairs* (December 2016), 131; Timur Kuran, "Turkey's electoral dictatorship," Project Syndicate [website] (April 10, 2014).

Bibliography

Books

Ahmad, Feroz, *The Turkish Experiment in Democracy, 1950–75* (London: Hurst, 1977).
—— *The Making of Modern Turkey* (London and New York: Routledge, 1993).
Barkey, Henri, and Graham Fuller, *Turkey's Kurdish Question* (Oxford: Rowman & Littlefield, 1998).
Başbakan Prof. Dr. Necmettin Erbakan'ın TBMM Grup Toplantısında Yaptığı Konuşmalar (4 Temmuz 1996–24 Aralık 1996) (Ankara: Başbakanlık Basımevi, 1997).
Cagaptay, Soner, *Islam, Secularism, and Nationalism in Modern Turkey: Who Is a Turk?* (London: Routledge, 2006).
—— *The Rise of Turkey: The Twenty-First Century's First Muslim Power* (Lincoln, NE: Potomac, 2014).
Çakır, Ruşen, *Ayet ve Slogan: Türkiye'de İslami oluşumlar* (Istanbul: Metis Yayınları, 1990).
—— *Ne şeriat ne demokrasi: Refah Partisini anlamak* (Istanbul: Metis Yayınları, 1994).
Çakır, Ruşen, and Fehmi Çalmuk, *Recep Tayyip Erdoğan: Bir dönüşüm öyküsü* (Istanbul: Metis Yayınları, 2001).
Çakır, Ruşen, and Semih Sakallı, *100 soruda Erdoğan x Gülen savaşı* (Istanbul: Metis Yayınları, 2014).
Çakır, Ruşen, İrfan Bozan, and Balkan Talu, *İmam Hatip Liseleri: Efsaneler ve Gerçekler* (Istanbul: TESEV Yayınları, 2004).
Çelik, Yasemin, *Contemporary Turkish Foreign Policy* (Westport, CT: Praeger, 1999).
Cook, Steven, *Ruling but Not Governing* (Baltimore, MD: Johns Hopkins University Press, 2007).
Davutoğlu, Ahmet, *Stratejik derinlik* (Istanbul: Küre Yayınları, 2001).
Eligür, Banu, *The Mobilization of Political Islam in Turkey* (New York: Cambridge University Press, 2010).
Erbakan, Necmettin, *Adil ekonomik düzen* (Ankara: Semih Ofset, 1991).
Göçek, Fatma Müge, *The Transformation of Turkey: Redefining State and Society from the Ottoman Empire to the Modern Era* (London: I.B.Tauris, 2011).
Hanioğlu, M. Şükrü, *The Young Turks in Opposition* (Oxford: Oxford University Press, 1995).
Heper, Metin, *İsmet İnönü: The Making of a Turkish Statesman* (Leiden: Brill, 1998).
Houston, Christopher, *Islam, Kurds and the Turkish Nation State* (Oxford: Berg, 2001).
Israeli, Raphael, *Muslim Anti-Semitism in Christian Europe* (New Brunswick, NJ: Transaction, 2009).
Jenkins, Gareth, *Political Islam in Turkey: Running West, Heading East?* (New York: Palgrave Macmillan, 2008).
Kaplan, Sefa, *Recep Tayyip Erdoğan* (Istanbul: Dogan, 2007).
Kayalı, Hasan, *Arabs and Young Turks: Ottomanism, Arabism, and Islamism in the Ottoman Empire, 1908–1918* (Berkeley, CA: University of California Press, 1997).

Kirişci, Kemal, and Gareth Winrow, *The Kurdish Question and Turkey: An Example of a Trans-State Ethnic Conflict* (Portland, OR: Frank Cass, 1997).

MacLean, Gerald, *Abdullah Gül and the Making of the New Turkey* (London: Oneworld, 2014).

Mango, Andrew, *Ataturk: The Biography of the Founder of Modern Turkey* (New York: Overlook Press, 1999).

Marcus, Aliza, *Blood and Belief: The PKK and the Kurdish Fight for Independence* (New York and London: New York University Press, 2007).

Martin, Lenore, and Dimitris Keridis, *The Future of Turkish Foreign Policy* (Cambridge, MA: MIT Press, 2004).

Mufti, Malik, *Daring and Caution in Turkish Strategic Culture: Republic at Sea* (New York: Palgrave Macmillan, 2009).

Okutan, Çağatay, *Tek parti döneminde azınlık politikaları* (Istanbul: İstanbul Bilgi Yayınları, 2004).

Pamuk, Orhan, *A Strangeness in My Mind* (New York: Vintage International, 2015).

Rubin, Barry, and Kemal Kirişci (eds), *Turkey in World Politics: An Emerging Multiregional Power* (Boulder, CO: Lynne Rienner, 2001).

Ünver, H. Akın, *Turkey's Kurdish Question: Discourse and Politics since 1990* (New York: Routledge, 2015).

VanderLippe, John M., *The Politics of Turkish Democracy: İsmet İnönü and the Formation of the Multi-Party System 1938–1950* (Albany, NY: SUNY Press, 2005).

White, Jenny, *Islamist Mobilization in Turkey: A Study in Vernacular Politics* (Seattle, WA: University of Washington Press, 2002).

Yavuz, M. Hakan, *Islamic Political Identity in Turkey* (New York: Oxford University Press, 2003).

Zurcher, Erik, *Turkey: A Modern History* (New York: I.B.Tauris, 2004).

Articles from newspapers, magazines, and news websites

"10 bin TL evlilik kredisi devlet destekli 2016," Habere Davet [website] (December 10, 2015).

"11 fugitive soldiers in Erdoğan assassination team captured," *Daily Sabah* (August 1, 2016).

"15 Temmuz gecesi meydanlara inenlerle ilgili önemli gelişme!" *Sabah* (August 16, 2016).

"55 milyon kişi 'etnik olarak' Türk. KONDA," *Milliyet* (March 22, 2007).

"ABD basını Kurtlar Vadisi'ne giden Emine Erdoğan'ı eleştirdi," Haber Vitrini [website] (February 16, 2006).

"AKP de ittihatçı çıktı," Odatv [website] (June 15, 2014).

Akyol, Kursat, "Will Turkey reinstate death penalty?" Al-Monitor [website] (July 29, 2016).

Akyol, Mustafa, "Whatever happened to the 'Turkish model'?" *New York Times* (May 5, 2016).

——— "How Morsi matters in Turkish politics," Al-Monitor [website] (May 17, 2015).

"Albright warns Turkey to guard its democracy," *New York Times* (June 14, 1997).

Alkan, A. Turan, "Başbakan'a mektup," *Zaman* (June 5, 2013).

Altan, Ahmet, "Gazetecilikten tutuklanmadılar," *Taraf* (March 7, 2011).

"Anayasa değişikliği 1'inci tur görüşmeleri," *Sabah* (April 28, 2010).

"Ankara'daki patlamada ölenlerin isim listesi," *Habertürk* (February 18, 2016).

Arango, Tim, "Kurds have bigger prize in mind after political gains in Turkey," *New York Times* (June 10, 2015).

——— "Nightclub massacre in Istanbul exposes Turkey's deepening fault lines," *New York Times* (January 1, 2017).

Arsu, Sebnem, "Intelligence chief must testify," *New York Times* (February 10, 2012).

Arsu, Sebnem, and Alan Cowell, "Turkey expels Israeli envoy in dispute over raid," *New York Times* (September 2, 2011).

Barkey, Henri, "Turkey's turmoil: why Erdogan and the Kurds are both to blame," *National Interest* (September 25, 2015).

"Başbakan Ahmet Davutoğlu'ndan 'beyaz toros' çıkışı," *Hürriyet* (October 20, 2015).

"Başbakan'dan ilk dershane açıklaması: Kararlıyız," *Sabah* (November 21, 2013).

Batuman, Elif, "Ottomania," *New Yorker* (February 17, 2014).

Baydar, Yavuz, "Family boycotts retrial for murder of Turkish-Armenian journalist," Al-Monitor [website] (September 20, 2013).

Bendern, Paul de, and Thomas Grove, "Turkish-Armenian editor shot dead in Istanbul," Reuters [news agency] (January 19, 2007).

Bilefsky, Dan, and Sebnem Arsu, "Sponsor of flotilla tied to elite of Turkey," *New York Times* (July 15, 2010).

Butler, Daren, and Nick Tattersall, "Turkey dismisses corruption case that has dogged PM Erdogan," Reuters [news agency] (May 2, 2014).

Cagaptay, Soner, "Ankara dispatch: eastern heading," *New Republic* (September 8, 2004).

——— "Turkish troubles," *Wall Street Journal* (July 31, 2007).

——— "Ending Turkey's nightmare," *Hürriyet Daily News* (August 3, 2011).

——— "Obama, Erdogan find shared interests," *Washington Post* (November 11, 2011).

——— "Next up: Turkey vs. Iran," *New York Times* (February 14, 2012).

——— "Turkey seeks to lock in long-term security," *Washington Post* (November 8, 2013).

——— "How the US military lost its favor for Turkey," Foreign Policy Concepts [website] (September 24, 2015).

——— "Erdogan's next act," *Wall Street Journal* (November 4, 2015).

——— "Kemal Erdoğan's second Turkish revolution," *Politico* [website] (January 27, 2016).

——— "The coup attempt is bad news for Turkey's democracy," *Washington Post* (July 16, 2016).

Çağaptay, Soner, and Cansın Ersöz, "AKP, alcohol, and government-engineered social change in Turkey," *Hürriyet Daily News* (May 10, 2010).

Cagaptay, Soner, and Duden Yegenoglu, "Left-wing monster: Abdullah Ocalan," FrontPage Magazine [website] (January 6, 2006).

Çakmaklı, Şahin, "İşte tarih tarih AKP'nin milli bayram yasakları," Odatv [website] (October 17, 2016).

Calamur, Krishnadev, "Jokes about Erdogan aren't funny in Germany," *Atlantic* (April 15, 2016).

Candemir, Yeliz, "Turkish soap operas: the unstoppable boom," *Wall Street Journal* (April 29, 2013).

"The capture of a Kurdish rebel," *New York Times* (February 17, 1999).

"Car bomb kills 18 at a military checkpoint in Turkey," *New York Times* (October 9, 2016).

Cetingulec, Mehmet, "Should they stay or should they go? Turkey leaves foreign investors at odds," Al-Monitor [website] (April 1, 2016).

——— "Where has Turkey's foreign direct investment gone?" Al-Monitor [website] (October 13, 2016).

"Ciller's chance," *The Economist* (June 19, 1997).

Çizmeci, Şule, "Tayyip Erdoğan'ın 75 bin kişilik seçim ordusu," *Milliyet* (February 15, 1994).

"Cumhurbaşkanı Erdoğan Kadın ve Adalet toplantısında konuştu," *Hürriyet* (November 24, 2014).

"Cumhurbaşkanı Erdoğan: Menderes gibi beyaz kefenimizi giyerek yola çıktık," *Sabah* (May 27, 2016).

"Cumhuriyeti asıl yıkacak şey işte bu," Odatv [website] (October 16, 2016).

Danforth, Nick, "Turkey's new maps are reclaiming the Ottoman Empire," *Foreign Policy* [website] (October 23, 2016).

"Danıştay kararları yatırımı engelliyor," *Yeni Şafak* (April 6, 2006).

"Death toll rises to 265 in failed Turkey coup: official," Reuters [news agency] (July 16, 2016).

"Debate on religion takes over politics in Ankara," *Hürriyet Daily News* (February 2, 2012).

Demirelli, Fatma, "Turkey not fretting over conservatives," *Hürriyet Daily News* (June 28, 2005).

Demirtaş, Serkan, "Sezer: the most criticized president ever," *Hürriyet Daily News* (August 29, 2007).

Dilipak, Abdurrahman, "En derin devlet," *Vakit* (October 16, 2009).

———"Lanetli süreç: 28 Şubat," *Yeni Akit* (February 27, 2015).

Dorsey, James M., "Judgment day: Islamists in Turkey make deep inroads in mainstream society," *Wall Street Journal* (June 18, 1997).

Durmuş, Yusuf Ziya, "Erbakan commemorated on anniversary of his death," *Daily Sabah* (February 27, 2015).

"DYP: Özal İdi Aminleşiyor," *Milliyet* (July 12, 1986).

"Egyptian, Greek military forces start joint exercise in Greece," Ahram Online [website] (December 7, 2015).

"Egypt, Russia to hold joint military exercises in mid-October," Reuters [news agency] (October 12, 2016).

"Eminonu Municipality and the Hizmet Foundation: serving the people of Eminonu?" *Hürriyet Daily News* (December 18, 1996).

Er, İsmail, and Emre Oktay, "Başbakan Erdoğan Başakşehir Stadı'nı açtı 3 gol birden attı," *Hürriyet* (July 27, 2014).

"Erdogan pulls it off," *The Economist* (September 13, 2010).

"Erdoğan, Menderes'in anıt mezarını ziyaret etti," *Cumhuriyet* (September 17, 2010).

"Erdoğan: Babam çok otoriter bir babaydı; yanlış yaptığımızda hesaplaşırdı," T24 [website] (September 3, 2013).

"Erdoğan: Simit ve su satar, kitap alırdım," NTV [website] (July 23, 2012).

"Erdoğan: Türbanda söz hakkı ulemanındır," *Hürriyet* (November 16, 2005).

"Erdoğan'ın karikatüre tazminat davasına ret," *Hürriyet* (November 17, 2006).

"Erdoğan'ın sözlerine ABD, İsrail ve Mısır'dan tepki," *Hürriyet* (August 21, 2013).

"Ergenekon'da dava sayısı Masonlarla 15 oldu," Haber7 [website] (February 6, 2011).

Ergin, Sedat, "O albaylar gitti darbeciler geldi," *Hürriyet* (July 23, 2016).

Erol, Reşat Nuri, "Erbakanın Adil Düzen söyleminin teorisi," *Milli Gazete* (March 2, 2016).

Fabian, Jordan, "Obama: Turkey has right to defend its airspace," *The Hill* (November 24, 2015).

"Farklı zamanlarda Haliç'e çok kafa yormak zorunda kalan üç kişi anlatıyor," *Hürriyet* (November 19, 1997).

Finkel, Andrew, "In Turkey, police arrest journalists and executives," CNN [website] (December 15, 2014).

"Fury after police pictured posing with Dink murder suspect," *Guardian* (February 2, 2007).

Göktepe, Cihat, "The Menderes period (1950–1960)," *Journal of Turkish Weekly* [website] (April 13, 2005).

Gurcan, Metin, "Why Turkey's coup didn't stand a chance," Al-Monitor [website] (July 17, 2016).

Gursel, Kadri, "AKP pursues scorched-earth tactics against Gulenists," Al-Monitor [website] (September 4, 2014).

—— "Erdogan Islamizes education system to raise 'devout youth,'" Al-Monitor [website] (December 9, 2014).

"'Hahambaşı'nın torunu imam hatibe yerleştirildi' iddiasi," T24 [website] (August 30, 2014).

"Hakaret davası bilançosu," *Hürriyet* (January 31, 2016).

Harvey, Benjamin, and Associated Press, "Mass protest at Turkish-Armenian editor Hrant Dink's funeral," *Guardian* (January 24, 2007).

Hauslohner, Abigail, Karen DeYoung, and Valerie Strauss, "He's 77, frail and lives in Pennsylvania. Turkey says he's a coup mastermind," *Washington Post* (August 3, 2016).

"Hem tatil hem siyaset için Bodrum'da," *Hürriyet* (August 5, 2008).

Humire, Joseph M., "Charter schools vulnerable to controversial Turkish movement," *The Hill* (March 10, 2016).

Idiz, Semih, "Islamists in disarray after Israeli apology," *Hürriyet Daily News* (April 11, 2010).

"İstanbul'da gözler Refah'ta," *Milliyet* (October 22, 1992).

"Kaddafi: Türkiye'nin hava sahası neden açık?" *Radikal* (March 9, 2011).

"Kadın belediye başkanının ilk icraatı 'kadın otobüsü,'" *Radikal* (October 4, 2014).

Kamm, Henry, "Cleanup is reviving Istanbul's Golden Horn," *New York Times* (June 1, 1986).

—— "Local elections in Turkey may set fate of sagging national cabinet," *New York Times* (March 28, 1994).

Kanter, James, "Gates criticizes Turkey vote against sanctions," *New York Times* (June 11, 2010).

Karaveli, Halil, "Erdogan's Journey," *Foreign Affairs* (December 2016).

"Kasımpaşa'dan Çankaya'ya, yoksulluktan yolsuzluk suçlamalarına Erdoğan'ın hayatı," T24 [website] (August 10, 2014).

Kenyon, Peter, "Turkey's president and his 1,100-room 'White Palace,'" NPR [website] (December 24, 2014).

Kinzer, Stephen, "Pro-Islamic premier steps down in Turkey under army pressure," *New York Times* (June 19, 1997).

Kireklo, Gül, "Yaprak hışırtısını yağmur sanıp cama koşardım," *Habertürk* (August 7, 2007).

Kirişci, Kemal, "Turkey and the international liberal order: what happened?" Brookings [website] (February 23, 2016).

Knickmeyer, Ellen, "In Turkish vote, ruling party wins by wide margin," *Washington Post* (July 23, 2007).

Knowlton, Brian, "US warns Iraq on new government," *New York Times* (March 21, 2005).

Kömürcüler, Güneş, "Tweet matters between Taksim–Tahrir squares," *Hürriyet Daily News* (June 7, 2013).

"Kronoloji: 28 Şubat'a giden yol," Al Jazeera Türk [website] (December 27, 2013).

Kucuksahin, Sukru, "Turkish students up in arms over Islamization of education," Al-Monitor [website] (June 20, 2016).

Kuran, Timur, "Turkey's electoral dictatorship," Project Syndicate [website] (April 10, 2014).

"Kurdish can be taught in Turkey's schools, Erdogan says," BBC News [website] (June 12, 2012).

Landler, Mark, "Obama's support of Erdogan is a stark reminder of Turkey's value to US," *New York Times* (July 20, 2016).

Letsch, Constanze, "Turkish doctors face fines for elective caesareans," *Guardian* (July 13, 2012).

Lister, Tim, "Ankara terrorist attack: what does it mean for Turkey?" CNN [website] (October 11, 2015).

"'Lozan'da masaya bunlar otursaydı ülkeyi "parsel parsel" satar, "Ne istediler de vermedik" der, sonra da "Kandırıldık" diyerek sıyrılmaya çalışırlardı,'" T24 [website] (September 29, 2016).

Merritt, Giles, "Europe should be doing more to bring Turkey into the fold," *International Herald Tribune* (June 28, 1994).

"Milli Eğitim Müdürü'nden skandal sözler!" *Cumhuriyet* (August 2, 2013).

Montalbano, William, "The army's prestige is growing amid political scandal," *Guardian* (November 4, 1994).

Moore, Jack, "Turkey YouTube ban: full transcript of leaked Erdogan corruption call with son," *International Business Times* (March 27, 2014).

Natali, Denise, "Turkey's protracted PKK problem," Al-Monitor [website] (September 1, 2015).

"Nedim Şener: Ramazan Akyürek, Dink soruşturmasında kilit isim," BBC Türkçe [website] (February 26, 2015).

Newman, Barry, "Turning eastward: Islamic party's gains in Istanbul stir fears of a radical Turkey," *Wall Street Journal* (September 12, 1994).

Nissenbaum, Dion, Emre Peker, and James Marson, "Turkey shoots down Russian military jet," *Wall Street Journal* (November 24, 2015).

"Obama reaches out to Muslim world," BBC News [website] (April 6, 2009).

Öktener, Aslı, "Nurdan Erbuğ'un pişmanlığı!" *Milliyet* (February 8, 2001).

Ortaylı, İlber, "Atatürk–İnönü çatışması," *Milliyet* (December 4, 2015).

Orucoglu, Berivan, "Why Turkey's mother of all corruption scandals refuses to go away," *Foreign Policy* (January 6, 2015).

"OSCE alarmed over Turkish PM's intimidation of female journalist," *Hürriyet Daily News* (August 10, 2014).

"'Ottoman Hearths' accused in attacks targeting parties, media," *Hürriyet Daily News* (September 12, 2015).

Özedincik, Sinan, "Artık eski Gülay yok," *Sabah* (September 7, 2012).

Özkök, Ertuğrul, "Beni maymun olarak çizseler," *Hürriyet* (March 2, 2009).

Parkinson, Joe, "Dogan shares jump on sale speculation," *Wall Street Journal* (October 14, 2010).

——— "Dismay over Turkish rates," *Wall Street Journal* (January 12, 2012).

Peker, Emre, "Turkish fight against Kurdish insurgency spreads," *Wall Street Journal* (February 21, 2016).

"PKK's organization game," Anadolu Ajansı [Turkish state-run press agency] (March 18, 2016).

Pope, Hugh, "Istanbul and Ankara set to fall to Islamists," *Independent* (March 29, 1994).

——— "Turkey's season of discontent: born-again democrats are disappointed with new prime minister Tansu Ciller, corruption and the army's grip on government," *Los Angeles Times* (August 2, 1994).

"Refah'tan yeni sesler," *Milliyet* (September 19, 1993).

Rugman, Jonathan, "Turkish PM fights off poll threat," *Guardian* (March 29, 1994).

Ryan, Yasmine, "Uncovering Algeria's civil war," Al Jazeera [website] (December 18, 2016).

Shehadey, Brett Daniel, "Is Turkey serving up Assad for Thanksgiving?" In Homeland Security [website] (November 23, 2014).

Smith, Roff, "Why Turkey lifted its ban on the Islamic headscarf," *National Geographic* (October 12, 2013).

Sokollu, Senada, "Mosque construction sparks controversy in Istanbul," Deutsche Welle [website] (August 23, 2013).

Stein, Aaron, "Turkey did nothing about the jihadists in its midst—until it was too late," *Foreign Policy* (July 1, 2016).

Steinvorth, Daniel, "Scandal and protests threaten Turkey's AKP," Spiegel Online [website] (March 19, 2014).

"Suruc massacre: at least 30 killed in Turkey border blast," BBC News [website] (July 20, 2015).

"Sweeping detentions of former top generals exempts Özkök," *Hürriyet Daily News* (February 22, 2010).

Tavernise, Sabrina, "Trial in editor's killing opens, testing rule of law in Turkey," *New York Times* (July 3, 2007).

Tharoor, Ishaan, "*Time* meets Turkish prime minister Recep Tayyip Erdogan," *Time* (September 26, 2011).

"Timeline of terrorism in Turkey," Euronews [website] (December 1, 2016).

Traynor, Ian, "Bitter Turkey finally lifts veto on Danish PM as Nato chief," *Guardian* (April 4, 2009).

——"Gaza flotilla raid draws furious response from Turkey's prime minister," *Guardian* (June 1, 2010).

Tremblay, Pinar, "Turkey's first presidential elections were no democracy," *Time* (August 17, 2014).

"The truce between Turkey and Kurdish militants is over," *The Economist* (July 26, 2015).

"Türban tartışmaları 60'larda başlamıştı," *Cumhuriyet* (October 5, 2010).

"Turkey builds nearly 9,000 mosques in 10 years," *Hürriyet Daily News* (September 16, 2016).

"Turkey Kurds: PKK chief Ocalan calls for ceasefire," BBC News [website] (March 21, 2013).

"Turkey's charismatic pro-Islamic leader," BBC News [website] (November 4, 2002).

"Turkey's first five referendums: a look back," *Hürriyet Daily News* (July 28, 2010).

"Turkey's Kurdish TV channel opens to mixed reviews," Reuters [news agency] (January 2, 2009).

"Turkey's top military leaders quit," Al Jazeera [website] (July 30, 2011).

"Turkish corruption probe row deepens," BBC News [website] (January 7, 2014).

"Turkish economy shrinks for first time since 2009," *Hürriyet Daily News* (December 12, 2016).

"Turkish general election 2015," *Hürriyet Daily News* (n.d.).

"Turkish officials hail Turkey's United Nations Security Council seat," *Hürriyet* (October 18, 2008).

"Turkish president Gül rules out becoming 'Erdoğan's Medvedev,'" *Hürriyet Daily News* (April 18, 2014).

Tuysuz, Gul, and Sabrina Tavernise, "Top generals quit in group, stunning Turks," *New York Times* (July 29, 2011).

Ünsal, Ünal, "Seçim barajı: Anayasa Mahkemesi'nin tarihi sorumluluğu," Diken [website] (December 12, 2014).

"Vali ve Jandarma Komutanı meydana birlikte seslendi," *Milliyet* (July 16, 2016).

"Vural Savaş: AİHM'in kararı doğru," *Hürriyet* (July 31, 2001).

Wilgenburg, Wladimir van, "Turkey's Gulen movement could endanger PKK peace process," Rudaw [website] (June 18, 2013).

"Yeni HSYK üyeleri göreve başlıyor," Anadolu Ajansı [Turkish state-run press agency] (October 26, 2014).

Yılmaz, Serpil, "Suriye ile yeni bir dönem," *Milliyet* (January 7, 2004).

Zeyrek, Deniz, "1 Mart mesajının adresi," *Hürriyet* (February 8, 2016).

Policy analysis and reports

"The 2013 Gezi Park protests," Harvard Divinity School [website] (n.d.). Available at http://rlp.hds.harvard.edu/faq/2013-gezi-park-protests.

Acemoglu, Daron, and Murat Üçer, "Why Turkish growth ended: an institutional perspective," Centre for Economic Policy Research [website] (November 18, 2015). Available at http://voxeu.org/article/why-turkish-growth-ended.

"Antisemitism and the Turkish Islamist 'Milli Gorus' movement: Zionists/Jews 'bacteria,' 'disease,'" Middle East Media and Research Institute [website] (September 1, 2007). Available at https://www.memri.org/reports/antisemitism-and-turkish-islamist-milli-gorus-movement-zionistsjews-%E2%80%9Cbacteria%E2%80%9D-%E2%80%9Cdisease%E2%80%9D.

Brinke, Koen, "The Turkish 2000–01 banking crisis," Rabobank [website] (September 4, 2013). Available at https://economics.rabobank.com/publications/2013/september/the-turkish-2000-01-banking-crisis/.

Cagaptay, Soner, "Turkey at a crossroads: preserving Ankara's Western orientation," Washington Institute for Near East Policy [website] (October 2005). Available at http://www.washingtoninstitute.org/policy-analysis/view/turkey-at-a-crossroads-preserving-ankaras-western-orientation.

——"What's really behind Turkey's coup arrests?" Washington Institute for Near East Policy [website] (February 25, 2010). Available at http://www.washingtoninstitute.org/policy-analysis/view/whats-really-behind-turkeys-coup-arrests.

——"Turkey after the constitutional referendum," Washington Institute for Near East Policy [website] (September 23, 2010). Available at http://www.washingtoninstitute.org/policy-analysis/view/turkey-after-the-constitutional-referendum-implications-for-washington.

——"Can Erdogan stay at the helm?" Washington Institute for Near East Policy [website] (May 2015). Available at http://www.washingtoninstitute.org/policy-analysis/view/can-erdogan-stay-at-the-helm.

Cagaptay, Soner, and Cem Yolbulan, "Assessing the new AKP cabinet," Washington Institute for Near East Policy [website] (May 31, 2016). Available at http://www.washingtoninstitute.org/policy-analysis/view/assessing-the-new-akp-cabinet.

Cagaptay, Soner, Christina Bache Fidan, and Ege Cansu Sacikara, "Turkey and the KRG: an undeclared economic commonwealth," Washington Institute for Near East Policy [website] (March 16, 2015). Available at http://www.washingtoninstitute.org/policy-analysis/view/turkey-and-the-krg-an-undeclared-economic-commonwealth.

Cornell, Svante, and M. K. Kaya, "The Naqshbandi–Khalidi order and political Islam in Turkey," Hudson Institute [website] (September 3, 2015). Available at http://

www.hudson.org/research/11601-the-naqshbandi-khalidi-order-and-political-islam-in-turkey.

Dalay, Galip, "The Kurdish peace process in the shadow of Turkey's power struggle and the upcoming local elections," Al Jazeera Center for Studies [website] (March 24, 2014). Available at http://studies.aljazeera.net/mritems/Documents/2014/3/2 5/2014325104448251734kurds-turkey%20new.pdf.

"Data of press freedom ranking 2016: index details," Reporters without Borders [website] (2016). Available at https://rsf.org/en/ranking_table.

"Eğitim Reformu Girişimi'nin Milli Eğitim Bakanlığı taslak öğretim programları inceleme ve değerlendirmesi," Eğitim Reformu Girişimi [website] (February 10, 2017). Available at http://www.egitimreformugirisimi.org/tr/node/1807.

"The future of world religions: population growth projections, 2010–2050," Pew Research Center [website] (April 2, 2015). Available at http://www.pewforum.org/2015/04/02/religious-projections-2010-2050/.

"Gezi Park protest: brutal denial of the right to peaceful assembly in Turkey," Amnesty International [website] (October 2013). Available at https://www.amnesty.org/en/documents/EUR44/022/2013/en/.

"Global gender gap report 2015: Turkey," World Economic Forum [website] (n.d.). Available at http://reports.weforum.org/global-gender-gap-report-2015/economies/#economy=TUR.

"Gross domestic product 2015, PPP," World Bank [website] (October 11, 2016). Available at http://databank.worldbank.org/data/download/GDP_PPP.pdf.

Hausmann, Ricardo, Laura D. Tyson, and Saadia Zahidi, *The Global Gender Gap Report 2006* (Geneva: World Economic Forum, 2006). Available at http://www3.weforum.org/docs/WEF_GenderGap_Report_2006.pdf.

"Historic inflation Turkey—CPI inflation," Inflation.eu: Worldwide Inflation Data [website] (n.d.). Available at http://www.inflation.eu/inflation-rates/turkey/historic-inflation/cpi-inflation-turkey.aspx.

Jahan, Selim, *Human Development Report 2015* (New York: United Nations Development Programme, 2015). Available at http://hdr.undp.org/sites/default/files/2015_human_development_report.pdf.

Makovsky, Alan, *Re-educating Turkey: AKP Efforts to Promote Religious Values in Turkish Schools* (Washington DC: Center for American Progress, 2015). Available at https://cdn.americanprogress.org/wp-content/uploads/2015/12/09115835/Re-EducatingTurkey.pdf.

Meyersson, Erik, "The reversal of (what little) liberal democracy (there ever was) in Turkey," Erik Meyersson [blog] (October 4, 2016). Available at https://erikmeyersson.com/2016/10/04/the-reversal-of-what-little-liberal-democracy-there-ever-was-in-turkey/.

Michek, Jessica, "Terror attacks in Turkey: what you need to know," Bipartisan Policy Center [website] (March 23, 2016). Available at http://bipartisanpolicy.org/blog/terror-attacks-turkey/.

"New World Bank report looks at Turkey's rise to the threshold of high-income status and the challenges remaining," World Bank [website] (December 10, 2014). Available at http://www.worldbank.org/en/news/press-release/2014/12/10/new-world-bank-report-looks-at-turkey-rise-to-threshold-of-high-income-and-challenges-remaining.

Özel, Soli, "The crisis in Turkish–Russian relations," Center for American Progress [website] (May 10, 2016). Available at https://www.americanprogress.org/issues/security/reports/2016/05/10/137131/the-crisis-in-turkish-russian-relations/.

"Quarterly national accounts: quarterly growth rates of real GDP, change over previous quarter," Organisation for Economic Co-operation and Development [website] (n.d.). Available at https://stats.oecd.org/index.aspx?queryid=350#.

"Reporters without Borders publishes the first worldwide press freedom index," Reporters without Borders [website] (October 2002). Available at https://rsf.org/en/reporters-without-borders-publishes-first-worldwide-press-freedom-index-october-2002.

Republic of Turkey Parliamentary Elections 3 November 2002 (Warsaw: Organization for Security and Co-operation in Europe/Office for Democratic Institutions and Human Rights, December 4, 2002). Available at http://www.osce.org/odihr/elections/turkey/16346?download=true.

Republic of Turkey Presidential Election 10 August 2014: OSCE/ODIHR Limited Election Observation Mission Final Report (Warsaw: Organization for Security and Co-operation in Europe/Office for Democratic Institutions and Human Rights, August 10, 2014). Available at http://www.osce.org/odihr/elections/turkey/126851?download=true.

Rodrik, Dani, "The plot against the generals," Dani Rodrik [website] (June 2014). Available at http://drodrik.scholar.harvard.edu/files/dani-rodrik/files/plot-against-the-generals.pdf.

Sayari, Sabri, and Bruce Hoffman, *Urbanization and Insurgency: The Turkish Case, 1976–1980* (Santa Monica, CA: RAND Corporation, 1991). Available at http://www.rand.org/pubs/notes/N3228.html.

Taşpinar, Ömer, and Gönül Tol, "Turkey and the Kurds: from predicament to opportunity," Brookings [website] (January 22, 2014). Available at https://www.brookings.edu/research/turkey-and-the-kurds-from-predicament-to-opportunity/

Telhami, Shibley, "The 2011 Arab public opinion poll," Brookings [website] (November 21, 2011). Available at https://www.brookings.edu/research/the-2011-arab-public-opinion-poll/.

"Turkey: freedom in the world," Freedom House [website] (2016). Available at https://freedomhouse.org/report/freedom-world/2016/turkey

"Turkey: freedom of the press 2016," Freedom House [website] (2016). Available at https://freedomhouse.org/report/freedom-press/2016/turkey.

"Turkey: freedom on the net 2016," Freedom House [website] (n.d.). Available at https://freedomhouse.org/sites/default/files/FOTN%202016%20Turkey.pdf.

"Turkey: GDP per capita (current US$)," World Bank [website] (n.d.). Available at http://data.worldbank.org/indicator/NY.GDP.PCAP.CD?locations=TR.

"Turkey's transitions: integration, inclusion, institutions," World Bank [website] (December 2014). Available at http://www.worldbank.org/en/country/turkey/publication/turkeys-transitions-integration-inclusion-institutions.

Zanotti, Jim, and Clayton Thomas, *Turkey: Background and US Relations* (Washington DC: Congressional Research Service, August 26, 2016). Available at https://fas.org/sgp/crs/mideast/R41368.pdf.

Journal articles and chapters from edited volumes

Akin, Erkan, and Ömer Karasapan, "The Turkish–Islamic synthesis," *Middle East Report* 153, no. 18 (1988), 18.

Akıncı, Uğur, "The Welfare Party's municipal track record: evaluating Islamist municipal activism in Turkey," *Middle East Journal* 53, no. 1 (1999), 75–93.

Belge, Ceren, "State buildings and the limits of legibility: kinship networks and Kurdish resistance in Turkey," *International Journal of Middle East Studies* 43, no. 1 (2011), 95–114.

Coleman, Heather, Gurdal Kanat, and F. Ilter Aydinol Turkdogan, "Restoration of the Golden Horn Estuary (Halic)," *Water Research* 43, no. 20 (2009).

Gunay, Zeynep, and Vedia Dokmeci, "Culture-led regeneration of Istanbul waterfront: Golden Horn Cultural Valley project," *Cities* 29, no. 4 (2012), 213–22.

Gunter, Michael M., "Abdullah Öcalan: we are fighting Turks everywhere," *Middle East Quarterly* 5, no. 2 (June 1998).

Jongerden, Joost, "Crafting space, making people: the spatial design of nation in modern Turkey," *European Journal of Turkish Studies*, no. 10 (2009).

Leder, Arnold, "Party competition in rural Turkey: agent of change or defender of traditional rule?" *Middle Eastern Studies* 15, no. 1 (1979), 82–105.

Moe, Christian, "Refah Partisi (the Welfare Party) and others v. Turkey," *International Journal of Not-for-Profit Law* 6, no. 1 (2003).

Reed, Howard, "Turkey's new Imam-Hatip schools," *Die Welt des Islams* 4, no. 2/3 (1955), 150–63.

White, Jenny B., "Islam and democracy: the Turkish experience," *Current History* 94, no. 588 (1995), 7–12.

Yegen, Beyhan, and Bihrat Önoz, "Management of water supply systems of metropoles: Istanbul example," in H. Gonca Coskun, H. Kerem Cigizoglu, and M. Derya Maktav (eds), *Integration of Information for Environmental Security*, NATO Science for Peace and Security Series C: Environmental Security (Dordrecht: Springer, 2008), 473–84.

Yeşilada, Birol A., "The Virtue Party," in Barry Rubin and Metin Heper (eds), *Political Parties in Turkey* (London: Frank Cass, 2002), 62–81.

Court decisions, documentaries, official documents, Ph.D. theses, videos, and web pages

Beyazıt, Hayrullah, "Hakkımızda," Osmanli Ocaklari [website] (n.d.). Available at http://osmanliocaklari.org.tr/hakkimizda.

"Case of Refah Partisi (the Welfare Party) and others v. Turkey" [judgment of the Grand Chamber of the European Court of Human Rights, February 13, 2003]. Available at http://minorityrights.org/wp-content/uploads/old-site-downloads/download-384-Refah-Partisi-v.-Turkey.pdf.

"Declaration by the presidency on behalf of the European Union on the banning of the Refah party in Turkey," European Commission [website] (January 21, 1998). Available at http://europa.eu/rapid/press-release_PESC-98-4_en.htm.

Demirci, Emin Yaşar, "Modernisation, religion and politics in Turkey: the case of the İskenderpaşa community," Ph.D., University of Manchester (1996).

Dündar, Can, *Lider Portreleri: Recep Tayyip Erdoğan* [NTV documentary, 2007].

"Fethullah Gulen: honorary chairman of the Rumi Forum," Rumi Forum [website]. Available at http://rumiforum.org/fethullah-gulen/.

"İlköğretim ve eğitim kanunu ile bazı kanunlarda değişiklik yapılmasına dair kanun: kanun no: 6287," *Resmi Gazete* [official gazette of the Republic of Turkey] (March 30, 2012). Available at http://www.resmigazete.gov.tr/eskiler/2012/04/20120411-8.htm.

Özallı Yıllar [online documentary series, January 13, 2016]. Available at http://32gun.com/video/konu/ozalli-yillar.

"Policy of zero problems with our neighbors," Republic of Turkey Ministry of Foreign Affairs [website] (n.d.). Available at http://www.mfa.gov.tr/policy-of-zero-problems-with-our-neighbors.en.mfa.

"Recep Tayyip Erdoğan address to the AKP youth branch," YouTube [website] (March 31, 2012). Available at https://www.youtube.com/watch?v=RICvSMHJ9q4a.

"Sevki Yilmaz konusmasi Almanya 1991," YouTube [website] (May 29, 2012). Available at https://www.youtube.com/watch?v=H8Gg0MgpAnY.

Turkish General Staff, "Press release no. BA-08/07" (April 27, 2007).

Ünlü, Mustafa (dir.), *12 Eylül* [documentary, Cine5, 1998].

Ustanın Hikayesi [Beyaz TV documentary, September 3, 2013].

"The world factbook: Turkey," CIA [website]. Available at https://www.cia.gov/library/publications/the-world-factbook/geos/tu.html.

Index